45 YEARS IN WALL STREET

A Review of the 1937 Panic and 1942 Panic,
1946 Bull Market with New Time Rules
and Percentage Rules with Charts
for Determining the Trend
on Stocks

By

WILLIAM D. GANN

Published by
LIBRARY OF GANN PUBLISHING CO. INC.
P.O. Box O
POMEROY, WA 99347

DEDICATED

To

The Memory of

SADIE H. GANN

A Good Wife and a Wonderful Mother

FOREWORD

In 1910 at the request of friends I wrote a small booklet entitled "Speculation a Profitable Profession." In this booklet I gave the rules that helped me to make a success in my personal trading.

January, 1923, I wrote, "Truth of the Stock Tape" to help those who were trying to help themselves in speculation and investment trading. This book was favorably received by the public and many proclaimed it my Masterpiece. The book fulfilled its mission as evidenced by letters from grateful readers. After predicting the great panic in 1929 there was a call for a new book to bring "Truth of the Stock Tape" up to date. I answered that call in the early part of 1930 by writing "Wall Street Stock Selector" giving my readers the benefit of practical experience in which I developed new rules since 1923. In "Wall Street Stock Selector" I predicted the "Investors Panic," and said that it would be the greatest panic the world had ever known. This prediction was fulfilled by the panic which ended in July, 1932, with some stocks declining to the lowest levels they had reached for the past 40 to 50 years.

A great advance followed the 1932 panic and my rules helped many people to make substantial profits.

In 1935 satisfied readers asked me to write a new book. I responded to that call by writing my third book "New Stock Trend Detector" in the latter part of 1935, giving the benefit of my experience and new and practical rules which I had discovered.

Since 1935 many changes have taken place; the market passed through the panic of 1937 which was forecast by me. The decline ended in March, 1928, and a minor Bull Market followed to November 10, 1938.

The second World War started September 1, 1939, and the United States entered the war in December, 1941. After we were in the war a further liquidation in stocks occurred and final lows were reached April 28, 1942, when stocks sold below the low level of 1938 at the lowest levels since 1932.

From the lows in 1942 a prolonged advance followed

which continued after the end of the Japanese War in August, 1945.

1946, May 29, stocks sold at the highest level they had reached since 1929. My rules and my forecast called the top of this advance and the sharp decline which followed to October 30, 1946, when final low was reached.

Fourteen years have passed since writing my last book and I have gained more knowledge through actual market operations. The world is upset and confused; investors and traders are puzzled over the business depression and the decline in the stock market. Many have written requesting me to write a new book. With the desire to help others I have written "45 Years in Wall Street" giving the benefit of my experience and my new discoveries to aid others in these difficult times. I am now in my 72nd year; fame would do me no good. I have more income than I can spend for my needs, therefore, my only object in writing this new book is to give to others the most valuable gift possible—KNOWL-EDGE! If a few find the way to make safer investments my object will have been accomplished and satisfied readers will be my reward.

W. D. Gann.

July 2, 1949

INTRODUCTION

In 1926 I read "Truth of the Stock Tape," written by W. D. Gann in 1923. To me it was a masterpiece. Then in 1927 I met Mr. Gann and since then I have read all the books he has written. The rules he has laid down have greatly benefited me when times were good, also when they were trying.

In one place he says "Remember when you make a trade, you can be wrong, therefore place a stop loss order for your protection." Another rule says, "When in doubt, get out of the market." Then again he says, "When you have nothing but hope to hold on to, get out of the market." That I am writing this, should indicate I have followed these rules and others in his books, and they have paid off.

It has been my pleasure and privilege to read Mr. Gann's latest book, "Forty-Five Years in Wall Street," before it goes to press, and I commend it to others. What he has written here is the result of many years of research and study. He is the only man I ever knew who I thought had worked as much as Mr. Thomas Edison.

In this his latest book, the rule on short time period price correction is a valuable one to any investor. Time period rules, three day and nine point charts and anniversary dates, are new discoveries by Mr. Gann, that I have never read about from anyone else.

This book contains rules that will help one make profits and keep them, if the rules are learned and applied without hope or fear.

CLARENCE KIRVEN.

July, 1949

45 YEARS IN WALL STREET

CONTENTS

CONTENTS (Continued)

CHARTS

45 YEARS
IN WALL STREET

CHAPTER I

IS IT MORE DIFFICULT TO MAKE PROFITS NOW THAN BEFORE 1932?

Many people write me and ask this question. My answer is—No, you can make just as great profits now as you ever could, provided you select the right stocks to buy and sell. Changed conditions have changed market actions somewhat. The laws passed by the government regulate trading in stocks and require higher margin. The income tax laws make it necessary to trade for the long pull swings in order to escape paying too much income tax. It no longer pays to try to scalp the market because swings in a short period of time do not warrant it. Remaining in the broker's office and trying to read the tape is out of date. You will benefit by spending your time making up charts and studying them.

Many stocks that have been listed for a long time have become seasoned and move more slowly. This cuts out the possibilities for quick profits in a short period of time. There is no longer a large list of stocks selling at high prices above $100 per share and making wide fluctuations.

1949, June 14, when stocks reached extreme Low there were about 1,100 issues traded in that day. There were only 112 stocks selling above $100 per share. Many of these were preferred stocks held by investors and this class of stocks moves in a narrow range. On June 14 there were 315 stocks selling below 20, 202 selling below 10, and 83 selling below $5.00 per share, making a total of 600 selling below 20 per share, or more than 50% of the total issues traded. With so many stocks selling at Low Levels, you can only make money by taking a long-pull trading position.

During recent years many of the high priced stocks have declared stock dividends, splitting up the stock and putting more stocks in the low price range.

Larger Profits on Same Amount of Capital

You can make more money today than you could several years ago using the same amount of capital. For example: When a stock was selling at $100 per share and you bought 100 shares you had to put up $10,000 or pay for it outright. And at the time you could buy it on the 50% margin, if it advanced 10 points, you made a profit of $1,000 or 20% on your capital. At the present time, suppose you should buy 1,000 shares of a stock selling at $10 per share on a 50% margin, this would require $5,000 capital. If the stock advances 5 points you will have made a profit of $5,000 or 100% on your capital investment. With so many stocks selling at Low Levels with good prospects for future enhancement, you have opportunities for making profits just as fast today as ever before.

Volume of Sales Smaller

The total volume of stocks traded on the New York Stock Exchange during recent years is much smaller. This is because people buy stocks and hold them longer. There are no longer any pools or manipulation in stocks since the passing of the Security Exchange Regulations. This does not mean that there cannot be Big Bull markets and large advances in the future. As time goes by stocks pass into the hands of investors who hold them for a long period of time. The floating supply is gradually absorbed. Then, when something suddenly happens to start a buying wave, buyers find the supply of stocks scarce and have to bid them up. It always happens that the higher prices go, the more people want to buy. This causes a final grand rush and a rapid advance in the last stages of a Bull Market. History repeats on Wall Street and what has happened in the past will happen again in the future.

In January, 1946, the U. S. Government made a rule compelling everyone who bought stocks to put up 100% margin, or in other words, pay for them outright. Stocks were already selling at very High Levels and had been advancing for three and a half years. Did this ruling by the government stop the public from buying stocks? It did not. The Averages advanced more than 20 points and the advance lasted five months longer to May 29, 1946, when final High was reached, which proves that the government could not stop the advance in stocks as long as the people were in the mood to buy. In fact, a lot of traders believe that the government took this action because it thought there would be a runaway advance in stocks and traders believing this continued to buy stocks regardless of the margin required. My experience has taught me that nothing can stop the Trend as long as the Time Cycle shows Up-Trend. Nothing can stop its decline as long as the Time Cycle shows Down. Stocks can and do go Up on bad news and go Down on good news.

1949 in March, the government reduced the marginal requirements on stock to 50% margin. Many people thought this was very bullish and that it would start a Bull Market, but it did not. Stocks rallied for two days to March 30, then declined over 18 points on the Averages until June 14. They went down because the Trend was down. The Time Cycle had not run out for Bottom.

Cross Currents in Stocks

In recent years the market has been more mixed than for a long time. Some groups of stocks advance while others decline at the same time. This is due to various causes and conditions in the different industries. You can determine these cross currents and get the Trend of any individual stock if you keep up a Monthly High and Low Chart and study it and apply the rules which I give you.

Why You Have Lost Money in Stocks
AND
How to Make It Back

Why do the great majority of people who buy and sell stocks lose? There are three main reasons:

1. They overtrade or buy and sell too much for their capital.

2. They do not place stop loss orders or limit their losses.

3. Lack of Knowledge. This is the most important reason of all.

Most people buy a stock because they hope it will go up and they will make profits. They buy on tips, or what someone else thinks, without any concrete knowledge of their own that the stock will advance. Thus they entered the market wrong and did not recognize this mistake or attempt to correct it until too late. Finally they sell because they fear the stock will go lower and often they sell out near low levels, getting out at the wrong time, making two mistakes, getting in the market at the wrong time and getting out at the wrong time. One mistake could have been prevented, they could have gotten out right after getting in wrong. They do not realize that operating in Stocks and Commodities is a business or a profession, the same as engineering or the medical profession.

Why You Should Learn to Determine the Trend of the Market

You may have tried to follow market letters and like many others either lost money or failed to make profits, because the market letters gave a list of too many stocks to buy or sell and you picked the wrong one and lost. A smart man cannot follow another man blindly even though the other man is right, because you cannot have confidence and act on advice when you do not know what it is based on. You will be able to act with confidence and make profits when you can SEE and KNOW for YOURSELF why STOCKS should go UP or DOWN.

That is why you should study all of my rules and make up charts for yourself on the individual stocks, as well as the averages. If you do this you will prepare yourself to act independent of the advice of others, because you will know from Time-Tested Rules what the trend of the market should be.

CHAPTER II

RULES FOR TRADING IN STOCKS

To make a success in trading in stocks you must get the knowledge first; you must learn before you lose. Many traders go into the stock market without any knowledge and lose a large part of their capital before they learn that it is necessary to go through a period of preparation before they start trading. I am giving you the benefit of more than 45 years of experience in the stock market and laying down rules which, if you learn and follow, will make you a success.

The first thing for you to realize is that when you make a trade you can be *wrong*; then you *must know* what to do to *correct* your *mistake*. The way to do that is to *limit* your *risk* by *placing* a *Stop* Loss Order 1, 2 or 3 points below the price at which you buy. Then if you are wrong you will automatically be sold out and will be in position to enter the market again when you have a definite indication. *Do not guess*; make a trade on definite rules and according to definite indications based on the rules which I lay down; this will give you a better chance to make a success.

Read all of the rules and examples in my books, "Truth of the Stock Tape", "Wall Street Stock Selector" and "New Stock Trend Detector", and study 12 and 24 rules which are bound with this book "45 Years in Wall Street". The rules are good and will benefit you if you study them. Remember that you can never learn too much. Always be ready and willing to learn something new; never have a fixed idea that you know it all. If you do, you will not make any more progress. Times and conditions change and you must learn to change with them. Human nature does not change and that is the reason history repeats and stocks act very much the same under certain conditions year after year and in the various cycles of time.

Rule 1. Determining the Trend

Determine the trend of the Dow-Jones 30 Industrial Averages or the 15 public utilities averages or the average on any group of stocks that you intend to trade in, then select the stock in the group in which you want to trade and see if its Trend indications conform to the Trend indicated by the Averages. You should use the 3-Day Chart for the Averages and the 9-Point Average Swing Chart as outlined later in the book, and apply all of the rules for determining the right time to buy or sell.

Rule 2. Buy at Single, Double and Triple Bottoms

Buy at Double and Triple Bottoms or on Single Bottoms when they are nearer previous Old Bottoms or Tops or resistance levels. Remember the rule: Tops or ceilings which are selling points become floors, supports or buying points after these tops have been crossed and the market reacts to them, or sells slightly below them. Sell at or against Single, Double or Triple Tops and, remember, that after an Old Top is broken by several points and the market rallies up to or near it again, it becomes a selling point. After you have made a trade, determine the proper and safe place to place a Stop Loss Order, and give it to your broker immediately. If you do not know where to place a Stop Loss Order, do not make the trade.

Do not overlook the fact that the 4th time the averages or an individual stock reaches the same level it is not as safe to sell, because it nearly always goes through. Reverse this rule at the bottom. When stocks decline to the same level the 4th time in most cases it breaks the bottom and continues down.

The Meaning of Double Tops and Bottoms

A Double Top on the Averages can be in a range of 3 to 5 points. However, most Double Tops form in a range of from 1 to 2 points except at great extremes. The same way at an extreme bottom. If there has been a previous bottom around this same level many years back, the Averages can decline 4 to 5 points below the previous bottom without indicating that they are going lower, and this can become a Double or a Triple Bottom.

Individual stocks usually make a Double Top in a 2 to 3 point range and sometimes within a 1 to 2 point range. The same at the bottom; they make a Double Bottom in a 2 to 3 point range and sometimes the range is only 1 to 2 points below the different bottoms. Stop Loss Orders should be placed on individual stocks 1 to 3 points above Double and Triple Tops, depending upon how high stocks are selling. Stop Loss Orders should be placed under Double and Triple Bottoms 1 to 3 points away.

A Triple Top or Bottom occurs when the Averages or an individual stock has reached the same level the 3rd time. This is often the safest place to buy or sell because the market moves away from a Triple Top or a Triple Bottom much faster.

Rule 3. Buy and Sell on Percentages

Buy or sell on a 50% decline from any high level or a 50% advance from any low level so long as these reactions or rallies are with the main trend. You can use the percentage of the individual stocks as well as the percentage of the Averages to determine the resistance levels and buying and selling points. You can use 3 to 5 per cent, next 10 to 12 per cent, next 20 to 25 per cent, 33 to 37 per cent, 45 to 50 per cent, 62 to 67 per cent, 72 to 78 per cent and 85 to 87 per cent. The most important resistance levels are 50% and 100% and the proportionate parts of 100%. (See examples under Chapter on Percentages of High and Low Prices.)

Rule 4. Buy and Sell on 3 Weeks' Advance or Decline

Buy on a 3 weeks' reaction or decline in a Bull Market when the main trend is up, as this is the average reaction in a strong Bull Market. In a Bear Market sell on a rally of around 3 weeks after you know the trend is down.

After a market advances or declines 30 days or more, the next time period to watch for tops and bottoms is around

6 to 7 weeks which will be a buying or selling level, protected, of course, with Stop Loss Orders according to resistance levels. After a market rallies or declines more than 45 to 49 days, the next time period is around 60 to 65 days which is about the greatest average time that a Bear Market rallies or a Bull Market reacts.

Rule 5. Market Moves in Sections

Stock market campaigns move in 3 to 4 Sections or waves. Never consider that the market has reached final top when it makes the first section in a move up, because if it is a real Bull Market it will run at least 3 Sections and possibly 4 before a final high is reached.

In a Bear Market, or declining market, never consider the market as final bottom when it makes the first decline or Section because it will run 3 and possibly 4 Sections before the Bear campaign is over.

Rule 6. Buy or Sell on 5 to 7 Point Moves

Buy or sell individual stocks on reactions of 5 to 7 points. When a market is strong, reactions will run 5 to 7 points but— will not decline as much as 9 or 10 points. By studying the Industrial Averages you will see how often a rally or reaction runs less than 10 points. However, it is important to watch 10 to 12 point rallies or declines for buying or selling levels on the average. The next important point to watch is 18 to 21 points up or down from any important Top or Bottom. Reactions of this kind in the Averages often indicate the end of a move.

When to Take Profits—After you have bought stocks or sold them, the next thing you need to know is when to take profit. Follow the rules and do not take profits until there is a definite indication of a change in trend.

Rule 7. Volume of Sales

Study the total volume of sales on the New York Stock Exchange in connection with the time periods and study the rules under volume of sales later on in the book. Study the volume of sales on individual stocks based on the rules given, as the volume of sales will help in determining when the trend is changing.

Rule 8. *Time Periods*

The time factor and time periods are most important in determining a change in trend because Time can over balance Price and when the Time is up the Volume of sales will increase and force prices higher or lower.

Dates for Change in Trend—The stock market averages and individual stocks follow a seasonal change in trend which varies in different years, but by knowing the important dates and watching them you will be able to determine a change in trend very quickly by applying all the other rules. The important dates are as follows:

January 7 to 10, and 19 to 24. These are the most important at the beginning of the year, and changes in trend that last for several weeks, and sometimes several months, occur around these dates. Check the records and prove it for yourself.

February 3 to 10, and 20 to 25. These are next important to the dates in January.

March 20 to 27. Minor changes occur around this date and sometimes major tops or bottoms occur.

April 7 to 12, and 20 to 25. Not as important as January and February, but the latter part of April is often quite important for a change in trend.

May 3 to 10, and 21 to 28. The changes this month are of as great importance as those that occur in January and February, and many major Tops and Bottoms have occurred around these dates in the past and a change in trend has taken place.

June 10 to 15, and 21 to 27. Minor changes in trend occur around these dates and in some years extreme highs and extreme lows occur. Example: 1948, June 14, extreme high; 1949, June 14, extreme low, up to the time of this writing.

July 7 to 10, 21 to 27. This month is next in importance to January because it is at the middle of the year when dividend payments occur and seasonal changes and crop conditions have some effect on the change in trend of stocks.

August 5 to 8, and 14 to 20. This month is as important in some ways as February for change. Check the back records and you will see how important changes occur around these dates.

September 3 to 10, and 21 to 28. These periods are the most important of any in the year, especially for Tops, or final highs in a Bull Market, as more highs have occurred in September than any other month. Some minor changes, both up and down, have occurred around these dates.

October 7 to 14, and 21 to 30. These periods are quite important and some major changes have occurred between these dates. They should always be watched if a market has been declining or advancing for some time.

November 5 to 10, and 20 to 30. These are very important for changes in trend as a study in past history will prove. In election years a change in trend often occurs in the early part of the month, and in other years low prices are recorded between the 20th and 30th.

December 3 to 10, and 15 to 24. The latter period and running into the January period for a change in trend has shown a high percentage of changes over a period of years.

Refer to the 3-day chart tables showing exact dates when extreme high and low price has been reached and check these past dates and watch them each month in the future.

When looking up dates for Change in Trend, consider whether the market has run from any high or low price 7 to 12 days, 18 to 21, 28 to 31, 42 to 49, 57 to 65, 85 to 92, 112 to 120, 150 to 157, or 175 to 185 days. The more important the top and bottom that these Time periods start from, the more important the change.

Market Over-Balanced—The Averages or individual stocks become over-balanced after they have advanced or declined a considerable period of Time, and the greater the Time period, the greater the correction or reaction. When a Time period on a decline exceeds the Time period of a previous decline it indicates a change in trend. When the price breaks a greater number of points than the previous decline or reaction it indicates that the market is Over-Balanced and a change in trend is taking place.

Reverse this rule in a Bear Market. When stocks have been declining for a long period of Time, the first time that a rally exceeds the Time period of a previous rally it is an indication that the trend is changing, at least temporarily. The first time that the price rallies a greater number of points than a previous rally, it indicates that the Space or Price movement is Over-Balanced and a change in trend has started. The Time change is more important than reversal in price. Apply all of the rules to see if a change in trend is due at the Time when these reversals take place.

When the market is nearing the end of a long upswing or a long downswing and reaches the 3rd or 4th Section, the swings upward will be smaller in price gains and the Time period will be less than the previous Section. This is an indication that a change in trend is due. In a Bear or declining market, when the loss in points becomes less than the previous Section and the Time period is less, it is an indication that the Time cycle is running out.

Rule 9. Buy on Higher Tops and Bottoms

Buy when the market is making higher Tops and higher Bottoms which shows that the main trend is up. Sell when the market is making lower Tops and lower Bottoms which indicates the main trend is down. Time periods are always important. Check the Time period from previous Top to Top and from previous Bottom to Bottom. Also check the Time required for the market to move up from extreme low to extreme high and the Time required for prices to move down from extreme high to extreme low.

Monthly High and Low Charts.—When markets are slow and narrow, and especially for low priced stocks, all you need to do is keep up the monthly high and low chart; when activity starts you can start keeping a weekly high and low chart and for stock selling at very high levels, keep the daily high and low charts, but remember that the 3-Day Swing

Chart is much more important as a Trend Indicator than a daily high and low chart.

Rule 10. Change in Trend in Bull Market

A change in trend often occurs just before or just after holidays. The following dates are important. January 3, May 30, July 4, the early part of September, after Labor Day, October 10 to 14, November 3 to 8 in election years, and November 25 to 30, Thanksgiving, and December 24 to 28. This latter period may run into the early part of January, before a definite change in trend is indicated.

When prices on the Industrial Averages or the individual stocks break the last low on a 9-Point Swing Chart or break the last low on the swing on a 3-Day Chart it is an indication that the trend is changing, at least temporarily.

Bear Market: In a declining market when prices cross the Top of the last upswing on a 9-Point Chart, or cross the top of the last upswing on a 3-Day Chart, it is the First Signal for a Change in Trend. When prices are at High Levels there are usually several swings up and down; then when the market breaks the Low of the Last Swing it indicates a reversal and change in Trend.

At low levels prices often narrow down and remain in a narrow trading range for some Time, then when they Cross the Top of the last upswing it is important for a Change in Trend.

Always check to see if the market is exactly 1, 2, 3, 4 or 5 years from any extreme High or Low price. Check back to see if the Time Period is 15, 22, 34, 42, 48 or 49 months from any extreme or low price, as these are important time periods to watch for Change in Trend.

Rule 11. Safest Buying and Selling Points

It is always safest to buy stocks after a definite Change in Trend has been established. After a stock makes bottom and has a rally, then follows the Secondary Reaction and it gets support at a higher bottom. When it starts to advance and crosses the Top of the First Rally, it is the safest Place to Buy because the market has already given an indication of uptrend. Stop Loss Orders can be placed under the Secondary Bottom.

Safest Selling Point—After a market has advanced for a long time and made Final High and has the First Sharp quick Decline, then rallies and makes the Second Lower Top, and from this Top declines and Breaks the Low point of the First Decline, it is then Safer to Sell because it has given the Signal that the main Trend has changed to the Down side.

2-Day Reactions and Rallies: This is a most important time period in very fast active markets. Reactions will only run 2 days and not decline into the third day. This will happen many times before there is any indication of a Change in Trend. When a stock or the Averages react only 2 days, it is in a very strong position. You will find some of these 2-day moves shown in the table for the 3-Day Chart.

In an active, Fast Declining Market, rallies will be sharp and fast, only lasting 2 days. Study the table for the 3-Day Chart and you will find many rallies of this kind during the fall of 1929 and during 1930-31 when the big Bear Market was under way.

Remember stocks are never too High to Buy as long as the Trend is Up and they are never too Low to Sell as long as the Trend is Down; but do not overlook the fact that you must always use a Stop Loss Order for your protection. Always Go With the Trend and not against it. Buy stocks in Strong Position and Sell Stocks in Weak Positions.

Rule 12. *Price Gains in Fast Moves*

When markets are very active and advancing or declining very fast they average about 1 point per calendar day. When the Movement on Averages or individual stocks is 2 points or more per day, it is far above normal and does not last very long. Movements of this kind occur when there are

Short Time Periods and a quick corrective reaction or decline in a Bull Market. When the Trend is down in a Bear Market these quick fast rallies correct the position in a short period of time. Read the information and examples under "Short Time Periods Correct Prices."

I want to impress upon you strongly that if you expect to make a success in the stock market you must put in plenty of time studying, because the more time you put in, the more knowledge you gain, the more profits you will take out later. Over 45 years of practical experience in trying and testing rules have proven to me what is required for your success. I have given you the rules that will work; you must do your part; you must learn the rules, act on them at the right time and put them into execution.

TWENTY-FOUR NEVER-FAILING RULES

In order to make a success trading in the stock market, the trader must have definite rules and follow them. The rules given below are based upon my personal experience and anyone who follows them will make a success.

1. Amount of capital to use: Divide your capital into 10 equal parts and never risk more than one-tenth of your capital on any one trade.
2. Use stop loss orders. Always protect a trade when you make it with a stop loss order 3 to 5 points away.
3. Never overtrade. This would be violating your capital rule.
4. Never let a profit run into a loss. After you once have a profit of 3 points or more, raise your stop loss order so that you will have no loss of capital.
5. Do not buck the trend. Never buy or sell if you are not sure of the trend according to your charts.
6. When in doubt, get out, and don't get in when in doubt.
7. Trade only in active stocks. Keep out of slow, dead ones.
8. Equal distribution of risk. Trade in 4 or 5 stocks, if possible. Avoid tying up all your capital in any one stock.
9. Never limit your orders or fix a buying or selling price. Trade at the market.
10. Don't close your trades without a good reason. Follow up with a stop loss order to protect your profits.
11. Accumulate a surplus. After you have made a series of successful trades, put some money into surplus account to be used only in emergency or in times of panic.
12. Never buy just to get a dividend.
13. Never average a loss. This is one of the worst mistakes a trader can make.
14. Never get out of the market just because you have lost patience or get into the market because you are anxious from waiting.
15. Avoid taking small profits and big losses.
16. Never cancel a stop loss order after you have placed it at the time you make a trade.
17. Avoid getting in and out of the market too often.
18. Be just as willing to sell short as you are to buy. Let your object be to keep with the trend and make money.
19. Never buy just because the price of a stock is low or sell short just because the price is high.

20. Be careful about pyramiding at the wrong time. Wait until the stock is very active and has crossed Resistance Levels before buying more and until it has broken out of the zone of distribution before selling more.
21. Select the stocks with small volume of shares outstanding to pyramid on the buying side and the ones with the largest volume of stock outstanding to sell short.
22. Never hedge. If you are long of one stock and it starts to go down, do not sell another stock short to hedge it. Get out at the market; take your loss and wait for another opportunity.
23. Never change your position in the market without a good reason. When you make a trade, let it be for some good reason or according to some definite plan; then do not get out without a definite indication of a change in trend.
24. Avoid increasing your trading after a long period of success or a period of profitable trades.

When you decide to make a trade be sure that you are not violating any of these 24 rules which are vital and important to your success. When you close a trade with a loss, go over these rules and see which rule you have violated; then do not make the same mistake the second time. Experience and investigation will convince you of the value of these rules, and observation and study will lead you to a correct and practical theory for success in Wall Street.

SAFETY OF CAPITAL

Your first thought must be how to protect your capital and make your trading as safe as possible. There is one safe, sure rule, and the man who will follow it and never deviate from it will always keep his money and come out ahead at the end of every year. This rule is divide your capital into 10 equal parts and never risk more than one-tenth or 10 per cent of your capital on any one trade. If you start with $1000 you should not risk more than $100 on your first trade, and the way to limit your loss is to place a stop loss order. It is much better to have 10 shares of stock and lose 3 points or $30 than to have 100 shares and lose $300. You can always find new opportunities to make profits, so long as you have capital to operate with. Taking heavy risks in the beginning endangers your capital and impairs your judgment. Trade in such a way that you will not be disturbed mentally by a loss, if it comes.

I feel that I cannot repeat too many times the value of using stop loss orders because it is the only safety valve to protect the investor and trader. An investor or trader will place a stop loss order and one time out of ten the stop will be caught at the exact top or bottom. After this he always remembers that and says, "If I place a stop loss order, they will just go down and catch it, or just go up and catch it and then the market will go the other way." So he does not use the stop loss order the next time. His broker often tells him that stop loss orders are always caught. The trader forgets that nine times out of ten the stop loss order was right and would have prevented big losses by getting him out at a time when the market was going against him. The one time that the stop loss order gets you out wrong it makes up for it in the next nine times that it gets you out right. So don't fail to use a stop loss order.

CHANGING YOUR MIND

A wise man changes his mind; a fool never. A wise man investigates and then decides, and a fool just decides. In Wall Street, the man who does not change his mind will soon have no change to mind. When once you have made up your mind to make a trade and you have a reason for it, do not change without a reason. The most important thing that I refer to is changing stop loss orders, or cancelling stops when the market is going against you. The first thing to do when you make a trade is to place a stop loss order, which is for your own protection. Once you have placed a stop, you have acted wisely and used good judgment. To change your mind from this decision is foolish and to cancel your stop, once you have placed it, is not based on good judgment but on hope, and hope can lead to nothing but losses in Wall Street. Nine times out of ten, when once you place a stop loss order, if you never cancel it, it will prove to be the best thing that ever happened, and the man who adheres to this rule will make a success. I reiterate, if you cannot follow a rule, do not start to speculate because you will lose all, and one of the rules that you must follow and never deviate from is to PLACE A STOP LOSS ORDER AT THE TIME YOU MAKE A TRADE AND DO NOT CANCEL IT.

OVERTRADING

History repeats because of the weakness of human nature. The greed for quick fortunes has cost the public countless millions of dollars. Every experienced stock trader knows that overtrading is his greatest weakness, but he continues to allow this weakness to be his ruin. There must be a cure for this greatest weakness in trading, and that cure is STOP LOSS ORDERS. The weakest point must be overcome, and the stop loss order is the cure for overtrading.

PROTECT YOUR PROFITS

It is just as important to protect profits as it is to protect your capital. When once you have a profit on a trade, you should never let it run into a loss. There are exceptions to this rule, and the amount of the profits should determine where stop loss orders should be placed. The following is about the safest rule that I can give you to use under average conditions. When once a stock has moved 3 points in your favor, place a stop loss order where you will be even if it is caught. In very active, high-priced stocks, it will pay you to wait until a stock shows a profit of 4 to 5 points; then move your stop loss order up to where you will have no loss should the market reverse. In this way, you will have reduced your risk to a minimum and the possibility of profits will be unlimited. As the stock moves in your favor, continue to follow up with a stop loss order, thus protecting and increasing your profits.

WHEN TO ENTER THE MARKET

It is very important to know when to buy or sell, and you must have some rule or some sign as your indication for the time to place your order to buy or sell. When you think the market is reaching bottom or top, you will find that 7 times out of 10 you will be wrong. It is not what the market does today or what you think it is going to do that is important; it is exactly what the indications are that it will do at a later date when you expect to make profits.

When a stock reaches low levels or high levels and you want to take a position, wait until it shows a sign that the trend has turned up or down. At times, you may miss the bottom or top by waiting, but you will save money by not making your trade until you have reason to believe that you are going with the trend and not against it.

One of the most important things that you should keep in mind is not how much profit or how much loss you are going to make. You should leave the money part out of the question. Your object should be to keep right on the market. Go with the trend of the market. Study all the time to determine the correct trend. Do not think about profits. If you are right on the market, the profits will come. If you are wrong, then use the old reliable protector, a stop loss order.

BUYING OR SELLING TOO SOON OR TOO LATE

Investors often get out of the market too soon, because they have held stocks for a long time, waiting for activity and higher prices, and then sell out on the first move up into new territory, which is a mistake. See Swing Charts on Atchison, American Tel. & Tel. and New York Central on page 113.

There is another type of investor who always gets out of the market too late, because when the big advance comes, he holds on and hopes that the stock will go higher than it ever does. It never reaches the price at which he wishes to sell. The first quick break comes, and he decides that if the stock advances again to its former high level, he will sell out. The stock does advance but fails to get as high, then declines still lower, and he again fixes a price in his mind at which he will sell, but this is only a "hope" price, and he sees the stock drift lower and lower until finally, in disgust, he sells out after the stock has had a big decline from the top. It is always well to wait until you can see a change in the trend before selling out, but when once you do see that the trend has changed, then sell out without delay. A good rule for this kind of a trader is to follow up with stop loss orders, even if it is 10 to 20 points away.

DELAYS DANGEROUS

Action, not delay, makes money in Wall Street. There is no use hoping, as that will not beat the game. Men who gamble on hope always go broke. You must stop hoping and start thinking. Then, after you think, unless you act at the proper time, good thinking is useless. Knowing when to act and not doing it will not help any. Delays are always dangerous. The longer you hope and delay taking action in the market, the worse your judgment gets and the surer you are to make mistakes. Stagnation is death and destruction. Action is life. Being right or wrong and not acting will never save your money or help you to make it. Remember, delays are always dangerous. It is much better to take action now than to trust to uncertain time. You should never trade when sick or depressed. Your judgment is always bad when you are below normal physically. One of the rules of a successful speculator should be to keep good health, for health is wealth.

WHEN TO PYRAMID

There are two ways of pyramiding. One is to buy more or sell more just as soon as the market breaks into new territory or makes a new high or a new low. In a fast running market, you can continue to buy or sell every 3, 5 or 10 points up or down when the market is moving in your favor, all depending on the stock or your method of pyramiding. My method is to determine the reaction levels and how many points a stock has reacted from temporary top levels or rallied from temporary bottoms. Find out whether these reactions are running 3, 5, 7, 10, or 12 points; then buy or sell your 1st, 2nd, 3rd, or 4th lot for pyramiding on reactions from the top, waiting for 3, 5, or 10 points according to the past reaction. Reverse the rule in a bear market. If you had followed this rule on General Motors from 1924 to 1929, you would find that your pyramid would have been safer than buying or selling the stock every so many points apart.

My time rule, which will help you in pyramiding, is to determine the time of the first important reaction. For example, General Motors reacted only 3 weeks from the time it started up in 1924 and was good to buy every time it reacted 2 to 3 weeks from any top, until it made the final top and the main trend turned down. Determining the time of the reactions and measuring them this way will greatly increase your profits and enable you to follow the main trend of the stock, sometimes for several years, and you can often make 100 to 200 points profit. This time rule, like other rules, works best on active high-priced stocks and should only be applied in active markets.

A pyramid should always be followed up with a stop loss order, no matter what method you use, because your profits must be protected. The more profit you have, the more room you can give the market to fluctuate, or have its reverse moves or reactions, that is, you can place your stop loss order further away from the market so that a natural reaction will not disturb your pyramid. For example, suppose you have followed a stock up and have 100 points profit on your original purchase. If the stock has had a previous reaction of 20 points, it could again react 20 points without changing the main trend, therefore your stop loss order could be 20 points under the market, because if it was caught, you would not be losing part of your capital, but only a part of your paper profits, while in the early stages of your pyramid your stop loss order would have to be closer in order to protect your original capital.

HOW MUCH PROFIT TO EXPECT

Most traders expect too large profits from the business of speculation. They do not stop to figure what a gain of 25 per cent a year means over a period of 10 to 20 years. Starting with $1000 a gain of 25 per cent per year for 10 years equals $9,313.25. $10,000 increased at the rate of 25 per cent a year amounts to $93,132.70 in 10 years. You can see how easy it is to accumulate a fortune in a reasonable length of time if one only is conservative and does not expect too much. Many traders come to Wall Street with the idea that they can double their money in a week or a month. It cannot be done. There are exceptional opportunities at times, when a large amount of money can be made in one day, one week, or one month, but these big opportunities are few and far between, and when once you have one of them and make big profits, do not let hope run away with your judgment and expect to continue to make profits right along on such an enormous scale. Remember that the market makes normal moves most of the time and that you must take normal profits the greater part of the time. Many traders buy or sell a stock without any thought of how much profit there is a possibility of them making and never think about the possibility of a loss. This should be one of your rules: Never buy or sell a stock when you don't think you can make more than 3 to 5 points' profit unless you use a stop loss order of only 1 to 2 points. It does not pay, on an average, to risk 3 to 5 points' loss for a possible gain of 3 to 5 points. Try to make a trade where you have opportunities, or at least where there is a promise of greater profits than losses. There is no use getting into a stock when you think there is only a chance of making 3 to 5 points, because you can be wrong and lose that much or more. It is better to wait until stocks cross Resistance Levels one way or the other and get in where the opportunities are for greater profits and longer swings. Scalpers do not make money; they simply get scalped. Remember that to make a success your profits must always be greater than your losses, and your rule must be to cut losses short and let your profits run.

HOW TO ANSWER A MARGIN CALL

When you make a trade and put up the required margin at the time and later the stock goes against you and the broker calls for more margin, the thing to do in most cases is not to put up more margin, but sell out at the market or buy in in case you are short. If you put up more margin, let it be on a new trade and one which you have a good reason for making when your judgment is better. Nine times out of ten after a customer puts up margin the first time, he will hold on until there is a second margin call and a third and put up as.long as he has money to put up and lose all of his capital on one trade. If the broker has to call you for margin, there is something wrong, and the best thing to do is to get out.

Never have a joint account or trade in partnership with others if you can possibly avoid it. When two men have an account together, they may agree upon the right time to buy for long account or the right time to sell short and may be exactly right when they agree to make the trade, but here is where the hitch comes—when it comes to closing the trade they will seldom ever agree on the time and price to take profits. The result will be that they will make a mistake in getting out of the trade. One man will hold on because the other one does not want to get out and finally the market reverses and the trade goes against them; then they hold on and hope, and finally take a loss on what was a trade that they started together profitably. It is hard for one mind to work on the stock market and keep right, but it is much harder for two to agree and work in the market. The only way that two could make a success with it would be for one to do the buying and selling and the other to do nothing but place the stop loss orders. Stop loss orders will protect both of them when they make mistakes. It is a bad rule for a man and his wife to have a joint account together. The action of getting in and out of the market should be up to one man, who should learn to act and act quickly and not be influenced by a partner in a speculative deal.

WHAT TRADERS DON'T WANT TO KNOW

The average trader does not want to hear a painful truth. They want something in accordance with what they hope for. When they buy a stock they believe all the news, rumors, views and lies that are bullish, but just let some report come out that is bad or let someone tell him something unfavorable about the stock he has bought and he refuses to believe it. It is the truth that will help him and truth that he should want to hear, not something that will build up his hopes and cause him losses later. A trader after he has made a mistake, says "I am going to do different next time," but he doesn't and that is why we always have old lambs in Wall Street to lead the young lambs down the same lane to losses that the old lambs have followed. Real inside truth about losses in Wall Street is seldom ever told. Traders, big and little, always talk about their profits and brag about their successful trades, but keep quiet about their losses. Therefore, the innocent lamb, when he comes to Wall Street, is led to believe that there is nothing but profits to be made, instead of hearing the other side of the story of how losses are made in Wall Street, which is a thing that would really help him and prevent him from making the same mistake. The new lamb should know that failing to place a stop loss order and overtrading have been the cause of over 90 per cent of the failures in Wall Street. Therefore, in order to make a success he must act in a way to overcome the weak points which have caused the ruin of others.

HUMAN ELEMENT THE GREATEST WEAKNESS

When a trader makes a profit, he gives himself credit and feels that his judgment is good and that he did it all himself. When he makes losses, he takes a different attitude and seldom ever blames himself or tries to find the cause with himself for the losses. He finds excuses; reasons with himself that the unexpected happened, and that if he had not listened to some one else's advice, he would have made a profit. He finds a lot of ifs, ands, and buts, which he imagines were no fault of his. This is why he makes mistakes and losses the second time.

The investor and trader must work out his own salvation and blame himself and no one else for his losses, for unless he does, he will never be able to correct his weaknesses. After all, it is your own acts that cause your losses, because you did the buying and the selling. You must look for the trouble within and correct it. Then you will make a success, and not before.

One of the main reasons why traders make losses is because they do not think for themselves and allow others to think for them and advise them, whose advice and judgment is no better than their own. To make a success, you must study and investigate for yourself. Unless you change from a "lamb" to a thinker and seek knowledge, you will go the way of all lambs,—to slaughter under the margin caller's axe. Others can only help you when you help yourself, or show you how to help yourself.

I can give you the best rules in the world and the best methods for determining the position of a stock, and then you can lose money on account of the human element which is your greatest weakness. You will fail to follow rules. You will work on hope or fear instead of facts. You will delay. You will become impatient. You will act too quickly or you will delay too long in acting, thus cheating yourself on account of your human weakness and then blaming it on the market. Always remember that it is your mistake that causes losses and not the action of the market or the manipulators. Therefore, strive to follow rules, or keep out of speculation for you are doomed to failure.

CHAPTER III

HOW TO SELECT INDEPENDENT MOVERS

Many stocks make new Highs while other stocks are making new Lows and start moves independent of the Averages and the different groups of stocks. You can determine when these independent moves start by studying the action on the chart for several years back.

For example—Cities Service. 1938 High 11. 1939 Low 4. 1942 Low 2, High 3½. The stock had held in a range between 11 and 2 for four years and during 1942 made a range of only 1½ points per share, indicating that it was thoroughly liquidated and no one but the insiders wanted to buy it. You could have taken a chance and bought the stock at this time because you could not lose but two or three dollars per share if it went off the board. But what you want to know is when to buy, when it is safe, and when it shows a definite Up-Trend. In 1943 the stock crossed 11, the 1938 High, after a period of five years which indicated much higher prices, and you should have bought it at once. It continued to make Higher Bottoms and Higher Tops, showing the main Trend Up.

1948, June High 64½. The stock had advanced 53 points after it showed main Trend Up. When you bought it at 11, a 3 point Stop Loss Order would have held it and you could have doubled your money four or five times without pyramiding.

1949, High 48. 1949, Low 38, which is still above the 1948 levels. As long as the stock can hold above 38 it is still in position to go higher as the earnings. are good.

Buying One Stock and Selling Another Short

I have stated before under "Cross Currents of the Market" that some stocks advance and make new Highs while others decline and make new Lows. There are many times when you can sell one stock short at a High Level and buy another stock that is selling at a Low Level and the prices of these stocks will come together and you will make profits on both.

Radio and Pepsi-Cola

1947, August 34½, for Pepsi-Cola. It had previously sold at 40 and was making Lower Tops and on all the rules the Trend was down. Suppose you sold short 100 shares of Pepsi-Cola at 32. At the same time Radio was selling at 8, showing good support around Low Levels. You bought 100 shares of Radio at 8 and placed a Stop Loss Order on it at 7. On the Pepsi-Cola short you would place a Stop Loss Order at 35, making a total risk of about $400 plus commissions if both Stops were caught. They were not. Pepsi-Cola continued to decline and Radio advanced.

1947 Low on Radio 7½. Using my rule of a 100% advance we would watch Radio at 15 for Top. 1948, June High, 15 up 100% and the volume of trading was very heavy and the stock failed to go through. You had plenty of time to sell it around 15.

In 1948, Pepsi-Cola was selling below 20, which was a 50% decline from the last highest selling price, 40½. Having broken this important support level you would remain short of Pepsi-Cola reducing Stop Loss Order to 21. 1948, December, Pepsi-Cola Low 7½, down to the 1939 Low Level where it received support. This would be the time to cover short Pepsi-Cola at 8. This would give you 24 points profit on Pepsi-Cola and approximately 7 points on Radio. Pepsi-Cola did not decline to 7 and advanced to 12. You could have bought it with a Stop at 7 which would not have been caught.

When to Buy Radio

Look up the chart for the High and Low in recent years. 1945, High 19⅝; 1947, Low 7½. 1948 High 15. The 50% point or half-way between 7½ and 15 is 11¼. The last extreme high was 19⅝, 50% of this high selling price would be 9.81 or approximately $10.00 per share. 1949, June 14, Radio declined to 9¾ and around June 29 was still selling as low as 9⅝, giving you an opportunity to buy all the stock you wanted at $10.00 per share. You could place a Stop-Loss Order at 8½. The next thing you want to know is: When will it show strong Up Trend. When it crosses 11¼ and closes above this level it will indicate higher. The next objective is the 1949 High of 15 and the 1945 High at 19⅝. Should Radio ever cross 20 it will then be in a very strong position and indicate very much higher prices. I belive in the future of Radio; it has great possibilities, and may again become a real leader in the future.

CHAPTER IV

PERCENTAGE OF HIGH AND LOW PRICES

One of the greatest discoveries I ever made was how to figure the percentage of high and low prices on the averages and individual stocks. The percentages of extreme high and low levels indicate future resistance levels.

There is a relation between every low price to some future high price. and a percentage of the low price indicates what levels to expect the next high price. At this price you can sell out long stocks and sell short with a limited risk.

The extreme high price or any minor tops are related to future bottoms or low levels. The percentage of the high price tells where to expect low prices in the future and gives you resistance levels where you can buy with a limited risk.

The most important resistance level is 50% of any high or low price. Second in importance is 100% on the lowest selling price on the averages or individual stocks. You must also use 200%, 300%, 400%, 500%, 600% or more, depending upon the price and the Time Periods from High and Low. Third in importance is 25% of the Lowest price or the Highest price. Fourth in importance is 12½% of the extreme Low or extreme High price. Fifth in importance is 6¼% of the Highest price, but this is only to be used when the averages or individual stocks are selling at very high levels.

Sixth in importance is 33 1/3 and 66 2/3%. These percentages should be calculated and watched for resistance next after 25% and after 50%.

You should always have percentage tables made up on the Industrial Averages and on the individual stocks you trade in in order to know where these important resistance levels are located.

1896, August 8, low 28.50 for the 12 Industrial Averages. This was the extreme Low price and the percentage on this price is very important.

1896, Aug. 8, low 28.50	1921, Aug. 24, low 64
50% is 42.75	25% is 80.00
100% is 57.00	50% is 96.00
200% is 85.50	62½% is 104.00
300% is 114.00	75% is 112.00
400% is 142.50	100% is 128.00
450% is 156.75	125% is 144.00
500% is 171.00	137½% is 152.00
550% is 185.50	150% is 160.00
575% is 192.75	162½% is 168.00
600% is 199.50	175% is 176.00
700% is 228.00	187½% is 184.00
800% is 256.50	200% is 192.00
900% is 285.00	212½% is 200.00
1000% is 313.50	225% is 208.00
1100% is 342.00	237½% is 216.00
1200% is 370.50	250% is 224.00
1250% is 384.75	275% is 240.00
	300% is 256.00
	400% is 320.00
	500% is 384.00

1932, July 8, low 40.56 for the 30 Industrial Averages. The percentages are as follows:

1932, July 8, low 40.56	1942, April 28, low 92.69
25% is 50.70	12½% is 104.27
50% is 60.84	25% is 115.86
75% is 70.98	37½% is 127.44
100% is 81.12	50% is 139.00
150% is 101.40	62½% is 150.58
175% is 111.54	75% is 162.16
200% is 121.68	100% is 185.38
225% is 131.82	112½% is 196.96
250% is 141.96	125% is 208.45

PERCENTAGE OF HIGH PRICES

275% is 152.10
300% is 162.24
325% is 172.38
350% is 182.56
375% is 192.66
400% is 202.80
425% is 212.94
1933, July 18, low 84.45
100% is 168.90
1933, Oct. 21, low 82.20
100% is 164.40
1934, July 26, low 84.58
100% is 169.16
1938, March 31, low 97.50
100% is 195.00

1919, Nov. 3, high 119.62
100% is 239.24
200% is 358.86
325% is 388.50
1929, Sept. 3, high 386.10
50% is 193.05
75% is 96.52
87½% is 48.32
1930, April 16, high 296.35
50% is 148.17
75% is 74.08
87½% is 37.04
1933, July 18, high 110.53
25% from this is 82.90

1937, March 8, high 195.50
50% is 97.75
1943, July 15, high 146.50
50% is 73.25
25% on this price is 183.27
50% on this price is 219.75
1946, May 29, last extreme high 213.36
25% off of this price is 160.02

Other percentages for resistance levels of this price can be calculated.

Stocks Selling Below 50 Per Cent Level

It is very important when a stock breaks 50% or one-half between the extreme high and extreme low level. When it does not get support and holds at this level, it is in a very weak position and indicates a decline to 75% down or more between extreme high and extreme low.

Fifty per cent of the highest selling price is of still greater importance. When a stock breaks this level it is in a very weak position because if it is going to get support and advance it will get it when the stock has declined 50% from the highest level. Do not buy stocks after they get below this level until you see an indication of support based on all of the rules.

Market Action Proves the Rules

After we have calculated the percentage on the extreme low prices and on the extreme high prices it is important to calculate the 50% or half-way point between the extreme low and extreme high prices.

Examples:

1896, Low 28.50 to 1919, High 119.62 gives the half-way point at 74.06. 28.50 low to extreme high in 1929 of 386.10 gives 50% or half-way point of 207.28. 1921, Low 64 to 386 high gives the 50% or half-way point of 225.00. 1930, high, 296.25, to the low of 64 gives the 50% or half-way point at 180.12. 28.50 low to 296.25 high gives the 50% or half-way point at 162.37. 1937 high 195.50 to 28.50 low gives the 50% or half-way point at 112. 1937 high 195.50 to 1938 low 97.50 gives the 50% or half-way point at 146.50. 1932 low 40.56 to 1946 high 213.36 gives the half-way point at 126.96. 1942 low 92.69 to 1946 high 213.36 gives the fifty per cent or half-way point at 153.02.

When all of these figures are completed for resistance levels we proceed to prove that they work in calling tops and bottoms. Up to 1919 the extreme high on the Dow-Jones 30 Industrial Averages was 119.62. After 1921 the price was moving up from the low of 64 and we find that 87½% on 64 gives 120.00, making the old top and this resistance level very important. When prices cross the extreme High level we look in the table of percentages above 64 to see the resistance levels indicated for tops. We find that 500% gives 384.00. On September 3, 1929, the Averages made high at 386.10. Looking over the table of percentages from 28.50 low we see that 1250% is 384.75. Next figuring the important percentages on the old high price of 119.62 we find that 225% added to 119.62 gives 388.50 which shows three resistance levels at 384.00, 384.75 and 388.50. The Averages made extreme High at 386.10 but the highest closing price was 381.10. The Three-Day Chart and the 9-Point Swing Chart both showed the market was Top at these important resistance levels.

After the extreme High was reached the next point is to figure where the important resistance level and buying level should be. Rule 3 says that 50% of the highest selling price is the most important. 50% of 386.10 gives 193.00 as a support and buying level. The fastest decline in history followed the high in September, 1929, running to November 13, low 195.35, holding 2½ points above the important support level making this a buying level. Because the market failed to reach the exact 50% point it showed greater strength. We next apply the same rule and add 50% to the low of 195.35 and this gives 293.02 as a possible rally point and selling level.

April 16, 1930, high 297.25, a little over 3 points above the important resistance level, but prices did not go five points above it, based on Rule 2 that it requires five points above a resistance level or 5 points below an Old Bottom or resistance level to indicate a definite change in Trend.

After this top was established and the Trend turned down, based on the 3-Day Chart and the 9-Point Swing Chart, we next figure the 50% or half-way point between the low of 195.35 and the high of 297.25. This gives 246.30. When this point was broken it indicated much lower prices and you will note that the last rally, on September 10, 1930, made high at 247.21, just above this important 50% point. Later when the low of November 13, of 195.35 was broken and the averages broke 193, the 50% point of 386.10 they were in a very weak position and indicated much lower prices. The decline continued subject to normal rallies until July 8, 1932, when extreme Low was reached at 40.56. If we take 87½% from 386.10 we get 48.26. If we look at the table from the extreme Low of 28.50 we find 50% gives 42.75 as resistance level. If we subtract 37½% from the 1921 low of 64.00 we get 40.00 as a support level. Going back to 1897, April 8, the high was 40.37 and on the 3-Day Chart this level was crossed on June 4, 1897, which turned the main trend up and the Averages never sold at that level again until July 8, 1932, when they made bottom at 40.56.

From the extreme Low of 40.56 we calculate where the first resistance level should be met. We add 100% to this low level and it gives 81.12.

On September 8, 1932, the Averages rallied to 81.50, making top exactly on this important 50% point.

1933, February 27, low 49.68. This was the low of the secondary decline. You will notice in the table that 25% on 40.56 gives 50.70 making this a very important support level and the Averages made Bottom just one point below this level. The upward Trend was resumed.

1933, July 18, high 110.53. Why did the Averages make Top at this level? 175% on 40.56 gives 111.54 as an important resistance level and 112.00 is 75% on 64 low, making this an important resistance level and a place to sell as the volume of sales and Time Periods indicated top for a reaction because it was one year from the low in July, 1932.

We apply the same rules to the high of 110.53 and subtract 25% from this high selling price and it gives 82.90 as a support and buying level. The market had one of the fastest declines in history for a period of three days, July 21, low 84.45, holding just above this important support level. A rally followed and if you bought stocks at this time you could have sold them when the Averages rallied back to 107.00.

1933, October 21, last extreme low 82.20, less than 1 point under the support level of 82.90. This extreme Low level was the last time the Averages sold that low until the time of this writing, June 30, 1949. It is important to figure 100% on 82.20 which gives 164.40 as an important resistance level.

1934, July 26, low 84.58. This was the third time around this low level and it indicated a big Bull Market to follow because prices had held above 100% on the low of 40.56. A big Bull Market followed and prices continued to work up until they crossed 110.53, the high of July, 1933. After crossing this high level what price should we figure the Averages to go to? We know that 50% of 386.10 is 193.05. We know that the Old Bottom of November, 1929, was 195.35 and we know that the Averages made top February 24, 1931, at 196.96; therefore, the logical resistance and selling level would be 193-195.

1937, March 8, high 195.50, at the important 50% point and at the Old Tops and Bottoms, the 3-Day Chart and the 9-Point Swing Chart confirmed that this was Final High. We wish to figure the logical point for the next decline. We apply the same rule and subtract 50% from 195.50 which gives 97.75 as a support and buying level.

1938, March 31, the Averages made low at 97.50 and another Bull Market started.

1938, November 10, high 158.75. This was 62½% on the last low. The main Trend turned down from this level and the Averages broke the important 50% point and continued on down, making lower tops and lower bottoms on the important swings and finally breaking back below 110 and breaking 97.50.

1942, April 28, low 92.69. This was less than 5 points under the low of 1938 and was a buying point as this was a Triple Bottom, which was confirmed by the 3-Day Chart and the 9-Point Swing Chart. It was the place to buy stocks for a big Bull Market. From this low level we figured the percentages on 92.69. 50% on this is 139. 12½% the first important resistance level was 104.27.

1942, August 7, last extreme low 104.58. Just above this important support level at 104.27 from 213.33 to 104.27 the 50% point is 158.80.

Next we figure the important resistance levels from which the Averages should react. 50% between 92.69 and 195.50 is 144.09. 50% between 1937 high of 195.50 and 1938 low 97.50 gives 146.50.

1943, July 15, high 146.50, exactly at these important resistance levels where top was indicated for reaction. The Time Period running out in July also called for top and a reaction just the same as it did in July, 1933. The Averages reacted but did not break back far enough to show that the main Trend had turned down. Note that 37½% on 92.69

gives 127.44, which level was never broken. 1943, November 30 last low 128.94. Later when the Averages advanced and crossed 146.50 the old top and important resistance level, they indicated the next top at 158.75 made November 10, 1938. When the Averages crossed this level they again indicated the most important 50% point at 193-195.

After the war ended in August, 1945, the averages had made a last low on July 27th of 159.95; having already crossed the old tops they indicated much higher prices. The advance continued and the averages finally crossed 195.50 indicating higher prices. The first important percentage resistance level was 207.50 which was 50% between 28.50 and 386.10. The averages made top at this level, February 4, 1946, and had a quick reaction to 184.04 on February 26, later crossing 208.00. The next and most important resistance level was the 50% point between the extreme High of 386.10 and the extreme Low of 40.56. This was 213.33 and on May 29, 1946, the Averages made high at 213.36 exactly on this important 50% point. Note also that 425% on 40.56 was 212.94 making this a doubly important resistance level.

From the high of 213.36 we subtract 25% to get the first resistance level and buying point which gives 160.03.

October 30, 1946, extreme low, 160.49, again May 19, 1947, low 161.32, June 14, 1949, low 160.62. This was three times the market made bottom at this important support level and prices were holding above July 27, 1945, when the last low was 159.95.

From these strong support levels the Averages made a higher bottom on February 11, 1948, and advanced to 194.49 on June 14, 1948. This was back to the old 50% selling level where Old Bottoms and Tops had occurred so many times, making this a selling level which was confirmed by the 3-Day Chart and the 9-Point Swing Chart.

Present Position of the Dow-Jones 30 Industrial Averages

They have received support for the third time at 25% down from 213.36 and the last Old Bottom of July 27, 1945, is at 159.95. Should the Averages break these levels and close under them it will indicate 152.00 which is 275% on 40.56 and the next resistance point is 146.50 the Old Top and important 50% point.

1942 low 92.69, 1946 high 213.36, 50% or ½ point is 153.02.

At the time of this writing, July 19th, 1949, the averages have crossed 175 and indicate 177½, a resistance level, because it is 50% of the range between 160.49 and 194.49; therefore, from around 177½ there could be a moderate reaction, and when the averages cross 182½, the high of January 7, 1949, they will indicate much higher prices.

When the averages reach important resistance levels, or advance to old tops or decline to old low levels, you should study the position of the individual stocks you trade in and apply all of the rules given to these individual stocks.

Let the Market Tell Its Own Story

When you start to study the stock market do not have any fixed ideas and do not BUY or SELL on HOPE or FEAR. Learn the three most important factors, TIME, PRICE and VOLUME OF SALES. Study my rules and apply them. Be ready to change quickly when the rules show that the market is making a change in TREND. Let the action of the market tell its own story and trade only on definite indications based on the rules and you will make profits.

CHAPTER V

TIME PERIODS OF SHORT DURATION CORRECT PRICES

You often hear people say the market needs a correction. Prices have advanced too fast or declined too fast. When this happens in an advancing market it becomes overbought, shorts have covered and the technical position of the market is weakened, therefore, a price correction is in order. This may be a sharp, quick decline in a very short period of time. The fact that the price declines very fast scares people, they lose hope and decide the market is going very much lower, when as a matter of fact a *short decline* in a very *short period* of *time* has corrected the technical position from a weak position to a strong one.

The same occurs when the market has been declining for some time and it has built up an over extended short interest and longs have liquidated leaving the market in a weak technical position. Then a sharp advance takes place on short covering in a very short period of time. This causes buyers to become over confident and buy at the top and decide that the movement is going to continue but the technical position has been weakened and the market has been corrected on the short side by this sharp rally. Then the main Trend continues on down.

Apply all of the rules at all times in order to prevent misjudging the Trend of the market or making mistakes. Remember, when you do make a mistake or see that you are wrong, the way to correct it is to get out of the market immediately, or best of all when you make trade, place a Stop Loss Order for the protection of your capital. Keep in mind at all times the greatest TIME PERIOD, or the greatest correction of the market when it is advancing, and when a market is declining keep in mind at all times the greatest TIME PERIOD that had occurred when the market had rallied in a Bear Market. Keeping up with these Time Periods will help you to determine the Trend of the market. That is why I am reviewing these market movements and pointing out the Time Periods which have brought about sharp, quick rallies or sharp, quick declines and ended the market movement for that period of time. The main Trend as outlined before continues. All of the prices referred to are the Dow-Jones 30 Industrial Averages.

The New York Stock Exchange closed on July 30, 1914, due to the outbreak of war and heavy selling. It did not open until December the 12th, 1914, when heavy liquidation carried prices to the Lowest Level of many years.

1914, December 24, low 53.17. From this Low Level the market continued to advance as we were in a war period with large orders and corporations were accumulating large profits. This Bull Market continued for about one year after the end of the World War, November 11, 1918.

1919, November 3. High 119.62 for the Dow-Jones 30 Industrial Averages. This was the highest price in history up to that time, and they had advanced from 53.17, an advance of 66.45 points. Therefore, when a sharp, quick decline occurred after November 3, 1919, especially after the market had been advancing for nearly five years, you would know this was a SIGNAL that the Final Top had been reached and the Trend was turning down. The Trend continued down subject to normal rallies until August 24, 1921, low 63.90; this decline lasted nearly 22 months. From the 1921 low, the main Trend continued up to March 20, 1923, high 105.50, an advance of 19 months. From this Top Level there was a down swing until October 27, 1923 low, 85.50. A decline of 20 points in seven months time. This was a normal, natural decline. Refer to 9 Point Swing Chart which says that the declines and advances run in 20, 30, 40 points and so forth. But 20 points is an average move in the normal market. Therefore, this would be a point to check on all the charts, especially the Three-Day Chart, and watch for Change of Trend. Watch for the first sharp, quick decline that made a correction and indicated the trend would continue up.

1924, February 6, high 101.50.   An advance of 16 points from the last low, and prices had not yet crossed the top of March 20, 1923, which would be a SIGNAL for higher prices.

May 14, low 88.75.   This was higher by more than 3 points above the low of October 27, 1923, indicating a better support and higher prices.   The time for this decline was 69 days.   Refer to Rule 8 TIME PERIODS which says market movements often run from 60 to 72 days.

1925, March 6, high 123.50.   This price crossed the 1919 high by nearly 4 points.   Our rule says that prices have to go five points or more into new High to give a definite indication that the market is going to continue up.   However, this was the first indication that prices were going higher.   But a corrective reaction was in order as the market had been advancing from the last extreme Low of 85.50.

1925, March 30, low 115, down 8½ points, not 10 points which was a normal reaction and indication of strength. Also the fact that the Averages did not go 5 points below the high of 1919 which was 119.62 was another good indication that they were going higher, and that this correction which lasted only 24 days was only a minor reaction in a Bull Market.

1926, February 11, high 162.50, up 47.50 from the last Low of 115.   Time period 355 days and time for a corrective reaction.

1926, March 30, low 135.25.   Down 37.25.   Time 17 days.   This was a rapid decline moving down much faster than one point per calendar day and was the proper correction of a Bull Market and the trend continued up.

1927, October 3, high 199.78, an advance of 60.25 in 186 days.   The fact that the Averages were just below 200, and Rule 3 says that at 100, 200 and 300 and all even figures there is always public selling and some resistance. This indicated there should be a corrective reaction and it did come in a short period of time.

1927, October 22, low 179.78, down 20 points in 119

days. This was a correction and an advance followed. Later prices crossed 200, which was an indication of higher prices as they were in a new High territory.

1928, November 28, high 299.35, up 119.50 points in 403 days, with the price just under the 300 level a resistance and Selling Level, where a corrective reaction should occur, especially after more than one year's time had elapsed from the previous Bottom.

1928, December 10, low 254.50, down 44 points in 12 days. This was one of the sharpest corrective reactions that ever occurred since the Bull Campaign started in August, 1921. In fact, the prices did not go lower after this sharp, quick decline, but started making Higher Bottoms, an indication that it was all over and that prices were going higher.

1929, March 1; high 324.50, up 70 points in 81 days. This price was close to 325, an even figure at which the public always sells, and a corrective reaction was again in order.

1929, March 26, low 281, down 43½ points in 25 days. Note this was almost the same decline that occurred between November 28, 1928, and December 10, 1928. The market received support at these Levels with the same price decline and an advance was resumed.

1929, May 6, high 331, up 50 points in 41 days. The market had now made a new High which was an indication that after a reaction it would go higher.

May 31, low 291, down 41 points in 25 days, the same time period as the previous reaction, but making a Bottom 10 points higher than the previous Bottom, an indication of good support and that the main Trend was up, and that it would continue to be up.

1929, September 3, high 386.10, up 95 points in 95 days. (One of our rules is that a fast advancing market will gain about one point per calendar day.) This proved to be final High for the greatest Bull Market which had gone up on the greatest volume in history with the greatest public buying. In fact, public buying occurred from all over the world and had been greatly overdone, and it was only natural after the market had been advancing from August, 1921, to September, 1929, a period of a little over 8 years, and with prices up from 64 to 386.10, it was time to watch for a SIGNAL of the end. And it came, suddenly and unexpectedly! Here is the place to study the 3-Day Chart and you will see where the first SIGNAL was given on this chart. The public was heavily loaded with stocks, shorts had covered, and when the public started to sell, there were no buyers and a wide open break occurred.

1929, November 13, low 195.50, a decline of 190.60 points in 71 days, the greatest decline in the shortest period of time in history. This was the corrective decline from an over bought market in a short period of time, and a natural rally which always occurs after the first sharp decline was in order. The SECONDARY RALLY always occurs after a prolonged advance and a sharp decline. Then, in a Bear Market, after a sharp decline, there is first a sharp rally and a SECONDARY DECLINE which marks final Bottom and the main Trend turns up.

1929, December 9, high 267, up $71\frac{1}{2}$ points in 27 days. This was a sharp advance from an oversold condition on short covering and a natural, quick reaction was in order.

1929, December 20, low 227, down 40 points in 11 days. This decline was too rapid and the rally was in order.

1930, April 16, high $297\frac{1}{4}$, up 102 points from the low of November 13 in 154 days' time. This was the SECONDARY RALLY in a big Bear Market which always occurs after an advance of this kind. Watch for the first SIGNAL of a sharp decline to indicate the rally was over and go short. Looking at the 3-Day Chart, you will see how it gave the SIGNAL that the advance was over and prices continued toward lower Levels subject to small reactions until 1930, October 22, low 181.50, a decline of $116\frac{1}{4}$ points in 188 days. The fact that prices broke below the low of November 13, 1929, was an indication that the Bear Market was going to continue, and that there would be nothing but sharp, quick rallies when the market became oversold, as it had at this time.

1930, October 28, high 198.50, up 17 points in 16 days. One of our rules that normal rallies will run around 20 points. The fact that this advance failed to reach 20 points in 6 days indicated the market was in a weak position, and would go lower, which it did.

1930, November 10, low 168.50, down 30 points in 13 days. This was a very rapid decline because a liquidation was increasing as prices worked lower. However, from all sharp declines quick rallies lasting only a short period of time must occur.

1930, November 25, high 191.50, up 33 points in 15 days' time. This was a sharp quick rally and prices were moving up too fast. And the fact that prices did not reach the old low of November 13, 1929, which was 195.50, was an indication of weakness and lower prices. Also the fact that they were below the high of October 28, 1930, of 198.50, another indication that the main trend was still down, and this was only a short rally in the Bear Market.

LIQUIDATION AFTER A PROLONGED DECLINE AND A SHARP RALLY IN A BEAR MARKET

1930, December 2, high 187.50. From this lower top the decline started, and it was very severe in this final wave of liquidation as the public had held on and hoped for a Bull Market which did not come.

December 17, low 154.50, down 33 points in 15 days. This was a decline of almost 2 points per calendar day which was much more rapid than a normal decline should be, and near old support levels and above 150, a natural point for support for a rally to follow.

1931, February 24, high 196.75. Note that this was near the old bottom of November 13, 1929, and was under the high of October 28, 1930, making it a natural resistance and selling Level based on our rules that Bottoms become Tops and Tops become Bottoms and when these old Levels are reached, selling or buying takes place. The time period from December 17, 1930, was 69 days. This compares with 71 days, the decline from September 3, 1929, to November

13, again confirming Rule 8 of 67 to 72 day Time Periods. At the Top, February 24, 1931, the price was up $42\frac{1}{4}$ points and below December 17, 1930. This sharp quick rally in the Bear Market soon died out. By reviewing and studying the three-day chart you can see how the indication was given for lower prices again caused by reviewing all of the starting points and main Tops which move started all the way down from 1929. Each Top had been lower and Bottoms were continuing to be lower. Therefore, the main Trend was still down.

1931, June 2, low 119.60. This was down to the old high of 1919. According to the Rules, a rally should always take place as old Bottoms become Tops and old Tops become Bottoms. Therefore, we would expect a rally from this level as the price was down $77\frac{1}{4}$ points from the high of February 24, 1931, in a Time Period of 98 days.

1931, June 27, high 157.50, an advance of 37.90 points in 25 days. This price was up just above the old Bottom of December 17, 1930, but went only 3 points above it, and not 5 according to the rules. Therefore, this would be a selling Level, especially as the advance had been in such a short period of time.

1931, October 5, low $85\frac{1}{2}$, down 72 points in 100 days, almost the same time period as the previous one.

1931, November 9, high 119.50. Back to the low of June 2, 1931, and to the old Top of 1919, making this a selling Level. The time of this rally was 35 days, and the advance was 34 points. Rule 12 states that a fast advance runs about 1 point per calendar day. Therefore, again you should go short on this rally, and by watching the three-day chart you would get a SIGNAL that the Trend was turning down again.

1932, February 10, low 70. The time of this fast decline was 92 days. Price decline $49\frac{1}{2}$ points.

1932, February 19, high $89\frac{1}{2}$, up $19\frac{1}{2}$ points in 9 days. This was four points above the Low of October 5, 1931, and a selling Level. The market slowed down and met resistance near this Level, and the three-day chart indicated that the market had made Top for another decline.

Final Liquidation in Great Bear Market

1932, March 9, high 89½, the same high as of the 19th of February. Time, 18 days from the last high, meeting resistance at this same high of February 19th indicated lower prices unless the Averages could close above these levels, which they did not.

1932, July 8, low 40.56, down 49 points in 121 days. During the period from March 9, 1932, to July 8, 1932, the greatest rally was 7½ and 8 points, not making as much as 10 points, which is the smallest normal rally based on our rules. None of these rallies lasted more than 1, 3, 4, 4 and 7 days. The last 7-day rally from June 9 low, 44½, to June 16 high 51½, was 7 days with a gain of only 7 points.

After the low of July 8, the first rally lasted 8 days, and the price was up 5 points. Then a reaction of three days and the market only declined two points on Averages. Following this there was a rapid advance with only 3 and 5 day reactions until September 8, 1932, high 81.50, up 41 points, time 62 days. This was an advance on percentage of 100 per cent on the Averages. Refer to Rule 8 which states that these SECONDARY DECLINES or advances last 60 to 67 days.

From the last high of April 16, 1930, the greatest time on rallies was 69 days. Most of them were 25, 35 and 45 days, which were the great rallies in a Bear Market.

From November 13, 1929, to April 16, 1930, the time was 154 days, the price advance was 101.25.

1932, September 8, high 81½. A sharp reaction followed. October 10, low 57½, down 24 points in 32 days. This was a corrective reaction and a moderate rally followed.

Secondary Decline After September 8 High

1933, February 27, low 49.50, down 32 points, time 172 days. Compares with the Secondary Time Period of 154 days in April 16, 1930. After this SECONDARY DECLINE,

President Roosevelt was inaugurated for the first time and closed all the banks. After the banks reopened, everything started to advance. Later we went off of the gold standard which was inflationary, and the prices of stocks continued to advance in very large volume indicating up trend and a Bull Market. After these SECONDARY DECLINES, which correct the technical position of the market, the advance which follows is nearly always more rapid and greater than the first advance which started from the Bottom when the main Trend first turned up.

1933, July 18, high 110.50, up 61 points, time 144 days from February 27 low. This was on greatly increased volume and the market became over bought. At this time Dr. E. A. Crawford failed. He was one of the largest speculators in grains and other commodities, and was also heavily long of stocks. The heavy selling in commodities after Dr. Crawford's failure started liquidation in stocks and brought about the most severe decline in a short period of three days' time that had occurred since 1929. This was a sharp corrective reaction in a short period of time.

July 21, low 84.45, down 26.08 points in three days. The price was still above the high level of September 8, 1932, indicating good support and a buying level for a rally after such a sharp severe decline on heavy liquidation.

Secondary Rally

After the stock market makes Top and has the first sharp decline, there is always a SECONDARY RALLY that carries prices up around the extreme high Level, and if this rally is considerably lower than the first extreme Top, it is an indication of greater weakness.

1933, September 18, high 107.68, up 23.23 points in 62 days. This price was 3 points below the high of July 18, and the three-day chart soon showed a reversal and the Trend turned down again.

1933, October 9, high 100½. October 21 low 82.20, a decline of 18¼ points in 12 days. This was a quick, sharp decline in a short period of time, and the decline did not run

20 points which was an indication of good support. This was the lowest Level that the averages sold from 1933 up to 1949. In fact, this was the beginning of another upswing of a Bull Market, and the time period from July 18, 1933, high to October 21 low was 95 days. Refer to Rule 8 which says that advances and declines often run 90 to 98 days.

Sharp, Corrective Declines

1934, April 20, high 107.50. This was below the 1933 and 1934 tops.

1934, May 14, low 89.50, down 18 points, time 24 days. The fact that the market again declined only about the same as it did October 21, 1933, not going down 20 points, was an indication prices were getting support and were going higher.

Final Low

1934, July 11, high 99½.

1934, July 26, low 84½, down 15 points in 15 days. Rule 12 says that a sharp decline often runs about one point per day, and as prices were low below $100.00 per share this was a normal market and a normal decline. The decline had run a little over one year from the high on July 18, 1933, and it was time for a Change in Trend. By studying the three-day chart you can see how it indicated the market had made Bottom and that by crossing three-day Tops the Trend had turned up. In fact, the last important Top was July 11, 99½, and crossing 100 is always an indication for higher prices.

July 26, 1934, was the starting of another big Bull Market, and the fact that the price held two points above the low of October 21, 1933, showed it was a continuation of the Bull Market which started in 1932.

1935, February 18, high 108½, just one point above the Top of April 20, 1934, and the resistance or selling Level.

1935, March 18, low 96, down 12½ points in 28 days. This was a normal reaction running a little over 10 points and indicated support and an advance to follow.

—48—

1936, April 6, high 163.25. This was up a little over one year from the low of March 18, 1935, and was time for a corrective reaction.

1936, April 30, low 141.50, down 21¾ points in 24 days. The market received support here and showed an up trend on the three-day chart. The fact that the decline ran only a little over 20 points indicated that it was a normal reaction in a Bull Market.

1936, August 10, high 170.50, again high enough for a corrective reaction.

August 21, low 160.50, down 10 points in 11 days' time. This was only a normal reaction, and it was time to buy stocks as the main Trend was still up.

Final High in the Bull Market

1937, March 10, high 195.50. This was up to the old Lows made in November, 1929, and just under the old Top Levels. A natural resistance level and selling point for the market to make final high. The Bull Market was started July 8, 1932, and resulted in an advance of 155 points in 56 months' time. The starting of the last leg of the Bull Market was July 26, 1934, to March 10, 1937. This was 31 months and 12 days, and the advance was 110 points. The decline started after March 10 and, based on the ·three-day chart and all of the rules, indications were plain that the market had made final Top, and that the main Trend had turned down. However, we always know that the SECOND-ARY RALLY must come after final Top is reached.

Secondary Rally in Bear Market

1937, June 14, low 163.75, down 32¾ points, time from March 10, 96 days, a normal Time Period based on Rule 8, and time for the SECONDARY RALLY to take place.

August 14, 1937, high 190.50, up 26¾ points in 61 days. Around 60 days is one of the important periods, and it was this same kind of a period that brought the SEC-ONDARY RALLY after the Bull Market ended July 8, 1932. The fact that prices were 5 points below the high of March

10 was an indication of weakness. The main Trend soon turned down.

1937, October 19, low 115.50, down 80 points from the high of March 10, and down 75 points from the high of August 14, and down to below the Old Bottom of 1919, but not 5 points below it. Time for a quick, corrective rally on an oversold condition.

October 29, high 141.50, up 26 points in 10 days' time. The advance died out quickly, and the three-day chart soon showed that the main Trend would continue down.

Final Liquidation in the Bear Market

Always watch the last decline or the last advance which shows the final end of the campaign.

1938, March 15, high 127.50.

March 31, low 97.50, down 30 points in 16 days. This was an average of nearly 2 points per calendar day for this decline and was too fast. This decline from March 10, 1937, had run a little over one year's time and the price decline had been 50 per cent of the highest selling price. A percentage of this kind is always important for a Change in Trend.

1938, July 25, high 146.50. Time from May 27, 65 days, with the price up 40 points, time for a corrective reaction.

1938, September 28, low 127.50, down 19 points in 19 days. This was a normal reaction and following our rules that declines and advances often run around 20 points in a normal market, this would be time to buy again for a further advance in the Bull Market.

End of Short Bull Market

1938, November 10, high 158.75. Time from March 31, 224 days, an advance of $61\frac{1}{4}$ points and time for a sharp, quick decline.

November 28, low 136, down $22\frac{3}{4}$ points. Time 18 days. This indicated by breaking back more than 20 points that the Bull Market was over and that a further decline would follow.

Sharp Decline and Clean Out

1939, March 27, high 143.50.

1939, April 11, low 120, a decline of 23½ points in 15 days. This was a clean out of an overbought position and laid the foundation for a better rally.

From November 10, 1938, to April 11, 1939, time 152 days, down 38¾ points, a normal decline for the prices at which the Averages were selling.

War Move

1939, September 1, low 127½. On this date Hitler invaded Poland, and the war started. People bought stocks right and left and shorts started to cover. People believed that we would have the same kind of a Bull Market we had during the war from 1914 to 1918.

September 13, high 157.75, up 30 points in 12 days. This advance was too rapid, and due to the fact that prices failed to cross the top of November 10, 1938, at 158.75, it was an indication that there was heavy selling around these old Levels, while the market held a narrow trading range for some time giving every indication that it had reached Final Top and was getting ready to go lower.

1940, May 8, high 149. From this level a sharp, severe decline occurred. May 21, low 110.50, down 38½ points in 13 days. The Averages made triple Bottoms around this level on May 21, May 28, and June 10, giving an indication of good support and indicating that this was a sharp drive when Hitler was invading France and making great success.

A rally followed to November 8, 1940, which was two years from the high in 1938.

November 8, 1940, high 138.50. After this rally the market continued to make lower Tops and lower Bottoms until the final Bottom came.

Final Lows—End of Bear Market

1942, April 28, low 92.69. From March 31, 1938, the time was 49 months. The low on March 31, 1938, was 97.50. The low on March 18, 1935, was 96. Therefore, at this time the Averages failed to go five points under the Old Bottom and made this a buying level which was confirmed in a short period of time by the three-day chart.

From the low of April 28, 1942, reactions in price and time were very short showing Up Trend and no 10-point reaction occurred until 1943.

1943, July 15, high 146.50, up in the old selling zone and under a series of bottoms. A reaction was overdue.

August 2, low 133.50, down 13 points in 18 days. This was a natural corrective reaction. The advance from 92.69 to 146.50 was up 53.81 points.

1943, November 30, low 128.50, down 18 points from July 15 high. Time 138 days. This was a normal reaction in a Bull Market, and the main Trend continued up.

1945, March 6, high 162.50. This price had crossed the high of 158.75 made November 10, 1938, and indicated that it was still a Bull Market and prices were going higher, but a sharp, corrective reaction was in order.

1945, March 26, low 151.50, down 11 points in 20 days. Note that the high on April 8, 1940, was 152, from which a big decline followed. Therefore, when prices declined on March 26, 1945, to 151.50 they were down to this old top level and a buying or support level.

1945, May 8, the German War came to an end. This was bullish on stocks, and the market started to advance.

1945, May 31, high 169.50. This was in a new high level for the present move.

July 27, low 159.95, down 9.55 points in 57 days. Failing to react 10 points was an indication of a Bull Market as this is one of our normal reaction points. Prices held above the highs of November 10, 1938, which showed strong up trend.

1945, August 14, the Japanese War came to an end. This was bullish, and an advance followed.

1945, November 8, high 192.75. This was up under Old Selling Levels, Old Bottoms and Old Tops, and a natural reaction was in order.

November 14, low 182.75, down 10 points in 6 days, the same reaction as occurred previously, and a normal reaction indicating that the main Trend was still up.

1945, December 10, high 196.50, up to the Old Tops and Bottoms and Levels where a reaction could occur.

December 20, low 187.50, down 9 points in 10 days, and a normal reaction. Note that the prices had crossed the 1937 high which indicated higher prices, especially as over 7 years' time had elapsed.

1946, February 4, high 207.49. The market at this time was advancing on the largest volume for many months indicating that a sharp, corrective reaction was due.

February 26, low 184.05, a decline of 23.44 points in 22 days. This was the sharpest reaction that had occurred since April 28, 1942, and was the First Warning that the Bull Market was nearing the end.

An advance followed to April 10, high 208.93, which was above the high of February 4 and an indication that prices were going higher. However, this was a temporary Double Top and a reaction followed.

May 6, low 199.26, a decline of 9.67 points in 26 days, a normal reaction and the fact that prices held above the 200 level indicated good support and a further advance to follow.

Final Top—End of Bull Market

1946, May 29, high 213.36. This was the end of the Bull Market which began April 28, 1942. It had lasted exactly 49 months, the same Time Period between the bottom in 1938 and the bottom in 1942. The price was up 120¾ points. The fact that prices advanced only about 6 points over the February 4 high was an indication that the first SIGNAL of the break in February was correct in warning that the Bull Market was coming to an end. The three-day chart after May 29 high soon confirmed that the main Trend had turned down.

June 21, low 198.50, down 13¾ points in 23 days. This was the FIRST SIGNAL that the Bull Market had ended, but a SECONDARY RALLY was in order.

July 1, high 208.50, up around the same level as the high in February, up 10 points in 10 days, a normal reaction in the Bear Market.

1946, July 24, low 195.50, down at the old 1937 tops and the top of December, 1945. A support level for a rally.

August 14, 1946, last high 205¼. A big decline followed, and the Averages broke 184, the low of February 26, showing the main Trend was down. Note also August 14, 1937, was the last high of the SECONDARY RALLY after the main Trend had turned down.

The Bull Market from April, 1942, to May, 1949, was one of the longest in time periods except 1929. Therefore, a sharp, corrective reaction in a short period of time was in order.

1946, October 30, low 160.49, down 53 points from May 29 high, time 154 days. Note that the last low on July 27, 1945, was 159.95 making this a support level and buying point. The decline from May high to October low was 25% of the highest selling price 213.36 and occurring in 154 days, was a correction of an overbought market which had only had normal reactions up to that time.

From the low of October 30, 1946, a rally followed.

1947, February 10, high 184.50, up 24 points in 103 days, and under the bottoms of February, 1946, a period of one year's time, making this important for a Change in Trend as February 5th to 10th always is important for a change.

Secondary Decline

1947, May 5, high 175.50, May 19, low 161.50, 14 points down in 14 days. This is all according to our rule that normal markets decline about one point per calendar day. The fact that this bottom was higher than October 30, 1946, made it a Double Bottom and a buying level, which was confirmed by the three-day chart.

—54—

1947, July 25, high 187.50, up 26 points in 67 days. This is one of our normal rally periods running from 60 to 72 days, and a reaction was in order.

1947, September 9, and September 26, lows 174.50, down 13 points in 46 days. A rally followed.

October 20, high 176.50, up 12 points in 24 days and a lower top than July indicated good selling and the Trend continued down.

1948, February 11, low 164.04, down 23.40 points from July, 1947. This was a higher bottom than October, 1946, and May, 1947, indicating good support and a buying level. Prices held in a narrow trading range for one month and then the Trend turned up, based on the three-day chart.

1948, June 14, high 194.49, up 34 points from February 11, time 126 days and no reaction lasted over 6 days, and no reaction over 4 points, making this an overbought market when a natural reaction was in order. The fact that the price was up to the Old Bottoms and Tops, 1937 highs and 1929 lows, made this a resistance and selling level.

1948, July 12, last high 192.50; July 19, low 179.50, down 13 points in 7 days, and a signal for lower prices.

September 27, low 175.50, down to an old support level indicating a rally as September is always important for a change in Trend.

October 26, high 190.50, up 15 points in 29 days, and a lower top. This was the same price at which stocks turned down on August 14, 1937. It is always important to keep in mind the Time Periods and these old prices. At this time the prices were lower than they were in June and July, 1948, and it was two years from October, 1946, which was important for a change in Trend.

After Election, Sharp, Quick Declines

November 1, high 190; November 30, low 170.50; down 18 points in 29 days, down to a support level for a rally.

1949, January 7 and 24th, high 182.50, up 11 points, time 38 days. Rule 8 says that when prices reach high between January 7 and 24 and then break the low made in the early part of January, the Trend will turn down. The fact that after January 24 prices could not cross the high of January 7, indicated the Top and it was time to sell.

February 25, low 170½ and only one point lower than the low of November 30, 1948, a support level for a rally.

March 30, 179.15, up 8.65 points from February 25 low, up less than 9 points in 33 days. The fact that the market could not advance 9 points was an indication of weakness and lower prices could be expected.

Remember Rule 8 which says that important changes occur around May 5 to 10. May 5 last high, 177.25, which was lower than the high on March 30, and lower than the high on April 18 indicating that the main Trend was still down. The decline continued.

1949, June 14, low 160.62, time from March 30, 76 days, down 18.43 points. This was the third time around this same low level.

1946, October 30, low 160.49. 1947, May 19, low 161.38. 1948, November 30, low 170.50. The last decline from May 5 to June 14 was a decline of 16.63 points in a period of exactly 40 days, and the fact that prices were at these low levels for the third time and exactly one year from June 14, 1948, high indicated a buying point and time for a rally.

The advance followed June 14 Low and up to this writing, July 17, 1949, the Averages have advanced to above 175, the greatest advance to date from any low during 1949.

CHAPTER VI

TIME PERIODS FOR IMPORTANT SWINGS ON THE AVERAGES

When you have a record of the time required for each important swing of the industrial averages and you know the amount of the advance or decline, you are able to tell something about how long a time period the market will run in the future and you can watch for a change in trend at the end of the important time cycle which has repeated the greatest number of times in the past.

Following the price the letter "A" means advance and the number of days follow. Where the letter "D" follows the price, the days following mean the days the market has declined from the last level.

1912	Oct.	8	high	94.25		Aug.	24	63.90 D	49 days
1913	June	11	low	72.11 D	246 days	1922	Oct.	14	103.50 A	52 days
	Sept.	13		83.50 A	94 days		Nov.	14	93.50 D	31 days
	Dec.	15		75.25 D	95 days	1924	Feb.	6	101.50 A	84 days
1914	Mar.	20		83.50 A	95 days		May	14	88.75 D	98 days
	Dec.	24		53.17 D	279 days		May	20	105.50 A	98 days
1915	Apr.	30		71.78 A	127 days		Oct.	14	99.50 D	55 days
	May	14		60½ D	14 days	1925	Jan.	22	123.50 A	100 days
	Dec.	27		99½ A	199 days		Feb.	16	117.50 D	25 days
1916	July	13		86½ D	198 days		Mar.	6	125.50 A	18 days
	Nov.	21		110½	A 30 days		Mar.	30	115.00 D	24 days
	Dec.	21		90½			Apr.	18	121½ A	19 days
1917	Jan.	2		99¼ A	14 days		Apr.	27	119.60 D	9 days
	Feb.	2		87 D	31 days		Nov.	6	159.25 A	192 days
	June	9		99¼ A	127 days		Nov.	24	148.50 D	18 days
	Dec.	19		65.90 D	192 days	1926	Feb.	11	162.50 A	78 days
1918	Oct.	18		89.50 A	304 days		Mar.	3	144.50 D	20 days
1919	Feb.	8		79.15 D	103 days		Mar.	12	153.50 A	9 days
	July	14		112.50 A	156 days		Mar.	30	135.50 D	18 days
	Aug.	20		98.50 D	37 days		Apr.	24	144.50 A	25 days
	Nov.	3		119.62	A 26 days		May	19	137.25 D	25 days
	Nov.	29		103.50			Aug.	24	162.50 A	97 days
1920	Jan.	3		109.50 A	35 days		Oct.	19	145.50 D	56 days
	Feb.	25		89.50 D	53 days		Dec.	18	161.50 A	60 days
	Apr.	8		105.50 A	42 days	1927	Jan.	25	152.50 D	38 days
	May	19		87.50 D	41 days		May	28	172.50 A	123 days
	July	8		94.50 A	50 days		June	27	165.50 D	30 days
	Aug.	10		83.50 D	33 days		Oct.	3	195.50 A	97 days
	Sept.	17		89.75 A	38 days		Oct.	22	179.50 D	19 days
	Dec.	21		65.90 D	96 days	1928	Jan.	3	203.50 A	73 days
1921	May	5		80.05 A	135 days		Jan.	18	191.50 D	15 days
	June	20		64.75 D	46 days		Mar.	20	214.50 A	62 days
	July	6		69.75 A	16 days		Apr.	23	207.00 D	34 days

	May	14	220.50 A	21 days		Dec.	3	55.50 D	21 days
	May	22	211.50 D	8 days	1933	Jan.	11	65.25 A	39 days
1928	June	2	220.50 A	13 days		Feb.	27	49.50 D	47 days
	June	18	202.00 D	16 days		July	18	110.50 A	141 days
	July	5	214.50 A	19 days		July	21	84.50 D	3 days
	July	16	205.00 D	11 days		Sept.	18	107.50 A	59 days
	Oct.	24	260.50 A	100 days		Oct.	21	82.20 D	33 days
	Oct.	31	249 D	7 days	1934	Feb.	5	111.50 A	107 days
	Nov.	28	298.50 A	28 days		Mar.	27	97.50 D	50 days
	Dec.	10	254.36 D	12 days		Apr.	20	107 A	24 days
1929	Feb.	1	325 A	53 days		May	14	89.50 D	24 days
	Feb.	18	293 D	17 days		June	19	101.25 A	36 days
	Mar.	1	325 A	13 days		July	26	84.50 D	37 days
	Mar.	26	281.50 D	25 days		Aug.	25	96.25 A	30 days
	May	6	331 A	41 days		Sept.	17	85.75 D	23 days
	May	31	291 D	24 days	1935	Jan.	7	106.50 A	112 days
	July	8	350.50 A	38 days		Feb.	6	99.75 D	30 days
	July	29	337 D	21 days		Feb.	18	108.50 A	12 days
	Sept.	3	386.10 A	36 days		Mar.	18	96 D	28 days
	Oct.	4	321 D	31 days		Sept.	11	135.50 A	177 days
	Oct.	11	358.50 A	7 days		Oct.	3	126.50 D	22 days
	Oct.	29	210.50 D	18 days		Nov.	20	149.50 A	48 days
	Nov.	8	245 A	10 days		Dec.	16	138.50 D	26 days
	Nov.	13	195.50 D	5 days	1936	Apr.	6	163.25 A	112 days
	Dec.	9	267 A	27 days		Apr.	24	141.50 D	18 days
	Dec.	20	227 D	11 days		Aug.	10	170.50 A	108 days
1930	Feb.	5	274 A	47 days		Aug.	21	160.50 D	11 days
	Feb.	25	259.50 D	20 days		Nov.	18	186.25 A	89 days
	Apr.	16	297.75 A	50 days		Dec.	21	175.25 D	33 days
	May	5	249 D	19 days	1937	Mar.	10	195.50 A	79 days
	June	2	275 A	28 days		Apr.	9	175.50 D	30 days
	June	25	207.50 D	23 days		Apr.	22	184.50 A	13 days
	July	28	243.50 A	33 days		June	14	163.75 D	53 days
	Aug.	9	234.50 D	12 days		Aug.	14	190.50 A	61 days
	Sept.	10	247 A	32 days		Oct.	19	115.50 D	67 days
	Oct.	18	183.50 D	38 days		Oct.	29	140.50 A	10 days
	Oct.	28	298.50 A	10 days		Nov.	23	112.50 D	25 days
	Nov.	10	168.25 D	13 days		Dec.	8	131.25 A	15 days
	Nov.	25	191.50 A	15 days		Dec.	29	117.50 D	21 days
	Dec.	17	154.50 D	22 days	1938	Jan.	15	134.50 A	17 days
1931	Feb.	24	196.75 A	59 days		Feb.	4	117.25 D	20 days
	Apr.	29	142 D	64 days		Feb.	23	133 A	19 days
	May	9	156.00 A	10 days		Mar.	31	97.50 D	36 days
	June	2	119.50 D	24 days	1938	Apr.	18	121.50 A	18 days
	June	27	157.50 A	25 days		May	27	106.50 D	39 days
	Aug.	6	132.50 D	40 days		July	25	146.50 A	59 days
	Aug.	15	146.50 A	9 days		Aug.	12	135.50 D	18 days
	Oct.	5	85.50 D	51 days		Aug.	24	145.50 A	12 days
	Nov.	9	119.50 A	35 days		Sept.	28	127.50 D	35 days
1932	Jan.	5	69.50 D	57 days		Nov.	10	158.75 A	43 days
	Jan.	14	87.50 A	9 days		Nov.	28	145.50 D	18 days
	Feb.	10	70 D	27 days	1939	Jan.	5	155.50 A	38 days
	Feb.	19	89.50 A	9 days		Jan.	26	136.25 D	21 days
	June	2	43.50 D	103 days		Mar.	10	152.50 A	43 days
	June	16	51.50 A	14 days		Apr.	11	120.25 D	31 days
1932	July	8	40.60 D	22 days		June	2	140.50 A	52 days
	Sept.	8	81.50 A	62 days		June	30	128.75 D	28 days
	Oct.	10	57.50 D	32 days		July	25	145.50 A	25 days
	Nov.	12	68.50 A	33 days		Aug.	24	128.50 D	30 days

	Aug. 30	138.25 A	6 days
	Sept. 1	127.50 D	2 days
	Sept. 13	157½ A	12 days
	Sept. 18	147½ D	5 days
	Oct. 26	156 A	38 days
	Nov. 30	144.50 D	35 days
1940	Jan. 3	153.50 A	34 days
	Jan. 15	143.50 D	12 days
	Mar. 28	152 A	73 days
	May 21	110.61 D	54 days
	May 23	117.50 A	2 days
	May 28	110.50 D	5 days
	June 3	116.50 A	6 days
	June 10	110.50 D	7 days
	July 31	127.50 A	51 days
	Aug. 16	120.50 D	16 days
	Sept. 5	134.50 A	20 days
	Sept. 13	127.50 D	8 days
	Sept. 24	135.50 A	11 days
	Oct. 15	129.50 D	19 days
	Nov. 8	138.50 A	24 days
	Dec. 23	127.50 D	45 days
1941	Jan. 10	134.50 A	18 days
	Feb. 19	117.25 D	40 days
	Apr. 4	125.50 A	44 days
	May 1	114.50 D	27 days
	July 22	131.50 A	82 days
	Aug. 15	124.50 D	24 days
	Sept. 18	130.25 A	34 days
	Dec. 24	105.50 D	97 days
1942	Jan. 6	114.50 A	13 days
	Apr. 28	92.69 D	112 days
	June 9	106.50 A	42 days
	June 25	102 D	17 days
1942	July 9	109.50 A	14 days
	Aug. 7	104.40 D	29 days
	Nov. 9	118.50 A	94 days
	Nov. 25	113.50 D	16 days
1943	Apr. 6	137.50 A	132 days
	Apr. 13	129.75 D	7 days
	July 15	146.50 A	93 days
	Aug. 2	133.50 D	18 days
	Sept. 20	142.50 A	49 days
	Nov. 30	128.50 D	71 days
1944	Jan. 11	138.50 A	42 days
	Feb. 7	134.25 D	27 days
	Mar. 16	141.50 A	38 days
	Apr. 25	134.75 D	40 days
	July 10	150.50 A	76 days
	Sept. 7	142.50 D	59 days
	Oct. 6	149.50 A	29 days
	Oct. 27	145.50 D	21 days
	Dec. 16	153 A	50 days
	Dec. 27	147.75 D	11 days

1945	Mar. 6	162.25 A	69 days
	Mar. 26	151.50 D	20 days
	May 31	169.50 A	66 days
	July 27	159.95 D	57 days
	Nov. 8	192.75 A	104 days
	Nov. 14	182.75 D	6 days
	Dec. 10	196.50 A	26 days
	Dec. 20	187.50 D	10 days
1946	Feb. 4	207.50 A	46 days
	Feb. 26	184.04 D	22 days
	Apr. 18	209.50 A	51 days
	May 6	199.50 D	18 days
	May 29	213.36 A	23 days
	June 12	207.50 D	14 days
	June 17	211.50 A	5 days
	June 21	198.50 D	4 days
	July 1	208.50 A	10 days
	July 24	194.50 D	23 days
	Aug. 14	205.25 A	21 days
	Sept. 19	164.50 D	36 days
	Sept. 26	176.50 A	7 days
	Oct. 10	161.50 D	14 days
	Oct. 16	177.25 A	6 days
	Oct. 30	160.62 D	14 days
	Nov. 6	175 A	7 days
	Nov. 22	162.50 D	16 days
1947	Jan. 7	179.50 A	46 days
	Jan. 16	170.25 D	9 days
	Feb. 10	184.50 A	25 days
	Feb. 15	172 D	5 days
	Mar. 28	179.50 A	41 days
	Apr. 15	165.50 D	18 days
1947	May 5	175.50 A	20 days
	May 19	161.50 D	14 days
	July 14	187.50 A	56 days
	Sept. 9	174.50 D	57 days
	Oct. 20	186 A	41 days
	Dec. 6	175.50 D	47 days
1948	Jan. 5	181.50 A	30 days
	Feb. 11	164.04 D	37 days
	June 14	194.49 A	124 days
	July 19	179.50 D	35 days
	July 28	187 A	9 days
	Aug. 11	176.50 D	14 days
	Sept. 7	185.50 A	27 days
	Sept. 27	175.50 D	20 days
	Oct. 26	190.50 A	29 days
	Nov. 30	171.50 D	35 days
1949	Jan. 7	182.50 A	38 days
	Jan. 17	177.50 D	10 days
	Jan. 24	182.50 A	7 days
	Feb. 25	170.50 D	32 days
	Mar. 30	179.15 A	33 days
	Apr. 22	172.50 D	23 days
	May 5	177.25 A	13 days
	June 14	160.69 D	40 days

CHAPTER VII

DOW JONES 30 INDUSTRIAL AVERAGES 3-DAY CHART MOVES

My reason for using the Dow-Jones 30 Industrial Averages as a trend indicator is not because the Dow theory is working perfectly, but that these industrial Averages do indicate the trend of most of the individual stocks. However, the time period on some individual stocks will run out sooner than the Averages on the up side and some will run later. The same in the Bear Market. Some stocks will make low sooner by several months, and some later than the Averages. But the Averages are a good guide to the dates when final highs and lows will be reached, and they are important in getting resistance levels for buying and selling prices. The railroads are slowly becoming obsolete and do not work in harmony with the industrial Averages any more. The public utility averages are in strong position and work more in harmony with the industrial Averages than the rails do. My advice is to keep up the Dow-Jones 30 Industrial Averages and follow the trend of these stocks and then watch individual stocks that conform to the same trend, and trade in them. The percentage between the railroad averages and the 30 Industrial Averages has not been maintained the same during the past few years because industrial stocks in most cases on advances are stronger and advance faster than the rails. Therefore, it is folly to try to watch the rails to confirm with the industrials as based on the Dow theory. But the thing to do is to watch individual stocks that show strong or weak positions and trade in them and use the Industrial Averages as a trend indicator applying all the rules which I have given.

These Averages are not a true average. From 1897 to 1914 they are figured on a basis of 12 stocks. Then in December, 1914, they were changed to 20 stocks and later changed to 30 stocks. Although the Averages work all right and do give a definite indication of the trend, they do not represent the actual value of stocks as they sell today, because these Averages as they are figured have the dividends and split-ups figured in the averages. What I call a true average is the cost of buying 100 shares of the 30 stocks at any time, leaving out all dividends and split-ups. For example, June 14, 1949, the Dow-Jones Averages showed a low of 160.69 based on the present way of figuring. But by taking the 30 stocks and using the extreme low that day, dividing by 30, we get an average of 52.27, which is the correct average and what it would cost to buy these stocks at that time.

After June 14 DuPont was split up and the price changed.

June 28, 1949, figuring the Averages on the low of that day after the split up of DuPont, the Averages were 48.59, against the regular way of figuring the averages showing a low of 164.65.

While the average figure on the basis of the Dow-Jones formula for figuring was 164.65, there was only one stock in the entire list that was selling higher than this level, which was Allied Chemical selling at 167. American Telephone was 139. The next highest price, American Can, was 89.25 and National Steel at 75. All of the other stocks were selling at much lower levels, some of them selling as low as $17.00 and $18.00 per share and several of them around 20. This way of figuring the averages, of course, distorts the picture and makes the price look much higher than it actually is based on the day's prices. However, you can go ahead and use the Dow-Jones Thirty Industrial Averages and get the trend just the same as you could if they were figured on the basis of actual selling price.

Three-Day Moves or More

These figures are to be used with the 3 day chart. They are recorded in 3-day moves or more, except when extreme highs or lows are reached and we wish to catch a turn when the market is very active; in this case we sometimes use 1 and 2-day moves. All of these moves are based on calendar days. The rules to use is, when any 3-day Bottom is broken, it indicates lower prices and when the top, or high levels, of a 3-day level is crossed, it is an indication of higher prices. However, all other rules must be applied and you must always consider the last low, or starting point, from which the market moves up and the last high from which the decline starts, as these major swings are of greater importance. An advancing market continues to make higher bottoms on the main swings. A declining market continues to make lower tops on the main swings, but there are times when the market will remain in a narrow Trading Range without breaking the low of a previous swing and not crossing the high of a previous top. Until the averages or an individual stock breaks out of the trading range, you must not consider that the main trend has changed.

The Time Period is most important. The longer the time which has elapsed when a Top is crossed, or a Bottom is broken, the greater the advance or decline should be.

Always consider the fact of how long a market has been advancing from the extreme low level, or how long it has been declining from an extreme high level. Often at the end of any campaign, prices may move up into new high levels, or decline to slightly lower levels and then not continue on, because the time cycle is running out.

Examples: March 31, 1938, the Dow-Jones 30 Industrial Averages declined to 97½. The last Bottom around this same price level was March 18, 1935, when the Averages sold at 96.

1942, April 28, the Dow-Jones Averages declined to 92.62. This was not quite 5 points below the 1938 lows and was less than 4 points under the 1935 low. Our rules say that prices can decline 5 points below an old Bottom, or advance 5 points above an old Top without changing the main trend.

In April, 1942, stocks had been declining from the extreme high of March 10, 1937, and were down over 5 years, running out a long time cycle. Therefore, when prices broke these old levels, and failed to go 5 points lower, you would buy stocks, figuring that the trend was getting ready to change. Note the moves on the 3-day chart, 1942, April 21, last high 98.02 and April 28, extreme low, 92.69. This was a 7-day decline and less than 6 points decline.

May 11, 1942, the Averages advanced to 99.49; this was above the last top of April 21 on the 3-Day Chart and indicated higher prices. From May 11th, a 3-day decline occurred, making a low of 96.39, or down 3.30 points. The price never sold lower than this level until May 29, 1946, when final high was reached. By studying the 3-Day Chart and the progressive, or higher Bottoms and higher Tops, you will see how this chart continued to indicate higher prices with nothing but normal reactions, both in time periods and in price reactions.

30 Industrial Averages 3-Day Chart Moves

The figures published in this book show all of the 3-day moves on the Averages from 1912 to July 19, 1949. The 3-Day Chart in the back of the book starts November 8, 1940, and shows every 3-day move during that period.

Rule for Keeping Up 3-Day Chart

When a market is advancing and starts up from a low point and makes higher Bottoms and higher Tops for 3 consecutive days, the Chart is moved up to the top of the third day. Should the market then react for 2 days, you would not record this movement on the chart, but when it moved up above the First Top, continue to move the line up to the top of each day until there were 3 days lower Bottoms. Then you would move the line down to the low of the third day and continue to follow it down as long as prices went lower. If 2-day rallies occurred, you would ignore them, except when the market is near extreme high or extreme low prices. In cases of this kind you would record the 2-day moves, especially if the fluctuations were very wide. After a market has been advancing for a considerable time and makes a Double or Triple Top and breaks the last low on the 3-Day Chart, you consider that the minor trends, at least, have turned down. When a market is declining and crosses the last Top on the 3-Day Chart, you would consider that the trend had turned up at least temporarily. You will find it helpful to apply all of the other rules given with the 3-Day Chart indication.

Examples of Three-Day Moves.

Starting from November 8, 1940, high 138.50, the trend turned down on the 3-Day Chart and continued to make lower Tops and lower Bottoms.

1941, April 23, May 1, 16 and 26, lows were reached. On May 26 the second higher Bottom was recorded. This was the time to buy with a Stop Loss Order under the low of May 1. When prices crossed the high of May 21, the trend showed up. July 22 high, 131½. The Averages broke under the 3-Day Bottoms, and on August 15 made a low of 124½. The market rallied to September 18, reaching high at 130¼, a lower Top than July 22 and a Selling Level. The trend continued down, and the lows of August 15 were broken indicating that the main trend was down. The decline continued with only one 3-Day Top being crossed on January 6, 1942. This was only 2 points above the high of December 16, 1941, and January 6 is around one of the dates that we always expect the trends to change. The trend continued down to April 28, 1942, extreme low, 92.69, down 38.31 points from July 22, 1941, and the 3-Day Chart would have kept you short all the time.

From April 28 lows, the Averages started making higher Bottoms and higher Tops. It was the time to buy anyway against the old Bottoms of 1935 and 1938.

June, 1942, the Averages crossed the high of 102½ made on April 7. This definitely showed up trend. The advance continued making higher Bottoms and higher Tops until July 15, 1943, high 146½. This was a Selling Level as shown by the rules. The 3-Day Chart turned down and prices declined to November 30, making low at 128.94. Note that on March 10 and 22 lows were around 128½, making 129 a Buying Level against Old Bottoms on the 3-Day Chart. The trend turned up after November 30, and each Swing Bottom was higher until February 4, 1946, high 207½, a

Selling Level. A sharp, quick decline followed to February 26, low 184.04. Note last low levels around 183 on October 30 and November 14, 1945, making 184 a Buying Level against Old Bottoms. From February the trend moved on up again to May 29, 1946, FINAL HIGH 213¼. This was a Selling Level on many of our rules. June 12, low 207½ at the top of February 4 and a Rally Point. June 17, high 208½, same level as February 4, a Selling Level. The decline started and the Averages broke the low of June 12, showing main trend down. There was no 3-Day Top crossed until FINAL LOW October 30, 1946, at 160.69, a Buying Level against the low of July 27, 1945, and also based on other rules explained under Time Periods and Percentage Points.

From October 30 low, no lows were broken on the 3-Day Chart by 3 points until February 10, 1947, high 184½. This was under the Old Bottoms of February 26, 1946, and a Selling Level. The main trend turned down again, and each Swing Top was lower until May 19, 1947, low 161½, a Buying Level against the old Bottoms of October 30, 1946. A rapid advance followed. July 14, high 187½, July 18, low 182, July 25, high 187½, a Double Top and Selling Level. The Averages broke the low of July 18 and continued down to September 9 and 26, making low at 174½, the same low as June 25, a Double Bottom and Buying Level.

October 20, high 186½, a lower Top than July 14 and 25 and a Selling Level. The trend turned down, prices making Lower Tops and Lower Bottoms on the 3-Day Chart until February 11, 1948, when low was reached at 164.07. Another Bottom was made on February 20 and March 17, making this a Double Bottom and Buying Level. When prices crossed the Top of March 3, the trend was definitely up, making this a SAFE BUYING LEVEL. The advance was rapid, and no 3-Day Bottom was broken until June 14, 1948, high 194.49 at the 50 per cent point of 386 and at Old Bottom and Top Levels, making this a place to sell out long stocks and go short. The trend turned down.

August 11 and 21 and September 27 lows were made at 176½ to 175½. Double and Triple Bottoms and a Buying Level. A quick rally followed until October 26, high 190.50. There was a reaction to October 29, and a rally to November 1. The lows of October 29 were broken showing down trend, and a fast decline followed after the election.

November 30, low 170½, a Support and Buying Level against Old Bottoms. A rally followed.

1949, January 7, high 182½, and after a reaction there was another rally to January 24, making this a Double Top and Selling Level, and based on our other rules when the Averages could not cross the Tops of January 7 by the 24th, they indicated lower.

February 25, low 170½, a Double Bottom against November 30 lows and a Buying Level. March 30, high 179.15. The fact that the Averages failed to rally 9 points was an indication of weakness based on the 9-Point Chart. The trend turned down after March 30, and Bottoms and Tops were lower on the 3-Day Chart until June 14, low 160.62. This was a Triple Bottom against October 30, 1946, May 19, 1947, and a Buying Point protected with Stop Loss Order. A rally followed to July 19, with the Averages up above 174 and no 3-Day Reaction has occurred. In fact, only 1-day Reactions have taken place. This indicates strength, but there will come a time when the Averages will react 3 days or more. After that when they cross the top of the First Reaction, it will be a definite indication that the main trend has turned up, and prices should go higher.

RECORD OF 3-DAY MOVES ON AVERAGES 1912 TO 1949

(See analysis of 3-Day Moves November 8, 1940 and Chart in Back of Book.)

1912	Sept. 30.... 94.15	1914	Feb. 25.... 81.31	1916	Mar. 25.... 93.23
	Oct. 4.... 93.70		28.... 82.26		Apr. 6.... 94.46
	8.... 94.12		Mar. 6.... 81.12		22.... 84.96

1912 Oct. 14.... 92.40	Mar. 20.... 83.43	May 1.... 90.30
16.... 93.70	30.... 81.64	May 4.... 87.71
Nov. 4.... 90.29	Apr. 2.... 82.47	15.... 92.43
7.... 91.67	25.... 76.97	17.... 91.51
11.... 89.58	May 1.... 80.11	25.... 92.62
14.... 90.40	8.... 79.16	June 2.... 91.22
18.... 89.97	19.... 81.66	12.... 93.61
21.... 91.40	22.... 80.85	26.... 87.68
Dec. 11.... 85.25	June 10.... 81.84	July 5.... 90.53
1913 Jan. 9.... 88.57	25.... 79.30	13.... 86.42
14.... 84.96	July 8.... 81.79	22.... 89.75
18.... 85.75	30.... 71.42	27.... 88.00
20.... 81.55	Dec. 12.... 54.72	Aug. 1.... 89.05
30.... 83.80	14.... 56.76	8.... 88.15
Feb. 18.... 79.82	24.... 53.17	22.... 93.83
20.... 80.20	1915 Jan. 23.... 58.52	Sept. 1.... 91.19
25.... 78.72	Feb. 1.... 55.59	Nov. 9....107.68
Mar. 5.... 81.69	11.... 57.83	13....105.63
20.... 78.25	24.... 54.22	21....110.15
Apr. 4.... 83.19	Mar. 8.... 56.98	23....107.48
19.... 81.00	13.... 56.35	25....109.95
22.... 81.46	Apr. 30.... 71.78	29....105.97
29.... 78.39	May 10.... 62.06	Dec. 6....106.76
May 5.... 79.95	12.... 64.46	21.... 90.16
15.... 78.51	14.... 60.38	1917 Jan. 2.... 99.18
24.... 79.88	22.... 65.50	13.... 95.13
June 11.... 72.11	26.... 64.42	20.... 97.97
18.... 75.85	June 22.... 71.90	23.... 96.26
21.... 74.03	July 9.... 67.88	26.... 97.36
July 28.... 79.06	Aug. 18.... 81.86	Feb. 2.... 87.01
Aug. 1.... 78.21	21.... 76.76	6.... 92.81
13.... 80.93	28.... 81.95	9.... 90.20
15.... 79.50	Sept. 3.... 80.70	13.... 92.37
29.... 81.81	Oct. 2.... 91.98	15.... 91.65
Sept. 4.... 80.27	6.... 88.23	20.... 94.91
13.... 83.43	22.... 96.46	Mar. 1.... 91.10
17.... 82.38	28.... 93.34	20.... 98.20
22.... 83.01	Nov. 4.... 96.06	Apr. 10.... 91.20
30.... 80.37	9.... 91.08	14.... 93.76
Oct. 2.... 81.43	16.... 96.33	24.... 90.66
16.... 77.09	20.... 95.02	May 1.... 93.42
21.... 79.60	29.... 97.56	9.... 89.08
23.... 78.40	Dec. 2.... 94.78	June 9.... 99.08
27.... 79.38	8.... 98.45	20.... 94.78
Nov. 10.... 75.94	13.... 95.96	25.... 97.57
18.... 77.25	27.... 99.21	July 19.... 90.48
Dec. 1.... 75.77	1916 Jan. 11.... 94.07	21.... 92.61
4.... 77.01	17.... 96.63	25.... 91.24
15.... 75.27	20.... 93.60	Aug. 6.... 93.85
26.... 78.85	25.... 94.24	Sept. 4.... 81.20
30.... 78.26	31.... 90.58	10.... 83.88
1914 Jan. 26.... 82.88	Feb. 11.... 96.15	17.... 81.55
29.... 81.72	17.... 94.11	25.... 86.02
Feb. 2.... 83.19	19.... 94.77	Oct. 15.... 75.13
11.... 82.50	Mar. 2.... 90.52	20.... 79.80
14.... 83.09	16.... 96.08	Nov. 8.... 68.58

1917 Nov. 12.... 70.65	21....107.24	Dec. 4.... 77.63
15.... 69.10	26....111.10	21.... 66.75
26.... 74.03	Aug. 7....100.80	1921 Jan. 11.... 76.14
Dec. 19.... 65.95	12....105.10	13.... 74.43
1918 Jan. 2.... 76.68	20.... 98.46	19.... 76.76
8.... 74.63	Sept. 3....108.55	21.... 74.65
10.... 76.33	8....106.51	29.... 76.34
15.... 73.38	16....108.81	Feb. 3.... 74.34
31.... 79.80	20....104.99	16.... 77.14
Feb. 7.... 77.78	30....111.42	24.... 74.66
19.... 82.08	Oct. 3....108.90	Mar. 5.... 75.25
25.... 79.17	Nov. 3....119.62	11....'72.25
27.... 80.50	12....107.15	23.... 77.78
Mar. 2.... 78.98	13....110.69	Apr. 4.... 75.16
11.... 79.78	19....106.15	6.... 76.58
23.... 76.24	25....109.02	8.... 75.61
Apr. 6.... 77.95	29....103.60	May 5.... 80.03
11.... 75.58	Dec. 4....107.97	June 20.... 64.90
20.... 79.73	12....103.73	July 6.... 69.86
30.... 77.51	17....107.26	15.... 67.25
May 15.... 84.04	22....103.55	25.... 69.80
June 1.... 77.93	1920 Jan. 3....109.88	Aug. 16.... 65.27
26.... 83.02	16....101.94	24.... 63.90
July 1.... 81.81	20....103.48	Sept. 10.... 71.92
6.... 83.20	23....101.90	20.... 69.43
15.... 80.58	30....104.21	Oct. 1.... 71.68
18.... 82.92	Feb. 11.... 90.66	6.... 70.42
23.... 80.51	21.... 95.63	11.... 71.06
26.... 81.51	25.... 89.98	17.... 69.46
Aug. 1.... 80.71	Mar. 22....104.17	Nov. 16.... 77.13
10.... 82.04	24....100.33	22.... 76.21
17.... 81.51	Apr. 8....105.65	Dec. 15.... 81.50
Sept. 3.... 83.84	23.... 95.46	22.... 78.76
13.... 80.29	26.... 97.20	31.... 81.10
Oct. 4.... 85.31	29.... 93.16	1922 Jan. 5.... 78.68
9.... 83.36	May 8.... 94.75	20.... 82.95
18.... 89.07	19.... 87.36	31.... 81.30
30.... 84.08	June 12.... 93.20	Feb. 6.... 83.70
Nov. 9.... 88.06	30.... 90.76	8.... 82.74
25.... 79.87	July 8.... 94.51	21.... 85.81
Dec. 10.... 84.50	16.... 89.95	27.... 84.58
26.... 80.44	22.... 90.74	Mar. 18.... 88.47
1919 Jan. 3.... 83.35	Aug. 10.... 83.20	27.... 86.60
11.... 81.66	13.... 85.89	Apr. 22.... 93.46
15.... 82.40	17.... 83.90	27.... 91.10
21.... 79.88	24.... 87.29	May 3.... 93.81
24.... 81.75	31.... 86.16	11.... 91.50
Feb. 8.... 79.15	Sept. 9.... 88.33	29.... 96.41
Mar. 21.... 89.05	13.... 86.96	June 12.... 90.73
26.... 86.83	17.... 89.95	20.... 93.51
Apr. 9.... 91.01	30.... 82.95	29.... 92.06
12.... 89.61	Oct. 6.... 85.60	July 20.... 96.76
May 14....100.37	11.... 84.00	24.... 94.64
19.... 99.16	25.... 85.73	Aug. 22....100.75
June 5....107.55	Oct. 28.... 84.61	28.... 99.21
16.... 99.56	Nov. 1.... 85.48	Sept. 11....102.05
21....106.45	19.... 73.12	21.... 98.37
24....104.58	23.... 77.20	23.... 99.10
July 14....112.23	27.... 75.46	30.... 96.30

1922	Oct.	14	103.43
		31	96.11
	Nov.	8	99.53
		14	93.61
		20	95.82
		27	92.03
1923	Jan.	3	99.42
		9	97.23
		13	99.09
		16	96.96
	Feb.	21	103.59
		26	102.40
	Mar.	7	105.23
		10	103.82
		20	105.38
	Apr.	4	101.40
		7	102.56
		11	101.08
		19	102.58
		23	100.73
		26	101.37
	May	7	95.41
		9	98.19
		21	92.77
		29	97.66
	June	1	95.36
		6	97.24
		20	90.81
		23	93.30
		30	87.85
	July	7	89.41
		12	87.64
		20	91.72
		31	86.91
	Aug.	18	92.32
		25	91.59
		29	93.70
	Sept.	4	92.25
		11	93.61
		25	87.94
	Oct.	3	90.45
		16	86.91
		20	87.83
		27	85.76
	Nov.	10	91.39
		17	89.65
		26	92.88
		30	92.34
	Dec.	17	95.26
		22	93.63
1924	Jan.	11	97.46
		14	95.68
	Feb.	6	101.31
		18	96.33
	Mar.	14	98.86
		29	92.28
	Apr.	4	94.69
		14	89.91
		17	91.34

		21	89.18
	May	7	92.47
		14	88.77
		24	90.66
		29	89.90
	June	3	91.23
		7	89.52
		16	93.80
		23	92.65
	July	12	97.60
		17	96.85
	Aug.	4	103.28
		12	101.58
		20	105.57
		28	102.67
		30	105.16
	Sept.	6	100.76
		24	104.68
		29	102.96
	Oct.	1	104.08
		14	99.18
	Nov.	18	110.73
		22	109.55
1925	Jan.	13	123.56
		16	121.71
		22	123.60
		26	121.90
		31	123.22
	Feb.	3	120.08
		9	122.37
		16	117.96
	Mar.	6	125.68
		10	122.62
		12	124.60
		18	118.25
		20	120.91
		30	115.00
	Apr.	18	122.02
		27	119.46
	May	7	125.16
		13	124.21
	June	2	130.42
		10	126.75
		17	129.80
		23	127.17
	July	8	133.07
		11	131.43
		27	136.50
		31	133.81
	Aug.	25	143.18
	Sept.	2	137.22
		19	147.73
		30	143.46
	Nov.	6	159.39
		10	151.60
		13	157.76
		24	148.18
	Dec.	5	154.63
		9	152.57

		14	154.70
		21	152.35
		24	157.01
		30	155.81
1926	Jan.	9	159.10
		19	153.81
	Feb.	4	160.53
		8	159.10
		11	162.31
		15	158.30
		18	161.09
	Mar.	3	144.44
		10	153.13
		30	135.20
	Apr.	6	142.43
		16	136.27
		24	144.83
	May	3	140.53
		6	142.13
		19	137.16
	June	21	154.03
		26	150.68
	July	17	158.81
		24	154.59
	Aug.	14	166.64
		25	160.41
	Sept.	7	166.10
		20	156.26
		25	159.27
		29	157.71
	Oct.	1	159.69
		11	149.35
		14	152.10
		19	145.66
		27	151.87
		30	150.38
	Nov.	16	156.53
		19	152.86
	Dec.	18	161.86
1927	Jan.	3	155.16
		10	156.56
		17	153.91
		21	155.51
		25	152.73
	Feb.	1	156.26
		7	154.31
		28	161.96
	Mar.	7	158.62
		17	161.78
		22	158.41
	Apr.	22	167.36
		28	163.53
	May	21	172.06
		24	171.06
		28	172.56
	June	3	169.65
		6	171.13
		14	167.63
		16	170.15

1927	June	27	165.73
	Aug.	2	185.55
		12	177.13
	Sept.	7	197.75
		12	194.00
		15	198.97
		28	194.11
	Oct.	3	199.78
		10	189.03
		13	190.45
		22	179.78
		25	185.31
		29	180.32
	Nov.	23	197.10
		28	194.80
	Dec.	3	197.34
		8	193.58
		20	200.93
		28	198.60
1928	Jan.	3	203.35
		10	197.52
		13	199.51
		18	194.50
		24	201.01
	Feb.	3	196.30
		9	199.35
		20	191.33
	Mar.	30	214.45
	Apr.	10	209.23
		13	216.93
		23	207.94
	May	14	220.88
		22	211.73
	June	2	220.96
		12	202.65
		14	210.76
		18	201.96
	July	5	214.43
		11	206.43
		14	207.77
		16	205.10
	Aug.	7	218.06
		14	214.08
		31	240.41
	Sept.	10	238.82
		12	241.48
		27	236.86
	Oct.	1	242.46
		3	233.60
		5	243.08
		9	236.79
		19	259.19
		22	250.08
		24	260.39
		31	248.76
	Nov.	28	299.35
	Dec.	3	283.89
		4	295.61
		10	254.36

		31	301.61
1929	Jan.	3	311.46
		8	292.89
		25	319.36
		30	308.47
	Feb.	1	324.16
		8	298.03
		13	316.06
		18	293.40
	Mar.	1	324.40
		6	302.93
		15	322.75
		26	281.51
	Apr.	5	307.97
		10	295.71
		23	320.10
		26	311.00
	May	6	331.01
		13	313.56
		17	325.64
		31	290.02
	June	7	312.00
		11	301.22
	July	8	350.09
		11	340.12
		12	350.26
		16	339.98
		19	349.19
		22	339.32
		24	350.30
		29	336.36
	Aug.	5	358.66
		9	336.13
	Sept.	3	386.10
		13	359.70
		19	375.20
	Oct.	4	320.45
		11	358.77
		21	314.55
		23	329.94
		24	272.32
	Oct.	25	306.02
		29	212.33
		31	281.54
	Nov.	7	217.84
		8	245.28
		13	195.35
		22	250.75
		27	233.59
	Dec.	9	267.56
		13	239.58
		14	254.41
		20	227.20
		27	246.35
		30	235.95
1930	Jan.	2	252.29
		7	243.80
		16	253.49
		18	243.37

	Feb.	5	274.01
		10	266.37
		13	275.00
		25	259.78
	Mar.	10	279.40
		17	268.94
	Apr.	11	296.35
		15	189.34
		16	297.25
		29	272.24
		30	283.51
	May	5	249.82
		14	277.22
		20	260.76
	June	2	276.86
		12	241.00
		13	251.63
		18	212.27
		20	232.69
		25	207.74
	July	1	229.53
		8	214.64
		18	242.01
		21	228.71
		28	243.65
		31	229.09
	Aug.	5	240.95
		9	218.82
	Sept.	2	242.77
		4	234.35
		10	247.21
		30	201.95
	Oct.	3	216.89
		10	186.70
		15	201.64
		18	183.65
		21	193.95
		22	181.53
		28	198.59
	Nov.	10	168.32
		15	187.59
		18	177.63
		25	191.28
		28	178.88
	Dec.	2	187.96
		17	154.45
		20	170.91
		29	158.41
1931	Jan.	8	175.62
		19	160.09
		23	172.97
		29	164.81
	Feb.	11	185.89
		14	178.20
		24	196.96
	Mar.	6	178.46
		10	188.10
		13	175.89
		20	189.31

1931	Apr.	2....168.30		19.... 43.53			31.... 86.50
		6....174.69	Aug.	8.... 71.49		Nov.	21....101.94
		17....158.50		13.... 60.89			28.... 95.31
		20....164.42		17.... 70.50		Dec.	11....103.97
		29....141.78		20.... 65.99			20.... 93.70
	May	1....153.82	Sept.	8.... 81.39	1934	Jan.	2....101.94
		6....145.65		15.... 64.27			8.... 96.26
		9....156.17		22.... 76.01		Feb.	5....111.93
	June	2....119.89	Oct.	10.... 57.67			10....103.08
		27....157.93		20.... 66.13			16....109.96
	July	1....147.44		26..:. 59.03		Mar.	1....101.93
		3....156.74		29.... 63.67			3....106.37
		15....134.39	Nov.	3.... 57.21			8....100.78
		21....147.69		12.... 68.87			13....104.89
		25....137.69		17.... 62.18			21.... 98.45
		28....142.12		21.... 64.68			26....102.67
		31....133.70	Dec.	3.... 55.04			27.... 97.41
	Aug.	3....139.35		15.... 62.89		Apr.	20....107.00
		6....132.55		23.... 56.07		May	14.... 89.10
		15....146.51		30.... 60.84			18.... 96.57
		24....135.62	1933	Jan. 3.... 58.87			23.... 92.23
		29....142.58		11.... 65.28			28.... 96.33
	Sept.	21....104.79		18.... 60.07		June	2.... 90.85
		23....117.75		26.... 62.69			19....101.11
	Oct.	5.... 85.51	Feb.	6.... 56.65		July	3.... 94.25
		9....108.96		9.... 60.85			11.... 99.35
		14.... 96.01		27.... 49.68			26.... 84.58
		21....109.69	Mar.	16.... 64.56		Aug.	2.... 91.12
		29.... 98.19		31.... 54.90			6.... 86.32
	Nov.	9....119.15	Apr.	20.... 75.20			13.... 92.56
	Dec.	4.... 85.75		21.... 68.64			20.... 90.08
		7.... 92.60		24.... 74.84			25.... 96.00
		17.... 71.79		28.... 69.78		Sept.	17.... 85.72
		19.... 83.09	May	11.... 83.61			27.... 94.02
		28.... 72.41		15.... 79.06		Oct.	4.... 89.84
		31.... 79.92		18.... 84.13			17.... 96.36
1932	Jan.	5.... 69.85		22.... 78.61			26.... 92.20
		14.... 87.78	June	13.... 97.92		Nov.	26....103.51
		23.... 77.09		17.... 89.10			30....101.94
		26.... 80.79		20.... 98.34		Dec.	6....104.23
		29.... 74.19		23.... 91.69			20.... 98.93
	Feb.	2.... 80.74	July	7....107.51	1935	Jan.	7....106.71
		10.... 70.64		12....101.87			15.... 99.54
		19.... 89.84		18....110.53			21....103.93
		24.... 79.57		21.... 84.45			29....100.24
	Mar.	9.... 89.87		27.... 97.28		Feb.	2....102.56
	Apr.	8.... 61.98		31.... 87.75			6.... 99.95
		9.... 66.81	Aug.	10....100.14			18....108.29
	May	4.... 52.33		16.... 92.95			27....101.27
		7.... 60.01		25....105.60		Mar.	2....103.67
		16.... 50.21	Sept.	6.... 97.74			18.... 95.95
		20.... 55.50		18....107.68			22....100.88
	June	2.... 43.49		22.... 95.73			26.... 98.61
		6.... 51.21		26....100.23		Apr.	25....111.52
		9.... 44.45	Oct.	3.... 91.93		May	2....107.82
		16.... 51.43		9....100.58			16....117.30
	July	8.... 40.56		21.... 82.20			18....114.13
		16.... 45.98		25.... 95.23			28....117.62

1935 June 1....108.64
24....121.30
27....116.91
July 9...123.34
16....121.00
31....127.04
Aug. 2....124.28
14....128.94
20....124.97
27....129.97
Sept. 4....126.43
11....135.05
20....127.97
Oct. 1....133.19
3....126.95
28....142.08
31....138.40
Nov. 8....145.40
13....141.60
20....149.42
Dec. 2....140.38
9....145.07
16....138.91
1936 Jan. 10....148.02
21....142.77
Feb. 19...155.69
26....149.08
Mar. 6....159.87
13....149.65
26....159.53
28....154.66
Apr. 6....163.07
30....141.53
May 15....152.43
19....147.21
June 1....154.02
5....148.52
24....161.15
July 1....156.82
3....159.13
8....154.85
28....168.23
Aug. 3....164.61
10....170.15
21....160.52
28....168.02
Sept. 1....165.24
8....170.02
17....164.82
23....170.72
25....165.91
Oct. 19....178.44
26....172.16
Nov. 18....186.39
23....177.91
30....184.01
Dec. 2....179.66
15....183.30
21....175.31

31....181.77
1937 Jan. 4....176.96
22....187.80
27....182.15
Feb. 11....191.39
24....185.15
Mar. 10....195.59
22....179.28
31....187.99
Apr. 9....175.86
13....183.43
16....179.70
22....184.33
28....168.77
May 5....176.81
18....166.20
24....176.25
June 1....170.72
5....175.66
14....163.73
25....170.98
29....166.11
Aug. 14....190.38
28....175.33
31....179.10
Sept. 13....154.94
15....165.16
24....146.22
30....157.12
Oct. 6....141.63
7....150.47
19....115.84
21....137.82
25....124.56
29....141.22
Nov. 8....121.60
12....135.70
23....112.54
Dec. 8....131.15
14....121.85
21....130.76
29....117.71
1938 Jan. 15....134.95
28....118.94
Feb. 2....125.00
4....117.13
23....132.86
28....128.63
Mar. 1....131.03
12....121.77
15....127.44
31....97.46
Apr. 18....121.54
20....112.47
23....119.21
May 1....109.40
10....120.28
27....106.44
June 10....116.08

14....111.54
July 7....140.05
12....133.84
25....146.31
28....139.51
Aug. 6....146.28
12....135.38
24....145.30
29....136.64
Sept. 7....143.42
14....130.38
21....140.20
28....127.85
Oct. 24....155.38
29....150.48
Nov. 10....158.90
28....145.21
Dec. 1....150.20
5....146.44
15....153.16
21....149.06
1939 Jan. 5....155.47
13....146.03
19....149.88
26....136.10
Feb. 6....146.43
10....142.70
16....146.12
21....142.05
Mar. 10....152.71
22....138.42
27....143.14
Apr. 11....120.04
15....130.19
18....124.81
28....131.42
May 1....127.53
10....134.66
17....128.35
June 9....140.75
16....133.79
21....138.04
30....128.97
July 25....145.72
Aug. 11....136.38
15....142.35
24....128.60
30....138.07
Sept. 1....127.51
13....157.77
18....147.35
20....154.96
Oct. 4....148.73
18....155.28
20....152.55
26....155.95
Nov. 10....147.74
20....152.58
30....144.85

1939 Dec. 7....149.57	23....115.33	24....105.84
12....146.43	29....117.48	27....106.97
15....150.11	May 1....114.78	Aug. 7....104.50
19....148.35	13....117.93	19....107.88
27....147.66	16....115.36	26....105.37
1940 Jan. 3....153.29	21....118.45	Sept. 8....:107.88
15....143.06	26....115.33	11....105.58
25....147.29	June 23....125.14	Oct. 13....115.80
Feb. 5....144.69	July 1....122.54	16....112.71
9....150.04	9....128.77	21....116.01
26....145.81	17....126.75	28....112.57
Mar. 12....149.45	22....131.10	Nov. 9....118.18
18....145.08	25....127.74	18....114.12
Apr. 8....152.09	28....130.37	21....115.65
19....145.86	Aug. 15....124.66	25....113.55
24....149.45	Sept. 2....128.62	Dec. 18....119.76
May 3....146.42	11....126.31	22....118.09
8....148.70	18....130.00	28....119.96
21....110.61	25....125.33	29....117.30
23....117.84	Sept. 30....127.31	1943 Jan. 4....120.82
28....110.51	Oct. 17....117.88	7....118.84
June 3....116.44	24....121.69	Feb. 2....126.38
10....110.41	31....117.40	4....124.69
18....125.31	Nov. 5....120.34	15....129.15
26....118.67	13....114.91	19....125.82
28....124.42	24....118.19	Mar. 4....131.20
July 3....120.14	Dec. 1....113.06	10....128.49
17....123.91	4....117.54	12....131.39
25....121.19	10....106.87	22....128.67
31....127.18	16....112.30	Apr. 6....137.45
Aug. 7....124.61	24....105.52	13....129.79
12....127.55	1942 Jan. 6....114.96	May 10....139.30
16....120.90	12....110.10	14....136.13
22....126.97	14....113.29	20....140.09
27....124.95	22....108.30	25....138.06
Sept. 5....134.54	27....111.20	June 5....143.19
13....127.22	Feb. 11....106.00	15....138.51
24....135.48	16....107.96	July 15....146.41
27....131.38	20....104.78	Aug. 2....133.87
Oct. 3....135.86	Mar. 3....107.16	19....138.83
15....129.47	12....98.32	23....134.40
23....132.79	18....102.73	Sept. 10....138.26
28....130.96	31....99.25	14....137.24
Nov. 8....138.77	Apr. 7....102.75	20....142.50
28....129.13	17....95.80	Oct. 7....136.01
Dec. 2....131.96	21....98.02	20....139.21
5....129.54	28....92.69	25....137.88
13....133.00	May 11....99.49	28....139.74
23....127.83	14....96.39	Nov. 9....130.84
1941 Jan. 10....134.27	21....100.21	12....133.07
Feb. 4....122.29	25....98.68	17....129.86
10....125.13	June 9....106.34	20....133.15
19....117.43	12....103.27	30..:..128.94
26....122.90	18....106.63	1944 Jan. 11..:..138.89
Mar. 5....119.98	25....101.94	13....136.99
19....124.35	July 9....109.26	17....138.60
24....121.82	14....107.40	28....136.65
Apr. 4....125.28	16....109.21	Feb. 1....137.69

1944	Feb.	7....134.10		Feb.	4....207.49			30....179.77
		17....136.77			13....197.65		Aug.	1....184.38
		21....135.52			16....205.35			11....178.22
	Mar.	16....141.43			26....184.05			15....181.58
		29....136.98		Mar.	9....194.70			26....176.54
	Apr.	10....139.45			13....188.86		Sept.	2....180.56
		25....134.75			26....201.85			9....174.02
	May	12....139.38			29....198.23			17....179.37
		16....138.23		Apr.	10....208.93			26....174.42
	June	20....149.15			15....204.57		Oct.	20....186.24
		24....147.12			18....209.36			24....181.55
	July	10....150.88			25....203.09			29....184.70
		24....145.26			30....207.23		Nov.	6....180.61
	Aug.	2....147.07		May	6....199.26			10....182.70
		9....144.48			29....213.36			17....179.57
		18....149.28		June	12....207.52			21....183.97
		25....146.42			17....211.46		Dec.	6....175.44
		30....147.69			21....198.98			22....181.78
	Sept.	7....142.53		July	1....208.59			29....177.93
		26....147.08			16....199.48	1948	Jan.	5....181.69
		28....145.67			18....203.46			14....176.50
	Oct.	6....149.20			24....194.33			17....177.59
		10....147.67		Aug.	14....205.01			26....170.70
		18....149.18		Sept.	4....173.64		Feb.	2....176.05
		27....145.33			6....181.67			11....164.07
	Nov.	10....148.39			10....166.56			17....169.23
		16....145.17			16....176.26			20....166.38
	Dec.	16....153.00			19....164.09		Mar.	3....169.28
		27....147.93			26....175.45			17....165.03
1945	Jan.	11....156.68		Oct.	10....161.61		Apr.	23....184.48
		24....150.53			16...:.177.05			29....179.33
	Feb.	21....160.17			30...:160.49		May	15....191.39
		26....157.45		Nov.	6....175.00			19....187.46
	Mar.	6....162.22			22....162.29		June	14....194.49
		9....155.96			30....170.66			28....186.44
		16....159.42		Dec.	3....166.20		July	12....192.50
		26....151.74			10....177.21			19....179.50
	May	8....167.25			13....172.57			28....187.00
		11....162.60			23....178.54			30....180.00
		31....169.41			27....173.88		Aug.	5....184.50
	June	12....165.89	1947	Jan.	7....179.24			11....176.50
		26....169.55			16..:170.13		Sept.	7....185.50
	July	6....163.47		Feb.	10....184.96			21....176.50
		10....167.79			26....176.34			24....179.50
		27....159.95		Mar.	6....182.48			27....175.50
	Aug.	10....166.54			15....171.90		Oct.	26....190.50
		21....162.28			24....177.61			29....186.50
	Sept.	13....179.33			26....174.11		Nov.	1....190.00
		17....173.30			28....179.68			10....172.10
	Oct.	18....187.55		Apr.	15....165.39			19....178.00
		30....182.98			23....171.71			30....170.50
	Nov.	8....192.78			29....167.42		Dec.	13....178.50
		14....182.82		May	5....175.08			17....175.50
		17....192.66			19....161.38			30....179.25
		24....185.83		June	23....178.08	1949	Jan.	3....174.50
	Dec.	10....196.59			25....173.93			7....182.50
		20....187.51		July	14....187.15			17....177.75
1946	Jan.	17....205.03			18....182.51			24....182.50
		21....195.52			25....187.66			27....177.50

1949	Feb.	3....180.75		23....174.50	May 5....177.25
		11....171.00		30....179.15	10....173.50
		16....175.50	Apr.	7....175.25	17....176.25
		25....170.50		18....177.50	June 14....160.62
	Mar.	14....177.75		22....172.50	July 19....175.00

9-Point Chart Swings or More of the Averages

In making a chart of this kind, when the market is advancing the chart continues to move up until there is a reaction of 9 points or more. When the market is declining, the chart moves down on the line until there is a rally of at least 9 points or more, which is a reversal on the 9-Point Chart. In a few cases where the market is near the top or bottom, or an important change in trend is indicated, we record moves of less than 9 points. By studying this chart you will see how often the market moves around 9 to 10 points. The next important period to watch is moves running around 18 to 20 points, the next one around 30 points, then around 45 points and next, 50 to 52 points. A study of this record will help you in determining future trends of the main long swings on the market which is useful for long pull trading. You must learn to trade for the long pull under present income tax laws because you must carry stocks for 6 months or more.

In the prices given below "A" means an advance of a certain number of points and "D" means a decline of a certain number of points from the last high level.

1912	October	8.... 94.12			June	9.... 99.08	A	12.07
1913	June	11.... 72.11	D	20.00	December	19.... 65.95	D	33.13
	September	13.... 83.43	A	11.31	1918 October	18.... 89.09	A	23.14
	December	15.... 75.27	D	8.16	1919 February	8... 79.15	D	9.96
1914	March	20.... 83.43	A	8.16	1919 July	14...112.23	A	33.08
	December	24.... 53.17	D	30.26		20.... 98.46	D	12.77
1915	April	30.... 71.78	A	18.61	November	3...119.62	A	21.16
	May	14.... 60.38	D	11.40		29...103.60	D	16.02
	December	27.... 99.21	A	28.83	1920 January	3...109.88	A	6.28
1916	July	13... 86.42	D	12.79	February	25... 89.98	D	19.90
	November	21...110.15	A	23.73	April	8...105.65	A	15.67
	December	21... 90.16	D	19.99	May	19... 87.36	D	18.29
1917	January	2... 99.18	A	9.02	July	8.... 94.51	A	7.15
	February	2... 87.01	D	12.17	August	10.... 83.20	D	11.31

1920	September	17....	89.75	A	6.55
	December	21....	66.75	D	23.00
1921	May	5....	80.03	A	22.28
	June	20....	64.90	D	15.13
	July	6....	69.86	A	4.96
	August	24....	63.90	D	5.96
1922	October	14....	103.43	A	39.53
	November	14....	93.11	D	10.32
1923	March	20...	105.38	A	12.27
	October	27...	85.76	D	19.62
1924	February	6...	101.31	A	15.55
	May	14...	88.77	D	12.54
	August	20...	105.57	A	16.80
	October	14...	99.18	D	6.38
1925	January	22...	123.60	A	24.42
	February	16...	117.96	D	5.74
	March	6...	125.68	A	7.72
		30...	115.00	D	10.68
	April	18...	122.02	A	7.02
		27...	119.46	D	2.56
	November	6...	159.39	A	39.93
		24...	148.18	D	11.21
1926	February	11...	162.31	A	14.13
	March	3...	144.44	D	17.87
		12...	153.13	A	8.69
		30...	135.20	D	9.22
	April	24...	144.83	A	9.63
	May	19...	137.16	D	7.67
	August	24...	166.64	A	29.49
	October	19...	145.66	D	20.98
	December	18...	161.86	A	16.20
1927	January	25...	152.73	D	9.13
	May	28...	172.56	A	19.83
	June	27...	165.73	D	6.83
	October	3...	199.78	A	34.05
		22...	179.78	D	20.00
1928	January	3...	203.35	A	23.57
		18...	194.50	D	8.85
		24...	201.01	A	6.51
	February	20...	191.33	D	9.68
	March	20...	214.45	A	23.12
	April	23...	207.94	D	6.51
	May	14...	220.88	A	12.94
		22...	211.73	D	9.15
	June	2...	220.96	A	9.23
		12...	202.65	D	18.31
		14...	210.76	A	8.11
		18...	201.96	D	8.80
1928	July	5...	214.43	A	12.47
		16...	205.10	D	9.33
	October	1...	242.46	A	37.36
		3...	233.60	D	10.86
		19...	259.19	A	25.59
		22...	250.08	D	9.11
		24...	260.39	A	10.29
		31...	248.96	D	11.43
	November	28...	299.35	A	50.59
	December	3...	283.89	D	15.46

	4...	295.61	A	11.72
	10...	254.36	D	41.25

NOTE: This was down 44.99 from the high of November 28 at 299.35, and as 45 points is one of our rules for resistance levels this would be another reason for covering shorts and buying for a rally.

1929 January	3...	311.46	A	57.10
	8...	292.89	D	18.57
	25...	319.86	A	26.97
	30...	308.47	D	11.39
February	1...	324.16	A	15.69
	8...	298.03	D	26.13
	13...	316.06	A	18.03
	18...	293.40	D	22.26
March	1...	324.40	A	30.60
	6...	302.93	D	21.47
	15...	322.75	D	20.18
	26...	281.51	D	41.24
	28...	311.13	A	29.62
April	1...	294.11	D	17.02
	5...	307.97	A	13.86
	10...	295.71	D	12.26
	23...	320.10	A	24.39
	26...	311.00	D	9.10
May	6...	331.01	A	20.00
	9...	317.09	D	13.82
	11...	328.01	A	10.92
	13...	313.56	D	15.55
	15...	324.38	A	8.72
	16...	314.51	D	9.87
	17...	325.64	A	11.13
	23..	300.52	D	25.12
	24..	313.30	A	12.78
	27..	291.80	D	21.50
	29..	302.32	A	11.52
	31..	290.02	D	12.32
June	7..	312.00	A	21.98
	11..	301.22	D	10.78
	18..	323.30	A	22.08
	20..	314.32	D	8.98
July	8..	350.09	A	35.77
	11..	340.12	D	9.93
	12..	350.26	A	10.12
	16..	339.98	D	10.28
	17..	349.79	A	9.81
1929 July	23..	339.65	D	10.14
	24..	349.30	A	9.65
	29..	336.36	D	12.84
August	5..	358.66	A	22.30
	9..	336.13	D	22.53
	26..	380.18	A	42.05
	28..	370.34	D	9.84
September	3..	386.10	A	15.76
	5..	367.35	D	18.75
	7..	381.44	A	14.09
	10..	364.46	D	16.98
	12..	375.52	A	11.06

1929	September	13....	359.70	D 15.82		8...214.64	D 14.89
		19....	375.20	A 15.50		18...242.01	A 27.37
		25....	344.85	D 30.35		21...228.72	D 13.29
		26....	358.16	A 13.31		28...243.65	A 14.93
		28....	341.03	D 17.13		31...229.09	D 14.56
	October	2....	350.19	A 9.16	August	5...240.95	A 11.86
		4....	320.45	D 29.74		13...214.49	D 26.46
		8....	349.67	A 29.22	September	10...247.10	A 32.61
		9....	338.86	D 10.81		30...201.95	D 45.15
		11....	358.77	A 19.91	October	3...216.85	A 14.90
		17....	332.11	D 26.66		10...186.70	D 30.15
		18....	343.12	A 11.01		15...201.64	A 14.94
		19....	321.71	D 21.41		18...183.63	D 18.01
		22....	333.01	A 11.30		20...194.44	A 10.81
		24....	272.32	D 39.31		22...181.53	D 12.91
		25....	306.02	A 35.76		28...198.59	A 17.07
		29....	212.33	D 93.69	November	1...181.26	D 17.33
		31....	281.54	A 69.21		3...187.23	A 5.99
	November	7....	217.84	D 63.70		10...168.32	D 18.91
		8....	245.28	A 27.44		15...187.59	A 19.27
		13....	195.35	D 49.93		18...177.63	D 9.96
		20....	250.75	A 55.40	21-25...191.28	A 13.65
		27....	233.39	D 17.46		28...178.88	D 12.40
	December	9....	267.56	A 34.17	December	2...187.96	A 9.08
		13....	239.58	D 28.08		17...154.45	D 33.51
		14....	254.41	A 14.83		18...171.64	A 23.19
		20....	227.20	D 27.21		29...158.41	D 13.23
		21....	237.26	A 10.06	1931 January	7...175.32	A 16.41
		23....	226.39	D 10.87		19...160.09	D 15.23
		27....	246.35	A 19.96		23...172.97	A 12.88
		30....	235.95	D 10.40		29...164.81	D 18.16
1930	January	10....	252.91	A 14.96	February	26...195.95	A 31.14
		18....	243.37	D 9.54	March	13...175.89	D 20.06
	February	13....	275.00	A 31.63		20...189.31	D 13.42
		17....	265.29	D 9.71	Apr.	7...166.10	A 23.21
		19....	273.35	A 8.06		14...173.24	A 7.14
		25....	259.78	D 13.56		29...141.78	D 31.46
	March	10....	279.40	A 19.62	1931 May	9...156.17	A 14.39
		15....	268.97	D 10.43	June	2...119.89	D 36.28
1930	March	21....	284.08	A 15.11		5...138.89	A 19.00
		22....	274.63	D 9.35		8...127.96	D 10.93
	April	16....	297.25	A 22.62		9...138.88	A 10.92
		22....	284.28	D 12.97		19...128.64	D 10.24
		23....	293.27	A 9.00		27...157.93	A 29.29
		29....	272.24	D 21.03	July	1...147.44	D 10.49
		30....	283.51	A 11.27		3...156.74	A 9.30
	May	5....	249.82	D 33.69		15...134.39	D 22.35
		7....	272.15	A 22.33		21...147.69	A 13.30
		8....	257.74	D 14.41		31...133.70	D 14.00
		14....	277.22	A 19.48	August	15...146.41	A 12.71
		20....	260.76	D 16.46	September	21...104.79	D 41.62
	June	2....	276.86	A 16.10		23...117.75	A 12.96
		12....	241.00	D 35.86	October	5... 85.51	D 32.24
		13....	251.63	A 9.37		9...108.98	A 23.47
		18....	212.27	D 39.36		14... 96.01	D 12.97
		20....	232.69	A 20.42		24...110.53	A 14.52
		25....	207.74	D 24.95		29... 98.19	D 12.34
	July	1....	229.53	A 21.79	November	9...119.15	A 20.96

—77—

1931	December	17.....71.79	D 47.36		June	1...108.64	D	8.98
		19.....83.09	A 11.30		September	11...135.05	A	26.41
1932	January	5.....69.85	D 13.24		October	3...126.95	D	8.15
		14.....87.78	A 17.93		November	20...149.42	A	12.47
	February	10.....70.64	D 17.14		December	16...138.91	D	10.51
		19.....89.84	A 19.20	1936	March	6...159.87	A	20.96
		24.....79.57	D 10.27			13...149.65	D	10.22
	March	9.....89.88	A 10.31		April	6...163.07	A	13.42
	May	4.....52.33	D 37.53			30...141.53	D	21.54
		7.....60.01	A 7.68		June	24...161.15	A	19.62
	June	2.....43.49	D 16.52		July	8...154.85	D	6.30
		15.....51.43	A 7.94		August	10...170.15	A	15.30
	July	8.....40.56	D 10.89			21...160.52	D	9.63
	August	8.....71.49	A 30.93		November	18...186.39	D	5.87
		13.....60.89	D 10.69		December	21...175.31	D	11.68
	September	8.....81.39	A 20.50	1937	March	10...195.59	A	20.28
		15.....64.27	D 17.12			22...179.28	D	16.31
		22.....76.01	A 11.74			31...187.99	A	8.71
	October	10.....57.67	D 18.34		April	9...175.86	D	12.13
		20.....66.13	A 8.54			22...184.33	A	9.57
	November	3....57.21	D 8.92			28...168.77	D	15.56
		12.....68.87	A 11.66		May	5...176.81	A	8.04
	December	3.....55.04	D 13.83			18...166.20	D	10.61
1933	January	11.....65.78	A 10.24			24...176.25	A	10.05
	February	27.....49.68	D 15.60		June	14...163.73	D	12.52
	March	16.....64.56	A 14.78	1937	August	14...190.38	A	26.65
		31.....54.90	D 9.66		September	13...154.94	D	35.44
	April	20.....75.20	A 20.30			15...165.16	A	10.22
		21.....68.64	D 6.56			24...146.22	D	18.94
	June	13.....97.97	A 29.33			30...157.12	A	10.90
		17.....89.10	D 12.87		October	6...141.63	D	15.49
	July	18....110.53	A 21.43			7...150.47	A	8.84
1933	July	21.....84.45	D 26.08			19...115.84	D	34.63
		27.....97.28	A 12.83			21...137.82	A	21.98
		31.....87.75	D 9.53			25...124.56	D	13.26
	August	25....105.60	A 17.85			29...141.22	A	16.66
	September	6.....97.74	D 7.86		November	8...121.60	D	19.62
		18....107.68	A 9.94			12...135.70	A	16.10
	October	3.....91.93	D 15.75			23...112.54	D	23.16
		9....100.58	A 8.65		December	8...131.15	A	18.61
		21.....82.20	D 18.38			14...121.85	D	9.35
	December	11....103.97	A 21.77			21...130.76	A	8.91
		20.....93.70	D 10.27			29...117.21	D	13.55
1934	February	5....111.93	A 18.23	1938	January	15...134.95	A	17.74
	March	1....101.93	D 10.00		February	4...117.13	D	17.82
		3....106.37	A 4.46			23...132.86	A	15.73
		27.....97.41	D 8.96		March	31...97.46	D	35.40
	April	20....107.00	A 9.59		April	18...121.54	A	24.08
	May	14.....89.10	D 16.90			20...112.47	D	9.07
	July	11.....99.35	A 10.25			23...119.21	A	6.74
		26.....84.58	D 14.77		May	1...109.40	D	9.81
	August	25.....96.00	A 11.42			10...120.28	A	10.88
	September	17.....85.72	D 10.28			27...106.44	D	13.84
1935	January	7....106.71	A 21.00		July	25...146.31	A	39.87
		15.....99.54	D 7.17		August	12...135.38	D	10.93
	February	18....108.29	A 8.75			24...145.30	A	9.98
	March	18.....95.95	D 12.34		September	14...130.38	D	14.92
	May	28....117.62	A 21.67			21...140.20	A	9.82

1938	September	28...127.85	D 12.35		February	4... 207.49	A 11.97
	November	10...158.90	A 31.05			13... 197.65	D 9.84
		28...145.21	D 13.69			16... 205.35	A 8.70
1939	January	5...155.47	A 10.26			26... 184.05	D 21.30
		26...136.10	D 19.37		April	18... 209.36	A 25.31
	March	10...152.71	A 16.61		May	6... 199.26	D 10.10
	April	11...120.04	D 32.67			29... 213.36	A 14.10
	June	9...140.75	A 20.71		June	21... 198.98	D 14.38
		30...128.97	D 11.78		July	1... 208.59	A 9.71
	July	25...145.72	A 16.85			24... 194.33	D 14.26
	August	24...128.60	D 17.12		August	14... 205.01	A 10.68
		30...138.07	A 9.47		September	4... 173.64	D 31.37
	September	1...127.51	D 10.56			6... 181.67	A 8.03
		13...157.77	A 30.26			10... 166.56	D 15.11
		18...147.35	D 10.42			16...176.26	A 9.70
1939	October	26...155.95	A 8.60			19...164.09	D 12.17
	November	30...144.85	D 11.10			26... 175.45	A 11.36
1940	January	3...153.29	A 8.44		October	10... 161.61	D 13.84
		15...143.06	D 10.23			16... 177.05	A 15.44
	April	8...152.07	A 9.01			30... 160.49	D 16.56
	May	21...110.61	A 41.46		November	6... 175.00	A 14.51
		23...117.84	A 7.23			22... 162.29	D 12.71
		28...110.51	D	1947	January	7... 179.24	A 16.95
	June	10...110.41	D 7.33			16...170.13	D 9.13
	November	8...138.77	A 28.36		February	10... 184.96	A 14.83
	December	23...127.83	D 10.94		March	15... 171.97	D 12.99
1941	January	10...134.27	A 6.44			28... 179.68	A 7.71
	February	19...117.43	D 16.84		April	15... 165.39	D 14.29
	April	4...125.28	A 7.85		May	5... 175.08	A 9.69
	May	1...114.78	D 10.50			19... 161.38	D 13.70
	July	22...131.10	A 16.32		July	25... 187.66	A 16.28
	December	24...105.52	D 25.58		September	9... 174.02	D 13.64
1942	January	6...114.96	A 9.44		October	20... 186.24	A 12.22
	April	28... 92.69	D 22.27		July	11... 164.09	D 22.19
1943	July	15...146.41	A 53.73		June	14... 194.49	A 34.40
	August	2...133.87	D 12.54		July	19... 179.50	D 14.99
	September	20...142.50	A 8.63			28... 187.00	A 7.50
	November	30...128.94	D 13.66		August	11... 176.50	D 10.50
1944	July	10...150.88	A 22.06		September	7... 185.50	A 11.00
	September	7...142.53	D 8.35			27... 175.50	D 10.00
1945	March	6...162.22	A 19.69		October	26... 190.50	A 15.00
		26...151.74	D 10.48		November	30... 170.50	D 20.00
	June	26...169.55	A 17.81	1949	Jan. 7 & 24... 182.50	A 12.00	
	July	27...159.95	D 9.65		February	25... 170.50	D 12.00
	December	10...196.59	A 36.64		March	30... 179.15	A 8.65
		20...187.51	D 9.08		June	14... 160.62	D 18.53
1946	January	17...205.03	A 17.52		July 18 high 174.44 advance 13.82.		
		21...195.52	D 9.51				

Total Moves of 9 points or More

1912, October 8, to June 14, 1949, a period of 37 years in which there were a total of 464 moves of 9 points or more. This was an Average of about one 9-point move per month. There were 54 moves recorded of less than 9 points.

From 9 to 21 points a total of 271 moves or over 50% of the total.

—79—

From 21 to 31 points there were 61 moves or about one out of 4 times.

31 to 51 total 36 moves or about one out of 8.

Moves above 51 points were only 6 and these occurred during 1929 when we had the wildest market in history.

The above figures prove that the most important trend moves run between 9 and 21 points, and these are of the greatest importance for trend indications.

Moves of less than 9 points are of minor importance and when the Averages fail to rally as much as 9 points from a low level it is a sign of weakness and indicates lower prices. The same applies in an advancing market. If the Averages react less than 9 points it is an indication that they are in a very strong position and going higher.

When the main trend turns up and the Averages advance 10 points or more under normal conditions, they should continue to advance 20 points or more from the low levels.

After a Bear Market starts and the Averages decline more than 10 points, they should continue to decline 20 points or more. After the Averages move more than 21 points the next important point to watch is 30 to 31 points from extreme high or extreme low, as only a small percentage of moves runs over 31 points, before a move of 10 points or more occurs in the opposite direction.

Examples of 30-Point Moves:

> 1938 March 15 high 127.50, March 31 extreme low 97.50—a decline of exactly 30 points.
>
> 1938 September 28 low 127.50, November 10 high for the year 158.75—an advance of 31.25 points.
>
> 1939 September 1 low 127.50. This was the day Hitler started the war.
>
> 1939 September 13 extreme high for the year 157.50, exactly 30 points advance.
>
> 1946 February 4 high 207½, February 24 low 184.04—a decline of practically 24 points.
>
> 1948 February 11 low 164.04, June 14 high for the year

194.49—an advance of 30.40.

1949 June 14 low 160.62—a decline of 33.87 points from 1948 high.

From these figures you can see how often a move of around 30 points calls extreme high or extreme low of that particular move. This is especially the case in normal markets. During abnormal markets such as 1928, 1929 and 1930 moves were greater than 30 points because prices were extremely high and the range in fluctuations was very wide. These were abnormal times, and you cannot expect the market under present conditions to make moves comparable to these abnormal periods.

CHAPTER VIII

MONTHS WHEN EXTREME HIGHS AND LOWS WERE RECORDED

Because stocks run according to seasonal changes and make extreme highs in certain months at the end of a Bull Campaign, or in a major or minor move, it is important to go over past records when extreme highs are made at the end of these important moves.

1881 January and June high	1923 March
1886 December	1929 September
1887 April	1930 April
1890 May	1931 July
1892 March	1932 September
1895 September	1933 July
1897 September	1934 February
1899 April and September	1937 March
1901 April and June	1938 January
1906 January	1938 November
1909 October	1939 September
1911 February and June	1940 November
1912 October	1941 July and September
1914 March	1943 July
1915 December	1946 May
1916 November	1947 February, July & Oct.
1918 October	1948 June
1919 November	1949 January

From the above, you can see that there were 35 swings, or campaigns, in the stock market between 1881 and 1949. Below we give you the months, showing how many times the top, or high prices, were reached in each month.

January—4 highs in this month.

February—4 highs in this month.

March—4 highs in this month.

April—4 highs in this month.

May—2 highs in this month.

June—4 highs in this month.
July—4 highs in this month.
August—no highs in this month.
September—8 highs in this month.
October—4 highs in this month.
November—4 highs in this month.
December—2 highs in this month.

From the above figures, you can see that out of 35 swings, 8 made tops in the month of September. Therefore, September is one of the most important months to watch for a top when a Bull Market has been running for a long period of time. The months of January, February, March, April, June, July, October and November all show 4 tops made in each month. The months of May and December show 2 tops and the month of August shows that no important Bull Campaign reached a final high in this month. These figures give you an indication of the months to watch for the endings of a major or minor Bull Campaign.

Months When Extreme Lows Were Recorded

The Bear Markets or declines in stocks culminate a greater number of times in some months than others. Therefore, it is important for you to know when these extreme low prices have been reached. We give them below:

1884	June	1914	December
1888	April	1916	April
1890	December	1917	December
1893	July	1919	February
1896	August	1921	August
1898	March	1923	October
1900	September	1929	November
1901	January	1930	December
1903	November	1932	July
1907	November	1933	February
1910	July	1933	October
1911	July	1934	July
1913	June	1937	November

1938 March	1943 November
1939 April	1946 October
1940 May and June	1947 May
1941 May	1948 July, & March—Nov.
1942 April	1949 June

From the above figures you can see that in 36 declines, or Bear Campaigns, they have culminated, or reached final bottom, in the months indicated below:

January—1 time extreme low.

February—3 times.

March—2 times.

April—4 times.

May—3 times.

June—4 times.

July—5 times.

August—2 times.

September—1 time.

October—3 times.

November—6 times.

December—4 times.

You will note that 6 Bear Campaigns have ended in November, and 5 in July. Therefore, when stocks have been declining for a considerable period of time, you would expect them to reach final lows in the months of July or November. The next months when the most lows have occurred are April, June and December. These are the next important months to watch for the end of a decline.

The months of January and September indicate only 1 out of the 36 moves. Therefore, these months are not important for the terminations of Bear Campaigns. March only shows 2 extreme lows. If a market had been declining for some time, you could expect that the possibilities were greater for the extreme low to occur in April than in March. Study the past time periods in connection with individual stocks, as well as with the industrial averages, and the public utilities averages.

Monthly High and Low Prices Each Year

It is important to have a record of when extreme High and Low prices are reached in each calendar year. Below we are giving a record of the months when the Highs and Lows were made, and after 1897 we are giving the exact date the extreme Highs and Lows were recorded:

HIGH	LOW
1881 January and May	February, September and December
1882 September	January and November
1883 April	February and October
1884 February	June and December
1885 November	January
1886 January & December	May
1887 May	October
1888 October	April
1889 September	March
1890 May	December
1891 January & September	July
1892 March.	December
1893 January	July 26 (extreme low)
1894 April and August	November
1895 September	December
1896 April 17	August 8
1897 September 10	April 19
1898 August 26 and December 17	March 25
1899 April 4 and September 2	December 18
1900 December 27	June 25 and September 24
1901 June 3	December 24
1902 April 18 and September 19	December 15
1903 February 16	November 9
1904 December 5	February 9
1905 December 29	January 25

1906	January 19	July 13
1907	January 7	November 15
1908	November 13	February 13
1909	October 2	February 23
1910	January 22	July 26
1911	February 4 and	
	June 14	September 25
1912	September 30	January 2
1913	January 9	June 21
1914	March 20	December 24
1915	December 27	January 24
1916	November 25	April 22
1917	January 2	December 19
1918	October 18	January 15
1919	November 3	February 8
1920	January 3	December 21
1921	May 5	August 24
1922	January 5	October 14
1923	March 20	October 27
1924	November 18	May 14
1925	November 6	March 6
1926	August 14	March 30
1927	December 20	January 25
1928	December 31	February 20
1929	September 3	November 13
1930	April 16	December 17
1931	February 24	October 5
1932	March 9	July 8
1933	July 18	February 27 and October 21
1934	February 5	July 26
1935	November 8	March 18
1936	December 15	April 30
1937	March 10	November 23
1938	November 10	March 31
1939	September 13	April 11
1940	January 3	June 10
1941	January 10	December 24
1942	December 28	April 28

1943 July 15	January 7
1944 December 16	February 7
1945 December 10	January 24
1946 May 29	October 30
1947 July 25	May 19
1948 June 14	February 11
1949 January 7	June 14

Number of Times Extreme Highs Have Been Reached
   January—14 highs in 69 years.
   February—5 highs in 69 years.
   March—5 highs in 69 years.
   April—6 highs in 69 years.
   May—5 highs in 69 years.
   June—3 highs in 69 years.
   July—3 highs in 69 years.
   August—3 highs in 69 years.
   September—10 highs in 69 years.
   October—3 highs in 69 years.
   November—8 highs in 69 years.
   December—13 highs in 69 years.

From the above you can see that 14 Highs occurred in the month of January and 13 in the month of December. Therefore, when stocks have been advancing for a considerable period of time the percentage is largely in favor of Highs being reached in December or January. During the month of September, Highs were made 10 times. This is the next month to December and January and is important to watch for Top or Change in Trend when prices have been advancing for some time. The next month for Highs is November—8 having occurred. Next, March, April and May which ran 5, 6 and 5. The months of June, July, August and October only record 3 Highs each, therefore, these months are the ones when you would least expect extreme Highs to be reached.

Number of Times Extreme Lows Have Been Reached

January—9 times in 69 years.
February—10 times in 69 years.
March—6 times in 69 years.
April—6 times in 69 years.
May—3 times in 69 years.
June—5 times in 69 years.
July—6 times in 69 years.
August—2 times in 69 years.
September—2 times in 69 years
October—7 times in 69 years.
November—6 times in 69 years.
December—13 times in 69 years.

From the above you can see that the greatest number of Lows occurred in the month of December and the next in February, therefore, December and February are the most important to watch for Lows and a Change in Trend. January comes next with 9 and October—7. The months of March, April and November all show 6. April—3, August and September—2, these months showing the least number of Lows.

Considering both the High and Low months we find September, December, January and February the months when the greatest number of Highs and Lows have occurred in the past 69 years, making these months the most important to watch for a Change in Trend either way, provided prices have been advancing or declining for a considerable period of time. By checking the months when the last High and Low have occurred will help you to determine when the next Change in Trend takes place. You should also study the exact dates each month when Highs and Lows have been reached in the past. Watch around these same dates for future Change in Trend.

Dow-Jones 30 Industrial Averages Time Swings

1912, October 8, to June 14, 1949. The swings recorded are mostly the major swings when there was a rapid advance or a rapid decline in a comparative short period of time.

During this period there was a total of 292 time swings.

3 to 11 days—41 swings in this time period or about 1 in 7.

11 to 21 days—65 swings in this time period or about 1 in 4½.

22 to 35 days—65 swings in this time period or about 1 in 4½.

The duration of time periods from 11 to 35 days was 130 or more than 1/3 of the total moves, making this time period very important to watch from any extreme high or extreme low level.

Moves lasting 36 to 45 days were 31 or about one in 9½ times.

Moves of from 43 to 60 days were 33 or about one in 9 times.

Moves of from 61 to 95 days were 20 or about one in 14½ times.

Moves of from 96 to 112 days were 13 or about one in 22½ times.

Moves lasting more than 112 days were 12 or about one in 22 times.

The knowledge of these time periods will help you in using the other rules and in determining when a change in trend is due.

CHAPTER IX

JUNE LOWS COMPARISON FOR FUTURE HIGHS

1949, June 14, the Dow-Jones 30 Industrial Averages declined to 160.62, and up to this writing, July 19, 1949, have advanced above 175. Suppose June 14, 1949 this turns out to be the low level and a Bull Market starts. By comparing the previous low levels in June and what followed them, we get a line on what is possible to expect in the future.

1913, June 11 low 72.11. September 13 high 83.43, an advance lasting 3 months.

1914, March 20, high 83.49, a Double Top against September 13 high. This was an advance of 9 months from the low in June, 1913. The main trend turned down from March, 1914 and in June, the price was 81.84, slightly lower than the Double Top. From this level the decline followed ending in a panic in December, 1914 with the Averages down to 53.17.

1921, June 20, low 66. This was the First Bottom in a Bear Market.

1921, August 24, low 64. This was Final Low, and a Bull Market started.

1923, March 20, high 105.25. Up 41 points in 21 months. This ended the First Section of the big Bull Market which lasted until 1929.

1930, June 25, low 208. This was a low in the first year of a Bear Market, and a Bull Market could not be expected to start.

September 10, high 247, up 39 points in 77 days. This was only a Rally in a Bear Market.

1937, June 14, low 163.75.

August 14, high 190.50, up 36.75 in 61 days. This was only a Rally in a Bear Market as the Bull Market had ended in March, 1937.

1940, June 10, low 110.50.

November 8, high 138.50. An advance of 28 points in 147 days. This was a Rally in a Bear Market. After this there were no more important low levels in June until June 14, 1949, which was a decline of one year from June 14, 1948.

By using the above Time Periods when lows were made in June, the most important one to consider would be the low in June, 1921 because it was at the end of a Bear Market which had lasted for about 20 months. Therefore, adding this same Time Period from 1921 to 1923 to June 14, 1949, we get March 14, 1951 as a possible time that a Bull Market would run. Assuming that from June 14, 1949 we would only get a Rally in a Bear Market, then the Time Period would run out August 14 and 31 and December 27. The other Time Periods would run out in April, 1950 and in June, 1950, which compares with previous Time Periods.

1945, July 27, last low to July 27, 1949, 48 months.

August 27, 1949, 49 months, the same time as from 1938 to 1942 lows and from April, 1942 to high in May, 1946.

July 27, 1949 will be very important for a Change in Trend, and if the trend is up at that time, or the trend turns up soon after that time, prices should go very much higher.

1938, November 10, high 158.75. Prices made Final Low April 28, 1942. This was approximately 42 months between the extreme high and low. In 1945 the Averages crossed 158.75 after having remained below this level for six years and three months. They have now remained above the level of 158.75 for a period of 50 months. Therefore, breaking below the 160 level now would indicate considerably lower prices due to the long period of time which has elapsed.

Considering that the Averages reached extreme high May 29, 1946 and now for a period of 37 months have remained in a range of 53 points and have not broken below the low levels which were recorded on the First Decline to October 30, ·1946, a period of five months, should the Averages advance and get into a strong position after holding above this low level for such a long period of time, it could mean a prolonged advance and very much higher prices.

Anniversary Dates

My object in writing this book "45 Years in Wall Street" is to give you some new and valuable rules on Time Periods which will help to guide you in determining high and low prices in the future. If you study and apply these rules, they will be very valuable to you in the future.

In my research work I have discovered that stocks make an important Change in Trend in the months where they have reached extreme high and low. These are what I call anniversary dates, and these important dates should be watched each year for important Changes in Trend.

1929, September 3, a record all time high.

1932, July 8, the lowest level for the Averages since 1897, making these two dates important to watch each year for Change in Trend. The record below proves the value of these dates.

1930, September 10, last high before a Big Decline.

1931, August 29, a Big Decline started. This was just five days before September 3, the anniversary date.

1932, July 8, extreme low.

1932, September 8, high of First Rally in Bull Market.

1933, July 18, high for the year. September 18, high of Secondary Rally, from which a decline followed.

1934, July 26, low for the year. September 17, the last low from which advance started.

1935, July 21, made new high for the move. Reacted to August 2 from which the advance continued.

1935, September 11, high of the year up to that time. Decline to October 3, then crossed September 11 highs and continued up.

1936, July 28, high for the year up to that time, reacted and then continued to advance.

1936, September 8, high, reacted on September 17, and then continued up.

1937, July, no important Top or Bottom.

1937, September 15, last high of a Rally before a Big

Decline followed.

1938, July 25, high for a big reaction. September 28, last low before a big advance.

1939, July 25, high for a reaction to September 1.

1939, September 1 low, September 13 high of a 30 point advance.

1940, July 3, last low before a 20 point advance. September 13, last low before an advance to November 8.

1941, July 22, high of last Rally. September 18, last high before a Big Decline.

1942, July 9 and 16, last high for a reaction. September 11 last low before a big advance.

1943, July 15, high for a 13 point decline. September 20, high for a decline to November 30.

1944, July 10, high for a reaction to September 7.

1944, September, last low for a big up swing.

1945, July 27, last low, 159.95. This low has not been broken up to the time of this writing, July 2, 1949.

1945, September 17, low before a big up swing.

1946, July 1, last high before a big decline.

1946, September 6, top of a small rally, then declined to October 30.

1947, July 25, last high before a decline. September 9 and 26, last lows before an advance to October 20.

1948, July 12, last high before a decline to September 27.

1948, September 27, last low. Market rallied to October 26.

1949, Watch July 8, 15, 25, 28 for important changes.

September 2 to 10, 15 and 20 to 27. Important to watch for Changes in Trend.

Watch these anniversary dates every year and also watch the other dates when extreme highs and lows have been recorded, like March 8, 1937, March 31, 1938, April 28, 1942, May 29, 1946 and so on. If you put in time studying and comparing Time Periods and at the same time follow all the other rules, you will find it of great value in determining the Changes in Trend in the future.

When important news is announced, such as the beginning of war, the ending of wars, the dates of the inauguration and election of presidents, it is important to consider the price of the Averages of the individual stocks at the time of news developments and whether the trend is already up or down and the change that follows these important news dates.

1914, July 30, the starting of war. Dow-Jones Industrial Averages 71.42. December 24, extreme low 53.17.

1915, April 30, high 71.78, up to the level where prices were when war broke out. There was a reaction to May 14, low 60.38. June 22, Averages again at 71.90. From this level the reaction was small to July 9, low 67.88, then crossing the high level at the time the war broke out, the advance continued on to new high levels.

1918, November 11, end of World War I. The Averages made the last high on November 9 at 88.07 and crossed this high for the first time in March, 1919 and advanced to a new high of 119.62 on November 3, 1919.

The next important war date was September 1, 1939, low 127.51, and September 13 high 157.77. We are giving the resistance levels that have occurred around 127 to 130.

1939, August 24, 128.60. September 1, 127.51.

1940, August 12, high 127.55. September 13, low 127.32. December 23, low 127.83.

1941, July 27, low 126.75. September 30, high 127.31.

1943, February 2, low 126.38. March 22, low 128.67. April 13, last low 129.79. April 30, last low 128.94. A big advance followed.

There is always a reason why the Averages make high or low levels so many times around the same price. It is because there are certain percentage points around these levels.

1896, low 28.50. Add 350% gives 128.25.

1921, low 64. Add 100% gives 128.

1929, high 386.10. 1/3 gives 128.70.

1929, high 386.10 to 40.56, 1932 low, $\frac{1}{4}$ of range gives 126.70.

1932, low, 40.56 to 213.36, 1946 high, $\frac{1}{2}$ gives 126.96.

1937, high 195.59. 2/3 gives 130.32.

1937, high 195.59 to 97.46 low in 1938, 1/3 gives 130.17.

1942, low, 92.69 to 1937 high, 195.59, 3/8 gives 130.40.

There were 8 resistance levels or percentage points around these levels and the market made important tops and bottoms 11 different times around these levels. This shows you the importance of calculating percentage points and resistance levels from each important high or low level.

Resistance Levels 193 to 196

1929, November 13, low 195.35.

1931, February 24, high 196.96.

1937, March 10, high 195.59.

1948, June 14, high 194.49.

Four important tops and bottoms around these levels. The following are the reasons:

1929, high, 386.10, 1/2 gives 193.05, a very important resistance level.

1921, low, 64, add 200% gives 192.

1930, April 16, high 297.25 to 92.69, low in 1942, 1/2 gives 194.97.

1932, low 40.56 add 375% gives 192.66.

1945, July 27, low 159.95 to 213.36, May 29, 1946, 2/3 gives 195.56.

1939, September 1, low 127.51 add 50% gives 191.26.

1939, low 127.51 to 92.69, low in 1942, add 200% of the range gives 197.15.

1945, March 26, low 151.74. This was the last low before the Averages advanced to new high levels for that move.

Final high 213.36, 2/3 of the range gives 192.74. This gives 8 important resistance levels and shows why Averages have made 3 important high levels and 1 low level around these prices. Should the bull market continue in 1949 or in 1950 and cross 196 and close above these levels, it will be an indication for higher prices and the next important resistance level.

The Japanese attacked at Pearl Harbor on December 7, which was Sunday. On December 6 the low on the Dow-Jones Averages was 115.74 and the close 116.60. December 8, the high was 115.46. Prices never sold higher until extreme low of 92.69 was reached April 28, 1942. Therefore, the high of December 8 was an important point and when the Averages crossed it, it was an indication of much higher prices.

1943, October 13, high 115.80, at the low of December 6 and the high of December 8, 1941. On October 28, 1943, low 112.57, only 3 point reaction in 15 days, indicating strong up trend.

1943, November 9, high 118.18. The Averages had crossed the high price of December 8, 1941 indicating higher prices. A reaction followed to December 24, low 113.46, not 5 points decline in 45 days and not 3 points under the prices when the war started. This was an indication of good support and higher prices followed. The advance continued, and in February, 1945 the Averages crossed 127.51, the low of September 1, 1939, when the German war started.

1945, May 6, the German war ended, and the Averages continued to move up. June 26, high 169.15. This was over 10 points above the high of 1938 and had crossed all of the resistance levels between 158 and 163, a definite indication of higher prices.

1945, July 27, low 159.95, down less than 10 points in 31 days and holding at the strong resistance levels indicating higher prices.

1945, August 14, the Japanese war ended. The last low had occurred on August 9 with the Averages at 161.14, making 159.95 and 161.14 important support levels because they occurred at the end of the war with prices above the 1938 high levels, where they have held for 3 different declines without reaching 160. These examples are given to prove to you the importance of figuring resistance levels and percentage points from all important tops and bottoms in order that you can determine where the next important high or low level is likely to occur. Use all of the time rules, the 3 day chart and the 9 point chart to help you in determining the time and the price for future buying and selling levels, applying all of the rules to the individual stocks as well as to the Averages.

Resistance Levels 158 to 163

The records prove that these levels are very important for tops and bottoms as shown by extreme high and low levels.
1937, June 14, low 163.75.
1938, November 10, high 158.90.
1939, September 13, high 157.77.
1945, March 6, high 162.22.
1945, July 27, low 159.95.
1946, October 30, low 160.49.
1947, May 19, low 161.38.
1949, June 14, low 160.62.

A total of four highs and four lows around these levels. The last three important bottoms from 1946 to 1949 occurred around these levels at which the market received support and rallied each time. Below we give the percentage points showing why there was support or buying and resistance or selling around these levels. There is always a mathematical proof of why bottoms and tops occur so many times around the same level.

1896, low 28.50 to 386.10, high in 1929, 3/8 of the range gives 162.60.

1921, low 64 add 150% gives 160.

1932, low 40.56 to 195.59, high in 1937, 3/4 of the range gives 156.84.

1932, low 40.56 add 300% of the base or low gives 162.24.

1932, September 8, high 81.39, add 100% gives 162.78.

1933, October 21, low 82.20. Add 100% gives 164.40.

1938, March 31, low 97.46 to 1937 high, 195.59. 5/8 of the range gives 158.90, the exact high point of November 10, 1938.

1939, September 1, low 127.51 to 92.69, low April 28, 1942. This was the range between the starting of the war and the extreme low afterward. The decline was 34.82. Add this to 127.51 gives 162.33.

1945, March 26, low 151.74 to 213.36, extreme high. $\frac{1}{8}$ of this range gives 159.47.

1946, high 213.36. 25% of this price gives 160.02.

This shows 10 resistance points and proves why the market has made high and low levels for 8 times around these prices. The fact that June 14, 1949 the Averages reached this level for the third time and up to this writing, July 18, have rallied to 174.40 indicates that they are in strong position, but should they ever close below 160, it will be a sure indication for lower prices because it will be the fourth time, and based on our rule, prices should continue on down.

CHAPTER X

VOLUME OF STOCK SALES ON NEW YORK STOCK EXCHANGE

With Review of Bull and Bear Markets

These sales are a continuation from New Stock Trend Detector, page 81, and brings the sales up to June 30, 1949.

The bull market which started July 8, 1932, continued to March 10, 1937, with the Averages up 155 points.

1936, the volume of trade continued heavy, the months of January and February showing the greatest volume. The total volume of sale for the year 1936 was 496,138,000.

1937. The volume was heavy for the first 3 months. The month of January showed the largest volume for the year. After the decline started in March the volume decreased to 17,213,000 in August. On the big break in October the volume ran over 51 million. The total for the year 1937 was 409,465,000, much less than 1936.

1938. Final low was reached March 31, a little over one year from the top of 1937. The total volume for this bear campaign was 311,876,000.

April, 1938, to November 10, 1938. Prices advanced 61 points in this minor bull market, and the total volume was 208,296,000. In the month of October the volume of sales was 41,555,000, the largest of the year and the greatest of any month since March, 1937. This was an indication of top and indicated that the public was buying heavily on the advance. The averages reaching the exact resistance level as explained in the new book "45 Years in Wall Street."

From the high of November, 1938, prices declined to April 11, 1939, down 39 points. The volume on this period was 111,357,000. The volume in March, 1939, was 24,563,000, and in April the volume decreased and reached the lowest of the year in June.

May, 1939, to September, 1939. A total advance of 37 points. Total volume for this period was 117,432,000. The war started on September 1 and the advance from September

1 to 13 amounted to 30 points. The volume during September was 57,089,000. This was the greatest of any time since January, 1937, and indicated that the public was buying stocks heavily on the advance, and that the insiders were selling. Prices failed to cross the high of November 10, 1938, an indication of top, and a selling level. Large volume always tells of the top.

September, 1939, to April 28, 1942. The averages declined 64 points. The total volume was 465,996,000. The volume continued to decrease during 1940 and 1941. From a total of 496,138,000 in 1936, the volume in 1941 was only 170,604,000 indicating that liquidation was about completed. During February, March and April, 1942, the volume was around 8 million shares and slightly lower. This indicated complete liquidation and that the market was laying the foundation for higher prices.

1942, May to August. The volume continued to average below 8 million shares per month, indicating small buying in a liquidated market. Later in the year the volume increased, but the total for the year 1942 was the lowest in many years, only 125,652,000.

1943. There was a big increase in volume, 278 million. 1944 was 263 million.

The market continued to advance in 1945, and the total volume was 375 million, the largest of any year since 1938. This enormous volume indicated that the bull campaign was nearing the end.

1946, January. Sales 51,510,000. This was the largest sale for any month since March, 1937, and indicated that the top was near. After the high in the early part of February, the Averages only advanced 5 points higher to final high May 29, 1946.

A bull campaign was begun on April 28, 1942, and ended on May 29, 1946, with an advance of 120 points. The total volume for this period was 1 billion and 179 million. The fact that the volume had increased enormously in the last year of the advance indicated the end of the bull market.

1946, June to October 30. The Averages declined 53

points on a total volume of 136,955,000. This was a big decline in a short period of time, and the volume ran around 20 million for June, July and August.

In September when the market was breaking rapidly, the volume was over 43 million, and in October when the bottom was reached, the volume was 30 million. After that the volume continued to run small.

October 30, 1946, to February, 1947, a total advance of 27 points. Volume of sales a little over 100 million shares.

1947, March to May 19. Market declined 27 points on a volume of 60,576,000. During May when low was reached, the volume was down 20 million, showing that liquidation was not very heavy.

1947, May 19 to July 25. The Averages rallied approximately 28 points. The total volume 42,956,000. The volume in July was 25,473,000, the largest for any month in the year, indicating that the public was again buying on top, and a reaction was in order.

July 25, 1947, to February 11, 1948. The Averages declined about 25 points. Total volume was 139,799,000. The volume during February was under 17 million, the smallest for several months. The market became very dull and narrow at this time and was of small volume indicating there was no heavy selling pressure, and a rally was due, especially as the Averages were holding higher support levels than May, 1947.

February 11, 1948, to June 14, 1948, an advance of 30 points. Total volume 131,296,000. The volume in February was slightly below 17 million, and in May the total volume was 42,769,000. This was the highest volume of any month since September, 1946. This heavy volume with the Averages up to an old selling level indicated the market was making top. During the month of June, the total volume was a little less than 31 million showing that the public had loaded up in May and that buying power was decreasing on the advance.

June 14, 1948, to June 14, 1949. The Averages declined around 34 points. Total volume was 246,305,000.

In February, 1949, the volume again dropped to around 17 million, and in June, 1949, total volume was 17,767,000. This compared with the volume of nearly 43 million in May, 1948, another indication that the market was liquidated and with prices of the Averages down the low levels of October, 1946, and the lows of May, 1947, indicated a buying level. You will note that in 1947 the total volume of sales was 253,632,000, and in 1948 the total volume was 302,216,000, and the biggest percentage of this volume occurred on the advance from February to June.

The first six months of 1949 the total volume was 112,403,000. This is much less than one-half the total volume of 1948.

Should the market advance during the balance of 1949, the volume will probably increase and by the end of the year be as great as 1948.

Remember it is always important to study the volume of sales monthly and weekly and use the volume in connection with all of the other rules.

MONTHLY AND YEARLY VOLUME OF SALES ON NEW YORK STOCK EXCHANGE

(000 omitted)

	1936	1937	1938	1939	1940
Jan.	67,202	58,671	24,154	25,183	15,987
Feb.	60,884	50,248	14,525	13,874	13,472
Mch.	51,107	50,346	22,997	24,563	16,272
Apr.	39,610	34,607	17,119	20,245	26,693
May	20,614	18,549	13,999	12,934	38,965
June	21,429	16,449	24,368	11,967	15,574
July	34,793	20,722	38,771	18,068	7,305
Aug.	26,564	17,213	20,733	17,374	7,615
Sept.	30,873	33,853	23,825	57,089	11,940
Oct.	43,995	51,130	41,555	23,736	14,489
Nov.	50,467	29,255	27,926	19,223	20,887
Dec.	48,600	28,422	27,492	17,773	18,397
Totals	496,138	409,465	297,464	262,029	197,596

	1941	1942	1943	1944	1945
Jan.	13,313	12,998	18,032	17,809	38,995
Feb.	8,970	7,924	24,432	17,099	32,611
Mch.	10,124	8,554	36,996	27,645	27,490
Apr.	11,187	7,588	33,554	13,845	28,270
May	9,669	7,231	35,049	17,229	32,025
June	10,462	7,466	23,419	37,713	41,320
July	17,872	8,375	26,323	28,220	19,977
Aug.	10,873	7,387	14,252	20,753	21,670
Sept.	13,546	9,448	14,985	15,948	23,135
Oct.	13,151	15,932	13,924	17,534	35,474
Nov.	15,047	13,436	18,244	18,019	40,404
Dec.	36,390	19,313	19,528	31,261	34,150
Totals	170,604	125,652	278,738	263,075	375,510

	1946	1947	1948	1949
Jan.	51,510	23,557	20,217	18,825
Feb.	34,095	23,762	16,801	17,182
Mch.	25,666	19,339	22,993	21,135
Apr.	31,426	20,620	34,612	19,315
May	30,409	20,617	42,769	18,179
June	21,717	17,483	30,922	17,767
July	20,595	25,473	24,585	
Aug.	20,808	14,153	15,040	
Sept.	43,451	16,017	17,564	
Oct.	30,384	28,635	20,434	
Nov.	23,820	16,371	28,320	
Dec.	29,832	27,605	27,959	
Totals	363,713	253,632	302,216	112,403

CHAPTER XI

15 PUBLIC UTILITY AVERAGES

During the Roosevelt administration the public utilities were depressed and the government did everything against them. Times have changed since President Roosevelt passed away in 1945, and the utilities now get a square deal, and their prospects look brighter. It is of interest to review the course of the Averages on the utilities from 1929 to date. (Refer to Chart in back of Book.)

1929, September High 144½. November Low 64½.

1930, April High 108½.

1932, July Low 16½. September High 36.

1933, March Low 19½. This was 3 points above the Low of July, 1932 and indicated higher prices, which followed.

1933, July High 37½. This was 1½ points above the High of September, 1932.

1935, March Low 14½. This was below the Low of 1932 and the Low of 1933, and liquidation had been completed at that time, and an advance followed.

1937, February High 37½. This was back to the High of 1933 where resistance could be expected.

1938, March Low 15½, one point above the 1935 Low.

1939, August High 27½. This was still below the Low of August, 1937 showing main Trend down. Prices continued to decline.

1942, April final Low 10½. The market remained in a narrow trading range for several months and finally crossed the High of June, 1942 in October, 1942 showing Up Trend. The advance continued and in 1945 the averages crossed the High of 1939 and continued to advance crossing the Highs of 1933 and 1937.

1946, April, final high 44½. This was exactly the same price as the last high in February, 1932, a natural resistance level.

1946, October Low 32½. 1947, January High 37½.

1947, May Low 32. July High 36¼.

1948, February Low 31½, one point under the Low of October, 1946, but back to the same Lows of August, 1945.

1948, June and July High 36½, back to the High of July, 1947.

1948, November and December Low, 32½, making a Higher Bottom than February, 1948.

1949, April and May High 36½, back to the old Top Level.

June 14 Low 33.75. This was a much higher Bottom than December, 1948, showing good support. As long as the Averages hold above 33, they are in position to go higher, and when they cross 36½ will be in a stronger position and closing above 38, which is above 1947 Tops, will be still stronger and will indicate 44½, the 1946 High. The public utilities are in a stronger position than the Rails and also in a stronger position than the industrial Averages. This group of stocks is in position to lead the advance in the next Bull Market. The public utility Averages would have to break the Bottom at 31½ to indicate Lower.

August, 1949, will be important for a change in Trend in the Averages and if they have crossed Top and show Up Trend at that time, they might continue up int the spring of 1950.

Barron's Air Transport Averages

This group of stocks is definitely one of the groups for leaders in the future, and each individual company should be studied in making long pull investments in it. The review of Air Transport Averages is important and gives an indication of the future trend of air lines.

1937, January High 27¾. 1938, March Low 7½.

1940, April High 34½. 1942, April Low 13½.

1943, July High 43½. 1943, December 32½.

In December 1943 holding just below the High Level of April, 1940 shows that they were in strong position, and a rapid advance followed.

1945, December High 91½. 1947, January Low 37½.

1947, April High 46½. 1947, December Low 30.

This was below the low of December, 1943 and indicated higher prices and lower prices later.

1948, April High 39¼. 1948, November Low 25½.

1949, March Low 25¾. 1949, June Low 32.09.

Holding above the low of November, 1948 indicated strength and a rally to follow.

It is interesting to review the progressive Bottoms that these Averages have made over the past few years.

1938, Low 7½, 1942 Low 13½, 1948 Low 25½, and up to this writing, June, 1949 Low 32.09, making progressive or Higher Bottoms over a series of years which is an indication of higher prices later. It is the writer's opinion that the air lines will lead the next Bull Market. Among those that I consider best for future leaders are American Airlines, Pan American Airways, Northwestern Airways, Eastern Airlines and Trans-continental and Western Airlines. If I should have to select two that I consider the very best I would select Eastern Airlines and Pan American. These companies are well managed and have shown good earnings throughout all the years, and will be future leaders. It is my opinion that in the not distant future there will be a merger of several of the big airlines with the weaker lines, and eventually there will be three or four strong companies that will control all the business in the country. When this takes place the earnings will increase and the airlines will make rapid progress and those who buy airline stocks and hold them should get a sub-stantial increase on their investment.

Stocks With Small Number of Shares

During the past years when Bull Markets have occurred, stocks with a small number of shares outstanding have had substantial advances, greater in proportion than corporations with a large amount of shares outstanding. It requires less money to buy up the controlling supply of stocks of this kind, and therefore, when they become scarce it does not require so much buying power to bring about an advance.

Joy Manufacturing Company

This is an old and substantial company. It is well managed and not over-capitalized. The earnings in 1949 are running very high, and the prospects of good earnings are excellent. This company with less than a million shares outstanding and with such favorable earnings has a chance for substantial advancement in a Bull Market. We review the price swing on this stock:

1941, September High 14.

1942, August Low 7½.

1943, June and July High, 12½.

1943, December Low 9¾.

1945, May High 30¼.

1945, August Low 22¾.

1946, April High 34. October Low 18¼.

1947, October High 40½. This was the record High up to this time. The price well above the 1946 High should place the stock in a strong position.

1948, February Low 31½, still above the Low of May, 1945.

1948, June High 43½. This was a new High three points above the High of October, 1947.

1948, September Low 30½, supported at the same low level as May 1945, and one point below the Low of February, 1948.

1949, March High 40. Just under the High of 1947.

1949, June Low 31½. At the same level as February, 1948 and one point above the Low of November, 1948. As long as this stock holds above 30½ it is in position to go higher. Crossing 36½ will be in a stronger position and at any time it closes above 40½ will indicate much higher prices possibly above 43 or 43½. A stock of this kind should be bought and a Stop Loss Order placed, limiting the risk. When the Trend turns up there are possibilities of substantial profits.

CHAPTER XII

PUTS, CALLS, RIGHTS AND WARRANTS ON STOCKS

Many people do not understand what PUTS and CALLS are and how to BUY and SELL them. A CALL is an option to buy a stock at a fixed price. for 30, 60, 90 or 180 days. For these options you pay a premium of anywhere from $140.00 to $250.00 based upon the price of the stock and the condition of the market. All you can lose on the option is the price you pay for the call, and it is good from the day you buy it to the day it expires. For example, suppose you buy a call on United States Steel at 22 good for six months, and pay, we will say, $140.00 for the call. Now no matter how low U. S. Steel declines in the six months, you can only lose your premium money of $140.00. But, on the other hand, should steel advance to 30 at any time, you can sell the stock at 30 and your profit will be $800.00 less the cost of the call and commission.

Another thing that you could do if you had a call on steel and you had a profit—suppose that it advanced from 22 to 26 and you thought it might not go any higher. You could sell 50 shares short against it, which would give you your money back with a small profit. Then if the stock continued to advance, you would be making money on 50 shares which you would still have long. On the other hand, let us suppose that steel declines to 23. You decide that it is low enough, and you buy in 50 shares of stock and make 3 points. Then it advances on and before the time the option runs out it is up to 30 or higher, and you still get a profit on the full 100 shares.

Another way to use puts and calls is for protection. Just suppose that you are long of United States Steel and it is sell-ing around 22. You think it might go to 16 or 15 in the next few months, and you want to be protected. So you buy a put and pay $140.00 for the premium. In the meantime, steel declines to 16 and your loss on your long stock would only be from the price of the put where you could deliver it. In the meantime, you could buy the stock and deliver against the short sale and still have your long stock with the cost reduced.

Puts

A PUT means that you buy the privilege to deliver or sell 100 shares of stock or more at a fixed price any time during the life of the option, whether it be 30, 60, 90 days or six months. Suppose that Chrysler is selling at 50, and you think it is going lower. You buy a put at 50, good for six months. You might have to pay $187.50 or $200.00 for this. That is all you can lose. Suppose that during the six months Chrysler declines to 40. You could then buy in the stock 'and deliver it on the put at 50 and make 10 points less the cost of the put and your commission. You could also, if you were in Chrysler, if it declined to 45 and you thought it was low enough, buy 50 shares against the PUT. Then if the stock continued to decline you would still be making on 50 shares. If it turned around and advanced over 50, you would have 5 points profit on the stock bought against the put. This is what is called trading against PUTS and CALLS.

When you buy a put or call, it is endorsed and guaranteed by a stock exchange house, and no matter how high or how low the stock goes, you can always get delivery at the price you bought a PUT or CALL. No margin requirements are due until you make a trade and then you put up the regular margins until the stock is delivered. Any broker will give you information about buying PUTS and CALLS and the margin required at the time you make delivery or accept delivery on a PUT or CALL. PUTS and CALLS are traded in through the put and call brokers in New York. You can usually get quotations any day on almost any active stock running from 30 days to six months in advance. I consider PUTS and CALLS a profitable, safe way to trade because you can risk a small amount of money and you cannot lose more than that, while your profits are unlimited if the stock goes your way.

Rights and Warrants

Many people do not understand rights and warrants or how to trade in them. You can buy the warrants for a very small amount of money covering a long period of time. Some warrants at the present time run for as long as 1955.

A warrant is a right issued to buy or call for a certain number of shares of stock in a company covering a certain fixed period of time. They are the same as calls on stocks except they run for a longer period of time.

Any broker who is a member of the New York Stock Exchange will give you information on warrants and buy and sell them for you. You will find it most profitable to buy warrants in periods of depression when stocks are selling at very low levels and the warrants are also selling at low levels. At the end of a bull market the stocks will be selling at high levels, and you will have bought the warrants at low levels during the depression and can sell the stocks at high levels.

The issuance of warrants by corporations desiring to increase their stock capitalization performs the function of not only assuring the maintenance of an equitable percentage ownership, but generally acts as a device for the sale of additional securities over a period of time at a price agreeable to the management.

Warrants generally extend far into the future and, as a result, become a medium by which investors and traders in effect are trading in a call or option on the stock, with the advantage of an increased leverage which is inherent in this type of instrument.

This leverage characteristic makes warrants suitable as a speculative medium as can be seen by the wide price range as compared to the range in the common stock over a period of years. This is even more marked when considered on a percentage basis.

Some warrants are useful, also, to investors who in uncertain times desire to accumulate an investment position, providing the general level of prices increases, and who, in the meanwhile, do not desire to tie up more than a limited capital. In effect, such investors will buy a call on the stock and pay a premium for the privilege.

Large Profits on Small Risks

When you buy a warrant on any stock, all that you can lose is the price that you pay for the warrant. If the stock advances, the warrants also advance, and you make profits on the warrants when you sell them without calling for the stock or exercising your warrant.

Below we give some examples of profits which could have been made buying warrants.

Tri-Continental Corporation

This is a general management investment trust, and the stock is actively quoted all of the time. In 1941 and 1942 the warrants sold as low as 1/32. In 1936 they sold as high as 5 3/8. Should you have invested $1,000.00 in 1941 or 1942 and bought the warrants you could have bought 32,000 warrants. If you had sold them at 5 in 1946, they would be worth $160,000.00, a profit of $159,000 on $1,000.00 in 4 years time, less a small commission.

Merritt-Chapman and Scott

One of the leading contractors of the United States which equipped for all kinds of construction work and also handles construction in foreign countries. There is an active market for the common stock and it pays a dividend of $1.60 per year.

In 1938-39-40-41-42 and 43 warrants on this stock sold as low as 1/4 and 3/8. In 1946 the rights sold at 12½. A $1,000.00 investment when the rights were selling at 1/4 would have bought 40,000 warrants. Should you have sold the warrants in 1946 at 12, they would be worth $48,000.00, or a profit of $47,000.00 on $1,000.00 investment.

Atlas Corporation

This is an investment, trust and holding company.
In 1941 and 1942 the warrants sold as low as 1/4, or 25

cents a share. In 1946 they sold as high as 13⅝. $1,000.00 in 1942 at ¼ would buy 4,000 warrants. In the early part of 1946 the warrants could have been sold for 13, which amounts to $52,000.00, or a profit of $51,000.00 on an investment of $1,000.00.

The above profits are not picked out as just an exception. Warrants on other stocks of different kinds have shown as great opportunities for profit.

Below we give a list of warrants and rights actively traded in on the New York Stock and Curb Exchange. These are approximately for June 30.

ACTIVELY TRADED WARRANTS ON THE NEW YORK STOCK AND CURB EXCHANGE

SECURITIES	COMPARATIVE PRICE RANGE STOCKS AND WARRANTS	CURRENT PRICE
	(Date) (Price Range)	
A. C. F. BRILL	1944-49	
Stock	19—2	2
Warrants (1 sh. at 12½ to 1/1/50 and at 15 to 1/1/55)	11½—¾	¾
AMERICAN & FOREIGN POWER	1929-49	
Stock	199¼—¼	1⅝
Warrants (1 sh. at $25 at any time) ..	174—1/32	
ATLAS	1936-49	
Stock	34⅜—5¾	20
Warrants (1 sh. at $25 at any time) ..	13⅝—¼	4⅜
COLORADO FUEL & IRON	1936-49	
Stock	25⅞—4½	12½
Warrants (1 sh. at 17½ to 2/1/50) ...	12½—½	⅞
COMMONWEALTH & SOUTHERN	1930-49	
Stock	20¼—⅛	3½
Warrants (1 sh. at $30 at any time) ..	6¼—1/256	1/16
ELECTRIC POWER & LIGHT	1926-49	
Stock	103½—⅝	24¾
Warrants (1 sh. at $25 at any time) ..	78⅛—1/16	8¼
HUSSMANN-LIGONIER	1945-49	
Stock ADJ for 2 for 1 split July, 1947	18½—9	10¼
Warrants (1 sh. at $8.45 to 5/15/50)	14¾—3½	4

MERRITT CHAPMAN SCOTT	1936-49		
Stock		27¾—1¼	18⅛
Warrants (1 sh. at $28.99 at any time)		12½—¼	4½—5½
NIAGARA HUDSON	1937-49		
Stock		16⅞—⅞	9½
Warrants (1 sh. at $42.86 at any time)		3⅜—1/32	5/32 B
TRI-CONTINENTAL	1930-49		
Stock		20¼—⅝	6¼
Warrants (1.27 shs. at $17.76 at any time)		9—1/32	2⅛
UNITED CORP.	1930-49		
Stock		52—3/16	3
Warrants (1 sh. at $27.50 at any time)		30⅞—1/256	⅛
WARD BAKING CO.	1945-49		
Stock		19⅞—8¾	12
Warrants (1 sh. at $12.50 to 4/1/51 and 1 sh. at $15.00 to 4/1/55)		9⅛—2¾	2¾

CHAPTER XIII

NEW DISCOVERIES AND INVENTIONS

During the past history of the world following each depression some new discovery or some new invention has stimulated business and progress and brought on another boom. Fulton's invention of the steam engine and Whitney's invention of the cotton gin started a new era of progress.

In 1849 the discovery of gold in California brought on a wave of prosperity. From that time on, the progress of the railroads opened up the central and the western part of the United States, and great progress was made through this new mode of transportation.

The Bible tells us that old things pass away and new ones come to take their places. The canal boats and stage coaches passed away to give way to the railroad, a more rapid mode of transportation. Then came new discoveries and new inventions and the new mode of making steel, and the United States became an industrial nation and made great progress. In the early 1900's the progress and invention of the automobile revolutionized transportation and started another wave of prosperity giving employment to thousands of people. Then followed chemical discoveries and inventions, Rayon, and other new discoveries along chemical lines which aided progress and prosperity. Often when we were in the depths of a depression and things looked the worst, some new discovery or invention has brought about a revival of business and another wave of prosperity.

The invention of the airplane by the Wright brothers started another wave of prosperity and brought on increased rapid transportation which has not yet reached its height. This greatest mode of transportation of all is bringing all parts of the world closer together and uniting people for peace and business purposes. How much the airplane will do in the future to bring about greater prosperity remains yet to be seen, but its usefulness in every field of transportation is increasing day by day and its possibilities are unlimited. There is one problem with the airplane. That is, cheaper fuel and lighter fuel. This problem will no doubt be solved. When the load of fuel has come down and it becomes a pay load, air transportation, both for express, freight and passengers will become the cheapest mode of transportation in the world as well as the fastest. This will help to revolutionize business and bring on another wave of prosperity.

Atomic Power

The United States won the war in 1945 by the use of atomic power which was developed by the United States. While this atomic power caused great destruction of Japan at the cost of many lives, it shortened the war and saved many lives which would have been lost should the war have been prolonged. This great invention of power has possibilities beyond the comprehension of the average man, and it may be the very power that will solve the most difficult problem with the airplane by giving them cheap fuel and a great reduction in weight thereby making the load now carried as weight for gasoline a pay load which would increase not only the speed but increase the amount of cargo and passengers carried. It would give greater space for passengers and for cargo when the fuel is limited to a small place with greater power. There is a possibility that *atomic* power can be produced once it is perfected cheaper than any other fuel that man has ever invented. This would revolutionize air transportation and help to bring about increased prosperity. Not only *atomic* power but the power from the sun or from the air has possibilities in the future which would give cheap power and revolutionize manufacturing in many lines. This would cut the cost of production benefiting the consumer and giving him more for his dollar, therefore increasing the purchasing power because it is a well known fact that when the cost comes down the consumption increases. We can always buy unlimited amounts of anything when the price is within our means. *Atomic* power for energy holds the key to the future for cheap power and undreamed possibilities for this new discovery.

CHAPTER XIV

GREAT MARKET OPERATORS OF THE PAST

This writer recalls the panic of 1893 to 1896, when cotton sold as low as 3 cents a pound in the south, and a panic swept across the country which the people said was one of the worst in history. The price of wheat and other commodities was low, and I remember the first corner that I ever read about. The corner in wheat by Lighter in Chicago. In this campaign Lighter forced wheat from below $1.00 a bushel to $1.85 per bushel. He had a vast fortune made in paper profits, but he went broke. The old and valuable lesson that we can learn from studying the history of past large operators is what causes them to go broke after they accumulate a large fortune. In the case of Lighter, it was the unknown that caused his downfall. He did not believe that wheat could be delivered in Chicago in sufficient quantities to depress the market, but Armour, who was smarter than Lighter had reckoned on, had wheat shipped in by express cars for delivery. He broke the corner and Lighter went broke. No man gets so smart but what the unknown or the unexpected can happen and cause him to lose all the money he has made or the greater part of his fortune. Therefore, the lesson to be learned by mistakes of others is, don't make the same mistake. Most operators lose their money because they lose all sense of proportion, and they have only the desire for the power that money can give and want to corner the markets. Corners force prices too high and inflicts suffering upon the consumer, and the result is that almost all of them who have tried this have gone the same way. They have gone broke.

I was in the cotton market during the Sully campaign of 1903 and 1904. Sully amassed millions of dollars in a short period of time by buying cotton. He made the mistake of all great operators of thinking that he had too much power and that he could begin to force prices higher. The result was that Sully went broke and went through bankruptcy.

Theodore H. Price, another great operator in cotton of his day, made the same mistake of buying too much and underestimating the unexpected, and he also went broke. But with due respect to his memory, it must be said that Price made one of the greatest comebacks of any man in history, and made back millions of dollars and paid his creditors dollar for dollar. Another operator who started from a few hundred dollars and amassed millions of dollars and then went broke was Eugene Scales. Why did Scales go broke in the cotton market after accumulating millions of dollars? He went broke because he had a greater desire for power and to run the market than he had for making profits and using extreme cautious judgment. A man uses one kind of judgment and caution when he starts with a very small amount of money and entirely different judgment when he amasses a large amount of money. He does not figure that the unexpected can happen. Scales was a chronic bull. He never thought the market was going to reach top, and he continued to buy cotton hoping and believing prices would go higher, until finally he went broke, and died with very little money.

Jesse L. Livermore, one of the most spectacular traders of his day, made millions of dollars in the stock and the commodity markets. He went broke several times and went through bankruptcy several times, and a few times he paid out after he had gone bankrupt. Livermore was an honorable man and believed in paying debts even after he had been relieved through the courts of bankruptcy. I first met Livermore in 1908 and again in 1913 when he was trading through the firm of Murray Mitchell and Company, which failed, and I lost all of my money. In 1917 when Livermore came back and made a fortune, he not only paid back my proportionate part of money which I lost through the Mitchell failure, but paid everyone else. This was an honorable thing to do, and because of Livermore's honor and honesty, in 1934 when he was broke, I backed him and got other people to raise money and back him. Livermore came back again and made money. But Livermore's one weak point was that he never studied anything, except how to make money. He never studied the rules for keeping money. He had the greed and the desire for power, and when he got a large amount of money, he could not trade conservatively. He tried to make the market go his way instead of waiting until the market was ready to follow the natural trend. Livermore, after making the many fortunes, committed suicide and died practically broke. Why did a man who made so many millions of dollars as Livermore not keep them? It is because each time he had the same greed, the same desire for power, to be a great man and run the market. He wanted to rule, and he did not figure that the unexpected could happen, which it did and always will, and the result was that he lost his money.

Doctor E. A. Crawford, another great character and a great trader, made and lost several fortunes. He started again with a few thousand dollars in 1932 and probably made money faster than any other operator who was ever in the market. It is reported that at the height of the market in 1933 that he had accumulated a paper profit anywhere between 30 and 50 million dollars. He was buying all food products. Not only in the United States, but in foreign countries. he was heavily involved in the stock market. Dr. Crawford failed July 18, 1933, and all commodity markets smashed wide open on his failure. Why·did a man who could amass so many million dollars as this go broke? Simply because he did not figure that the unexpected could happen and that somebody could sell more grain and commodities than he could buy. He figured that prices were going to continue up without any reaction, which they always have to have. The result was he kept on buying until the fatal day came and he was forced to sell. He had thrown caution to the winds in buying, forgotten all the rules which he used in making money when he started on a small amount of capital, and the result was that without obedience to the rules of finance there could be but one result. Failure. He, like all other operators, made the great mistake of overtrading. This is the greatest sin of all speculative operators—overtrading, throwing caution to the winds and not figuring that the unexpected can happen. Last but not least of all of the great market operators was Jordan of New Orleans, who, it is reported, started with $300.00 a few years before 1946 and by operating in the cotton market accumulated many millions of dollars. Jordan went the way of all operators. He went broke. Why? Because he believed that cotton would keep on going up. He could not see any top, and he did not take profits. I am told that Jordan talked about cotton going as high as it went in the Civil War, $1.89 a pound. He forgot or did not know the rules of supply and demand. He continued to buy until he could buy no more. He had a great following. The public was buying. So finally, when the day came to try to sell, there were no buyers, and everybody became sellers. The collapse came from a high of 3928 for October Cotton on October 9, 1946 prices declined in less than one month's time to 2310 on November 7, 1946. Not only Jordan lost all of his fortune, but his followers lost millions of dollars and even the United States Government could not stop the decline in the cotton market. The Government and members of exchanges and other operators were forced to call in Anderson and Clayton and get them to take over the contracts of cotton held by Jordan and his followers in order to save the day. Jordan, like all of the other great operators, had not studied the market to know when prices were at abnormal levels. If he had carefully studied the prices of previous wars, especially the World War when cotton went to 43 cents a pound, July option selling at 4375, he would have known that prices were at abnormal levels. Again if he had reviewed the year 1923, he would have found that prices made high on November 30 around 37½ cents, and should have known by these records that when prices advance anywhere between 37½ cents and 39 cents a pound that they were at abnormal levels brought about by war conditions which always create abnormal prices. Had he considered well these facts, he would have started selling out long cotton in time to protect his profits and could have gone short and made another vast fortune. Had he understood the rules and fundamental principles of the market, he would have known the small gain that the cotton prices made in the last few weeks indicated that somebody was selling in almost unlimited quantities, and he should have started to sell at the time when he could have gotten out. But man's greatest enemy, hope, kept him holding on until the disaster came, and he went down the same as all the others because the unexpected happened, and someone was able to sell more cotton than he could buy. He was in bad company, the public was with him on a large scale. When he tried to get out, everybody else was trying to get out.

What can the ordinary man, speculator, investor or trader, learn from the history of great operators who have amassed millions of dollars and have lost them? He can learn the lesson of why they lost it, and what rules they failed to follow, and not do the same things that they did. Then he has a chance to make money and keep it. The greatest thing he must learn, and the most important, is not to overtrade. The next thing he must learn to do is to use *stop loss orders,* protecting both his principal and his profits by an automatic *stop loss order.* He must trade on facts eliminating both hope and fear, the trader's greatest enemies. If a man buys and holds on on hope, eventually he will sell when he fears the worst, and then it is too late.

Facts are stubborn things, but they must be faced and hope must be eliminated by any man who expects to make success by trading in stocks or commodities. A man must remember that the trend of markets change and he must change when the trend changes. He must learn the rules that have worked in the past and apply them in the market in the future in order to make a success.

We have reviewed the history of great market traders who have made millions of dollars and lost them. There must be exceptions to all rules. There are men who have made the money and kept it by following the right rules of finance.

Who are some of these great market operators who made the money and kept it? Bernard Baruch is one. He is an old man, retired and still worth millions of dollars, the greater part of it which he made out of investments and speculations in the stock market. Ben Smith, another operator of recent years, made the money and kept it. Bert Castles, another large operator, made money and kept it and died with it. How did Castles do it? When he bought he always placed a *stop loss order* on stocks not more than 5 points from the price at which he bought or sold. This limited his loss if he was wrong. When he was right, he let his profits run until he had a definite reason to cash in.

Successful investors have definite plans and rules, and follow them. If you expect to succeed, you must learn the right rules first; then follow them.

I could mention many more successful investors and traders who made millions of dollars and have kept it. What different rules did they follow from the rules followed by the plungers who made millions and then lost it? These wise operators, speculators or investors, if you please to call them that, were men who followed definite rules of finance. They learned how to determine the trend of stocks and commodities and bought at the right time. They were not hogs. They knew when to take profits. They knew that the unexpected could happen. They did not overtrade, and they sold when everybody else was buying and bought when everybody else was selling. This could not be done by ordinary human judgment or guess work. They had to follow well formulated rules, secure all the information possible and use the proper caution and not overtrade. This is the reason that they made a success and did not go broke. It is well for any trader to remember that when he makes a trade, he can be *wrong*. Then how can he correct that *mistake?* By putting on a *stop loss order* and taking a small loss. Unless a man knows the risk he is going to take and how much of his capital he can risk on a trade, he should never start speculating. Because without knowing these fundamental rules, sooner or later the unexpected will happen and he will go broke. It is not my object in writing this book after 45 years experience, to paint a rosy picture of an easy way to get rich, because there is no easy road to riches. My object is to tell you the truth and give you practical rules that will work if you put in the time to study and have the patience to wait for opportunities to *buy* and *sell* at the *right time,* you can make a success. Every man takes out of life just exactly according to what he puts in. We reap just what we sow. A man who pays with time and money for knowledge and continues to study and never gets to the point where he thinks he knows all there is to know, but realizes that he can still learn, is the man who will make a success in speculation or in investments. I am trying to tell you the truth and give you the benefit of over 45 years of operating in stocks and commodity markets and point out to you the weak points which will prevent you from meeting with disaster. Speculation can be made a *profitable profession.* Wall Street can be beaten and there is money operating in commodities and the stock market if you follow the rules and always realize that the unexpected can happen and be prepared for it.

CHAPTER XV

STOCKS LIQUIDATED

While the Dow-Jones 30 Industrial Averages have declined only 25% from the 1946 Highs, many individual stocks are down 75 to 90% from the Highs recorded in 1945 and 1946. The stock market discounts business six months or more in advance. Can stocks go up while a business depression is on? They can. It has happened in the past and it can happen again.

Airline Stocks

This group of stocks has been liquidated more than almost any other group. The air industry is a growing industry. It is not going out of business, and airline stocks will go up and sooner or later have sensational advances. They *will* become future leaders.

The following are the High and Low prices for recent years:

American Airlines	1945 High 95½	1948 Low 6
Bell Aircraft	1946 High 35½	1948 Low 10¾
Bendix Aviation	1945 High 63	1949 Low 26
Braniff Airlines	1945 High 37½	1948 Low 6
Eastern Airlines	1945 High 134	1949 Low 13
(1946 High 31½ after stock dividend)		
National Airlines	1945 High 41¾	1938 Low 4
Northwest Airlines	1945 High 63¾	1949 Low 7
Pan American World Airways	1946 High 29	1948 Low 8
Trans-World Airways	1945 High 79	1948 Low 9½
United Airlines	1945 High 62½	1948 Low 9½

Among the very best to buy are Eastern Airlines, Pan American and United Airlines.

Miscellaneous Stocks That Have Been Liquidated

The following stocks have declined to very Low Levels and show possibilities of advancing in the next Bull Market:

Gimbel Bros.	1946	High	73¾	1949 Low	12
Lockheed	1946	High	45½	1947 Low	10½
				1949 Low	16½
Martin, G. L.	1946	High	47¾	1949 Low	7
Montgomery Ward	1946	High	104	1949 Low	47½
Pure Oil	1948	High	42	1949 Low	24⅝
Philco Radio	1948	High	46½	1949 Low	25¼
Standard Oil of New Jersey	1948	High	93	1949 Low	60½
Sperry	1946	High	40½	1947 Low	17
U. S. Rubber	1946	High	80½	1949 Low	33
General Motors	1946	High	80½	1946 Low	47½
	1947	High	65¾	1948 Low	15½
	1948	High	66	1949 Low	51⅞

(In 1943 the Low was 48¾. The Lows have been progressively higher since that time, showing good support and unless General Motors breaks 51⅞ and closes below this level it is in a position to go higher. 1947 and 1948 is a Double Top, and should General Motors ever close above 66 it will indicate very much higher.)

Special Stocks

Admiral Corporation	1945	High	22½	1947 Low	6
	1948	High	22⅝	1948 Low	7
	1949	High	20¼	1949 Low	14¾

(This company is well managed and is showing good earnings. The stock was well supported on the decline in June 1949 and shows possibilities of going higher, especially if a Bull Market develops.)

Columbia Pictures	1945	High	45½	1948 Low	7½
Consolidated Vultee	1946	High	37	1948 Low	7¾

Columbia Gas Has been making Higher Bottoms each year

since 1942 and is in a position to go higher.

Electric Bond & Share   1946 High 26½ 1947 Low   9

This stock is in a strong position. Cash assets of the Company are much greater than the price for which the stock is selling. There is a possibility of a cash distribution of 12 and 14 dollars per share before the end of 1949. The stock is making progressively Higher Bottoms and is holding around 13¼ which is a 50% decline from the 1946 High, making this a safe, sure Buying Point. When the stock advances above 16 it will be in a very strong position and will indicate higher prices, possibly 25 to 26.

The above list of Special Stocks is in a position to become leaders in the next Bull Market. Remember, when you buy a stock, protect it with a Stop Loss Order and if it does not act right within a reasonable length of time, sell it and take a small loss.

CHAPTER XVI

CAN UNITED STATES AFFORD ANOTHER WAR?

In 1918 when we finished the World War, it was supposed to be the war that would end all wars. In 1939 Hitler started war again, and in 1941, we were forced into the war. The United States financed Russia and all of the other countries to help defeat Germany with the object that it was to end war for all times and that we were to have peace and prosperity.

What happened? Just as soon as the war was over, the United States started preparing for another war and propaganda has been circulated from time to time that sooner or later we would have to fight Russia. 15 to 16 billion dollars is being spent in 1949 in preparation for war. If we fought two wars to end wars and are now getting ready for another war, would that end war for all time? It would not; because wars have never settled anything and until men learn to settle differences without resorting to war, there can be no permanent peace. No matter who wins in war, they lose. War is a destructive, losing business. It costs the manhood of a country as well as the vital food products and necessities from manufacturing lines. The United States now has a debt of over 250 billion dollars. How can the United States afford to fight another war? Where would they get the money to finance it? Who would or who could afford to buy the bonds to finance another war? If we go into another war, it simply means complete bankruptcy and destruction of the United States. Wars are too costly. The United States is already mortgaged for more than can be liquidated, considering all government and private debts. What we need in Washington is men of vision and brains who will talk and work for peace and not waste money and prepare for war.

Why did we go to war in December 1941? Because our liberty was threatened and was insecure, we risked our lives and our resources to win a war and make our liberty secure.

We thought we were making it secure. But is it secure? And do we have the liberty that we had before the war? We do not, because the New Deal is taking the liberties away as fast as they can. The New Deal continues to talk of security. They are going to take care of people from the cradle to the grave; provide social security, provide medical treatment, provide everything. What this country needs, and the people as individuals, is not security, because security does not make progress. Security breeds defeat and worklessness. The country worked hard and risked everything when they were insecure. A man will work harder and make greater progress when he is insecure, and it is better that he is that way. If the government could provide everything for the people, which, of course, is impossible, it would then create nothing but a nation of loafers and everything would soon go to decay. The New Deal thrives on promises, promising everybody something for nothing, and the fellow who wants to get something for nothing is the man who will not give or produce. What this country needs is not more promises, but more production. The problems of this country can only be solved by more work and more saving, not by less work and more pay. If we are to have a free and independent country and retain the liberty for which our forefathers fought, then the rights for all must be equal. When our soldiers go to war, if they disobey orders or refuse to fight, they are shot down. They cannot go on a strike and refuse to fight; yet while the war was on, union labor continued to strike while our boys were risking and losing their lives. Why had union labor more right than the soldier who risks his life? He has not. The right to union labor leaders is given by politicians who have betrayed the rights of the people who elected them. Why has union labor the right to strike and cut off the necessities of life, to cause people to go hungry, cold and suffer all kinds of privations? Just because union labor leaders are trying to force business to give more pay for less work. This cannot make a prosperous country.

What caused France to lose the war? It was union labor and communism. The workers would not work and produce.

The result was France lost the war because the German people were not only willing to work, but they were forced to work and produce, and they won the war against France. Who gives to union labor the rights not enjoyed by capital or the private citizen? The law makers, who are elected by the people. They make laws to favor those whom they think can keep them in power? Is this justice? Is this liberty?

War or Peace

With our government preparing for war and talking about having to fight Russia sooner or later, war could come. If things get worse for the New Dealers, which they probably will, and they see a possibility of being defeated in 1952 they may bring on the war and then tell the people that they can't change horses in the middle of a stream and thereby try to scare the people into voting to keep them in power. What the investor wants to know is: What effect would war have on the price of stocks? It all depends upon the price stocks are selling at at the time war should start. It is my opinion that another war would be very bearish on stocks and might mean that the government would confiscate all stocks as well as other property, because with the present heavy debt it might be impossible to sell bonds to finance another war. In a case of this kind the government would have to resort to any means to obtain funds to finance a war.

Neither this country or any other country can stand another war without becoming bankrupt, and civilization could go back hundreds of years. We should all hope, pray, and vote for men who will keep us out of war.

How to Stop Wars

Wars in any country can be prevented. People have the right and have the power in their own hands to stop war. If our lawmakers can be prevailed upon to pass a law that no government can go in debt or sell bonds for war purposes, there certainly would be no war. If the government had to start a war out of its income, and not go in debt there would be no war. It has no right to go in debt, and to risk the people's lives and their money and mortgage their future. Nothing can be gained by war. This country needs to get on a cash basis and spend only its income and let that income be an excuse for cutting down government expenses.

THE GOVERNMENT CANNOT PREVENT DEPRESSION

GREAT PANIC COMING

The depression and panic will come before the New Deal goes out of office in 1953. Nothing can prevent it. Panic and depression have always followed war. The second World War cost the United States more money than any war in history. Our government debt is almost as great as the debts of all the balance of the world put together. With this burden of debt and the government expenses, how can a panic and depression be prevented? Wars have created nothing and added nothing to the value of any country. The United States has been the greatest spender and the greatest waster, and the taxpayers will be the greatest losers. I believe the Bible when it says that you shall reap just what you sow. New Dealers did not stop spending when the war ended, in fact, increased spending. They have given away tens of billions of dollars, and the result will be a panic and depression which will shake the foundation of this country and cause the voters to vote out the New Deal boys in 1952. It will be too late to do anything after the crash comes. Taxpayers have it in their power to stop this expense if they will organize and do something about it before it is too late. If New Deal spending and giving away continues as it is at the present time, it will just be a matter of a short time before the government will begin to confiscate property and everything else. Then the sons of liberty will march to fight for the liberty that they have lost in fighting wars before. The government, as Will Rogers said, never lost a war, but never won a conference.

What Will Cause the Next Depression or Panic

There will be many causes of the next great depression. England is broke as a result of the two great wars and most all of the other countries in Europe are in the same fix.

Japan, China, and India are in a bad financial condition and are likely to get worse if Communism continues to dominate China.

The United States debt is a great burden which cannot be overcome. The wasteful spending by our government has already caused irreparable damage and even if it should stop now panic would come anyway.

Foreign investors are already selling stocks in our market and have been for some time.

The investors in the United States nearly always sell in the last stages of a bear market. This causes a wide open break. In the future, as things get worse, insurance companies will have to liquidate stocks and bonds. Investment trusts will try to support stocks for a time and buy on a scale down but as conditions get worse they may get scared and become sellers in the last stages of the bear market after it has run for several years.

When the business men and investors in the United States lose confidence in the government's ability to prevent a depression then matters will get worse because business and the stock market hold up as long as people have confidence.

If the day comes, and it is not impossible, when the government can no longer support bond prices, this will be the last straw that will destroy public confidence and bring on the worst panic this country has ever seen. Effects always follow causes. The causes already exist and the government has sown the seed for another panic and depression and the cycles of business and the stock market prove that a panic is inevitable.

Future Trend of Stocks

Many economists and market experts all believe that a depression and panic is coming. Just when it will come they do not know because they do not understand time cycles. The Master Time cycle which I have used to forecast every important boom and depression or panic for more than 30 years, will in my opinion accurately forecast the next panic.

The New Dealers at Washington claim that they have the

magic formula for stopping inflation and preventing depressions and panic. The next few years will prove whether or not they can do it, because the acid test will come.

My cycle theory indicates that the business boom following the war ended in 1948 and that the trend is now down. As a rule, business has the first down swing and then a rally or a moderate up swing which fools most of the people and makes them believe that a business boom is coming again.

My study of time cycles indicates that the business depression will get worse in the last half of 1950 and in 1951 and 1952 we will run into real panicky and depressing conditions which the government will be unable to cope with. This will cause declines in stocks, bonds, commodities and everything else. Just how low stocks will go depends upon how much they rally in the next up swing and how high they are selling when the last down swing starts. Below I outline the approximate dates when changes in trend can be expected in the stock market.

There is a possibility, based on past cycles, that stocks will advance in the latter part of 1949 and continue on up into 1950. The stock market often runs six months or more ahead of business.

Outlook for 1950

1950, January 3 to 7 should be low for stocks, and the trend should turn up. The advance should continue in February with the market active.

March 18 to 22 may be top for reaction, which could run for a short period of time, possibly March 30 to 31, when a change in trend is indicated.

April. The advance should continue this month, and it is possible that final high for the year could be reached around April 25 to 30, especially if June 1949 proved to be low, this would mean that the bull wave had run 10 months, which is often the length of a short swing. Another reason is that this will be six years from April 1942 low and that the month of May and June will be 48 and 49 months from the 1946 high, making it very important for a change in trend.

June 14 to 21, important because it will be two years from the 1948 low and one year from June 14, 1949, if this proves to be extreme low. Around June 24 to 30, watch for important change in trend. The market could be bottom for a rally.

July. Stocks should advance this month even if the market is on the down trend there should be a rally in the bear market.

July 7 to 10 and 18 to 30, important for tops and a change in trend.

August. Some declines, but the market may be slow and narrow.

August 5 to 10, 14 to 18, 23 to 27 are dates for change in trend.

September. Remember this is one of the important anniversary months. You should watch for a change in trend the early part of the month and again around September 23 to October 3, which could be low for a rally. If the advance starts at this time, prices could rally up to around November 2 to 4, election time.

November 14 to 21, the time cycles indicate a decline and a possible low near the end of the month for a rally.

December. If the rally started in November, it could last to around December 15 to 20, when you should watch for top and a change in trend.

Preview of 1951 to 1953

1951 and 1952 indicate very depressing years for business and a bear market in stocks. Many stocks will go much lower than people ever dreamed they could go. The United States Government will have many difficult problems to face, and they will find it hard to solve them, as the majority of people will have lost confidence in the New Deal and their powers to prevent a panic. When once the people lose confidence, conditions get worse very fast.

The time cycles indicate a strong possibility that a Republican president will be elected in November, 1952, and it is possible that October and November, 1952 may mark the end of the bear market in stocks.

1953, January 20, a new president will take office, and if this is the Republican party, it will mean an improvement in business and starting of a new cycle. However, the cycles indicate that business is likely to be slow until April or June, and then during the summer and fall stocks will advance and business conditions will show a big improvement.

CONCLUSION

"45 Years In Wall Street" is finished. My actual experience on Wall Street dates back to 1902—47 years ago. These years have taught me my most PRECIOUS POSSESSION is TIME. The best use I can make of TIME is to use it to secure KNOWLEDGE which is more valuable than money.

In this book I have revealed some of my most valuable rules and secret discoveries never published before, in hopes that others will work and study hard to learn and apply these rules. If they do, speculation and investing will no longer be gambling but will become a PROFITABLE PROFESSION.

W. D. GANN

July 18, 1949

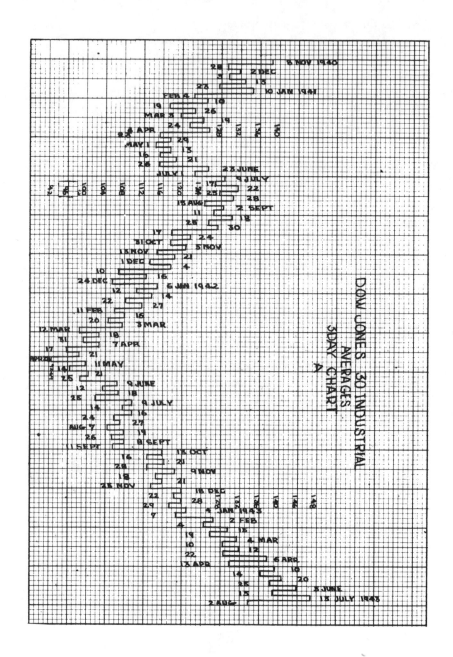

DOW JONES 30 INDUSTRIAL
AVERAGES
5 DAY CHART
A

5 NOV 1940
28
3
2 DEC
25
15
10 JAN 1941
FEB 4
19
10
MAR 5
26
24
14
8 APR
132
130
136
132
150
29
MAY 1
13
16
21
26
23 JUNE
JULY 1
9 JULY
98
100
106
108
112
116
120
171
163
23
22
28
15 AUG
11
2 SEPT
25
30
12
17
31 OCT
24
13 NOV
5 NOV
21
1 DEC
4
10
24 DEC
16
5 JAN 1942
12
4
22
27
11 FEB
15
20
3 MAR
12 MAR
18
31
7 APR
17
21
APR 28
11 MAY
4
27
25
21
12
9 JUNE
25
18
14
9 JULY
24
16
AUG 7
27
14
25
8 SEPT
11 SEPT
13 OCT
16
21
28
9 NOV
19
21
25 NOV
15 DEC
22
29
28
4 JAN 1943
7
134
136
140
146
148
2 FEB
4
19
15
10
4 MAR
22
12
13 APR
6 APR
14
10
25
20
15
3 JUNE
2 AUG
13 JULY 1943

—134—

3 DAY CHART
B

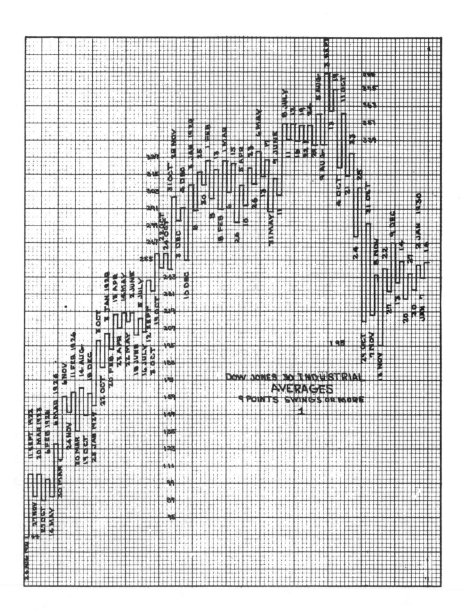

DOW JONES 30 INDUSTRIAL
AVERAGES
9 POINTS SWINGS OR MORE
1

9 POINTS SWINGS 2

9 POINTS SWINGS

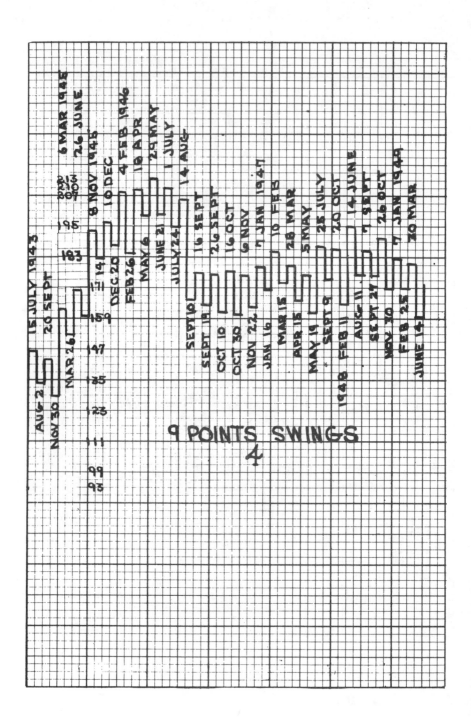

9 POINTS SWINGS

4

—140—

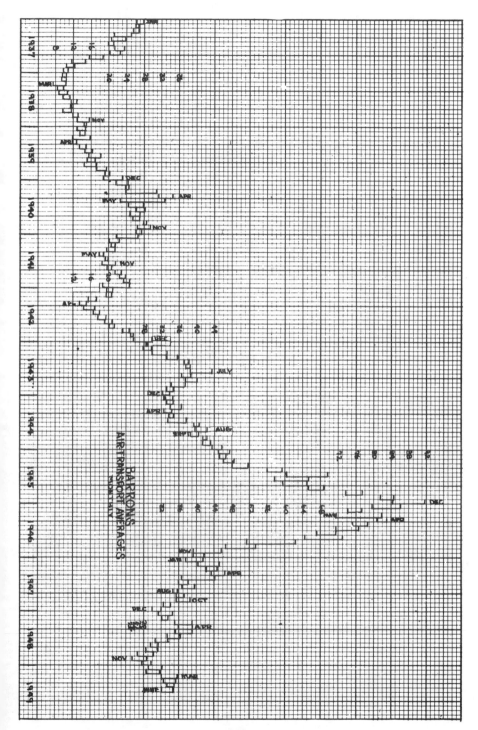

BARRONS
AIR TRANSPORT AVERAGES
MONTHLY

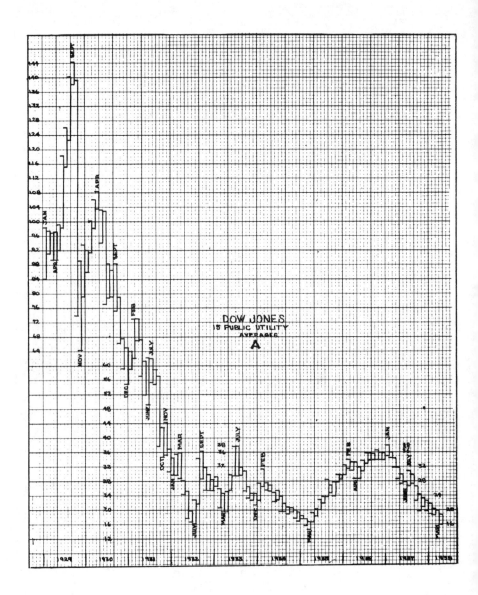

DOW JONES
15 PUBLIC UTILITY
AVERAGES

A

15 PUBLIC UTILITY
AVERAGES

PAN AMERICAN AIRWAYS
MONTHLY

RADIO CORP.
QUARTERLY

ANSWERS TO INQUIRIES

Hundreds of people write in from time to time asking for different kinds of information. In order to avoid having to answer a lot of unnecessary correspondence, we are answering frequent inquiries below.

MAGAZINES

Many people write and ask what magazines we consider best for an investor or a trader to read.

We consider the *Magazine of Wall Street* one of the best magazines for information pertaining to the stock market. *B. C. Forbes Magazine* is also good. It contains many valuable articles on financial affairs. The *Annalist*, published weekly by the *New York Times*, specializes on financial affairs and contains information valuable to traders and investors.

NEWSPAPERS

Investors and traders often want to know what newspaper we consider best for them to read.

The Wall Street Journal—This is the best financial newspaper published. It specializes in presenting all facts and information pertaining to corporations throughout the country, as well as major foreign corporations. Pertinent national news, especially agricultural and political, is equally stressed. This was one of the first papers to publish a set of averages or railroad and industrial stocks. These averages go back to 1896. Since 1914, it has published an average of bond prices and, since 1928, a public utility stock average. All of these averages are published daily and are very valuable to investors and traders who want to keep up charts on these various groups. Another feature of the *Wall Street Journal* is that it publishes each day a list of stocks which make a new high for the year and a list that makes a new low for the year. The *Wall Street Journal* does not publish any tips, rumors or misleading information. It publishes only reliable facts which are helpful to investors and traders. From time to time the *Wall Street Journal* publishes various charts on stocks, which are very helpful to traders and would cost them a lot of money if they had to secure the records and make up the charts themselves.

The New York Herald Tribune—This paper carries averages on various groups of stocks, as well as other information which is helpful to traders.

The New York Times—This also has a special set of averages and is a good paper for investors and traders to read.

What investors and traders want are the facts about the different companies and reports, and not tips or rumors. The newspapers, all of which are published in New York City, strive to give facts and reliable information.

STOCKS AND COMMODITIES

Baron's Magazine is one of the very good financial magazines published covering financial affairs and giving facts valuable to every investor and trader. The subscription rate is very low, compared to its value. This magazine is published weekly and is well worth subscribing to.

Chicago Journal of Commerce—This paper covers the commodity field better than most any other newspaper. Continuous quotations are given daily on all grains traded in on the Chicago Board of Trade. Continuous quotations on eggs on the Chicago Mercantile Exchange are also reported. Stock prices are covered daily and weekly and all facts pertaining to stocks and commodities are covered and commented on by an able staff of writers.

Commodity Year Book, published by Commodity Research Bureau, Inc., 76 Beaver Street, New York City. This book covers general statistical information on almost every commodity, and is one of the best of its kind for reliable, accurate statistical information.

Odd Lot Trades In Stocks and Job Lots In Grain

Traders often inquire whether they can buy and sell odd lots of stocks. Most of the brokers who are members of the New York Stock Exchange accept orders for odd lots. Most of them will buy stocks outright or for cash in any amount from one share on up. Job lots or 1,000 bushels of grain are traded in on the Chicago Board of Trade. Some of the brokers handle job lots and some do not. You can inquire from any broker who is a member of the Chicago Board of Trade and find out about trading in job lots or less than 5,000 bushels, which is a round lot or a contract. The Chicago Board of Trade and New Orleans Cotton Exchange trade in 50 bales of cotton. No other reliable exchange will trade in less than 50 bale lots of cotton. Those that are trading in or soliciting business for odd lots of cotton in 10 bales or more are, as a rule, bucket shops. Traders should be careful about placing their accounts with firms who are not members of the leading stock exchanges or commodity exchanges.

Brokers

People write and ask if we consider such and such a firm of brokers reliable. We consider all members of the New York Stock Exchange, the New York Cotton Exchange and the Chicago Board of Trade reliable, and advise traders to always keep their accounts with members of these responsible exchanges. If in doubt about your broker, get a report through Bradstreet, R. G. Dunn, or Bishop Service. For Brokers not members of one of the leading Exchanges, you should get a private report through your banker or some commercial agency before placing your account with them. You might be trading with a bucket shop and not know it.

NOTES

NOTES

NOTES

NOTES

NOTES

NEW STOCK TREND DETECTOR

A REVIEW OF THE 1929–1932 PANIC
AND THE 1932–1935 BULL MARKET

*With New Rules and Charts for Detecting Trend
of Stocks*

BY

WILLIAM D. GANN

W. D. GANN, *Publisher*
820 S. W. 26th Road
MIAMI, FLORIDA

FOREWORD

A man writes the best and does the most good for others when his object in writing is not to make money or gratify ambition or gain publicity, but to help others who need help and appreciate his efforts.

When I wrote TRUTH OF THE STOCK TAPE in 1923, it was because there was a demand for a book of that kind. People needed the help that I could give them and the benefit of my experience and knowledge. In that book I gave the best I had and received my reward. People appreciated my efforts. They bought the book then and they are still buying it. They say it is a good book and more than worth the money. That is very gratifying to me.

After the 1929 bull market culminated there was a demand for a new book to meet changed conditions under the so-called "New Era," so I wrote WALL STREET STOCK SELECTOR in the Spring of 1930. I gave freely of my knowledge and the benefit of years of experience. This book helped others to protect their principal and make profits. People who read the book pronounced it one of the best. It is still selling, and again I have been rewarded.

No man can learn all there is to know about forecasting the trend of stocks in 3, 5, 10, or 20 years, but if he is a deep student and hard worker, he learns more and knowledge comes easier after years of experience. I knew more about determining the trend of stocks in 1923 than I did in 1911. Seven more years of experience gave me more knowledge and enabled me to write the WALL STREET STOCK SELECTOR in 1930 and give my readers the benefit of my increased knowledge. Now, after five more years have elapsed, my experience and practical test of new rules have enabled me to learn more of value since 1930.

The 1929–1932 panic and what has followed since, gave me valuable experience and I have gained more knowledge about detecting the right stocks to buy and sell. I cannot lose if I pass this knowledge on to those who will appreciate it.

Hundreds of people who have read my books have asked me to write a new book. Again, I answer the call and meet the popular demand with NEW STOCK TREND DETECTOR. I believe the book will help others to avoid some of the pitfalls of reckless speculation. If I can lead a few more to the field of knowledge, I shall again be amply repaid for my efforts.

W. D. GANN

January 3, 1936,
88 Wall Street, New York.

NEW STOCK TREND DETECTOR

CONTENTS

CHARTS

NEW STOCK TREND DETECTOR

CHAPTER I

A NEW DEAL IN WALL STREET

Since writing TRUTH OF THE STOCK TAPE in 1923 and WALL STREET STOCK SELECTOR in 1930, the greatest panic that the world has ever seen has taken place, culminating with the greatest stock decline in history, reaching extreme low levels on July 8, 1932. Conditions have changed since 1929 and new laws have been passed affecting stock market movements. The passing of the law supervising stock exchanges has made a great change in the action of the stock market and made it necessary to formulate new rules to meet the changed conditions. The Bible says, "Old things pass away and new ones come to take their places." "A wise man changes his mind, a fool never." The man who refuses to change when conditions change, or to see the new way of doing things is doomed to failure.

This is an age of progress. We move forward, not backward. We cannot stand still. We must go ahead with progress or retrograde into the list of the "has beens." Henry Ford made hundreds of millions of dollars with the old Model "T" car. It was a good car in its day and Ford was satisfied with it, but time and conditions changed. The public changed and demanded an up-to-date, better car. Henry Ford, being a wise man, saw the "handwriting on the wall" and changed his mind. In the midst of the world's greatest depression, Ford closed his factory and spent over $100,000,000 to develop a new and better car, or as the

1

boys say, "He made a lady out of 'Lizzie.' " He was not actuated by the desire for more money when he developed this new car. It was pride and ambition and not greed that urged him to keep the public's good will by giving them a better car at a lower price. The public responded quickly and the new Ford became a leader. Each year Ford has improved his car until the 1936 Model is the best car yet produced.

Politicians with selfish motives have always preached against Wall Street and misled the public in regard to the way business is handled on the New York Stock Exchange and the type of men who handle it. There is no business in the world where a higher type of honor exists than among the men who are members of the New York Stock Exchange. No business men in the world live up to their contracts like the brokers on the floor of the New York Stock Exchange. In other lines of business contracts are made for future delivery of different classes of goods, lumber, textiles and mercantile products of various kinds. In cases of this kind, when prices advance, the buyer calls on the seller to make delivery of the products, but when prices decline he cancels his contract and leaves the seller to get out the best way he can. I quote from a letter received from a prominent lumberman:

> In marketing lumber it is impossible to profit from future price changes even should one be fortunate enough to anticipate them, for the reason the purchaser may cancel the contract if prices decline, but the saw mill is expected to fill the contract at the sale price even if prices advance above it. With few exceptions, this is the general rule governing sales by saw mills to factories that consume the major part of hardwood lumber in the United States. In the decline of the lumber market the first part of 1934, my company had lumber orders cancelled, amounting to 1,400,000 feet. I know this must seem strange to you, having operated so long where all contracts are made binding on both buyer and seller.
>
> "I have a high regard for the business methods used in Wall Street. After trading there ten years, it is my opinion there is probably no place or business so free of repudiations or acts of dishonesty."

Such a thing as a member of the New York Stock Exchange ever attempting to cancel his contract for a stock he buys or sells is unheard of. When a broker buys or sells stocks on the New York Stock Exchange by raising his hand or nodding his head, he is bound by his honor to live up to the contract and he does. No matter how much the stock goes against him or what the loss is, he never welches. He does not attempt to cancel his contract. He makes his delivery. The brokers and the managers of the New York Stock Exchange are honest and reliable men. The public has been confused as to the position of the New York Stock Exchange, which is but the means and the machinery for carrying on transactions between buyer and seller. The brokers on the floor of the New York Stock Exchange are in no way responsible for the actions of pools or outside deals which at times have been handled by unscrupulous manipulators in the past, but the public has been led to believe that the Stock Exchange and its members were working against them. The brokers simply buy and sell for a commission and give the best service possible to their customers. The New York Stock Exchange serves a useful purpose. The greater part of the manufacturers of this country have their stocks listed on the New York Stock Exchange and every buyer and seller can know every day what the prices are. Without the New York Stock Exchange there would be no Clearing House, no place where people who need money could instantly turn their securities into cash. The fact that the New York Stock Exchange has been in existence since 1792 proves that it fills an economic need, or it would have long since been out of business.

For years Wall Street and the New York Stock Exchange and its rules and way of doing business were considered the best and needed no changes. Then came the "New Deal" and the Securities Exchange Law which compelled changes in rules. Before these laws were put into effect, the New York Stock Exchange saw the need of a new way of doing business and keeping the public thoroughly informed of the way business was carried on.

Why Blame Wall Street and the New York Stock Exchange?

The man who makes profits never gives credit to Wall Street brokers or any one else for his profits. He takes credit for making them himself. Then, why should he blame his losses on someone else?

If you make a trade in stocks and lose money, do not let politicians lead you to believe that pool managers, manipulators, Wall Street, or the New York Stock Exchange are the cause of your losing money, because they are not. No one forces you to make a trade. You buy or sell stocks because you hope to make profits, and you would not kick if you made them; therefore, don't play the "baby act" and blame someone if you lose. If you had carelessly run in front of an automobile and were injured, would you blame the automobile or the driver for your carelessness? Just because people have been killed by cars is no reason why laws should be passed to keep automobiles off the roads and streets. Politicians have tried to pass laws for years to restrict the useful operations of the Stock Exchange and Commodity Exchanges just because people who lost money have complained to Congressmen against the Exchanges which serve a useful purpose.

The Law of Supply and Demand

The prices on the New York Stock Exchange, New York Cotton Exchange and the Chicago Board of Trade are governed by Supply and Demand. No matter whether the buying or selling is by the public, by pools, or by manipulators, prices decline when there are more sellers than buyers and prices advance when stocks are scarce and when there are more buyers than sellers. The members of these Exchanges do not make the markets; they only do the buying and selling for the public and large operators. The pools and large operators in the past have manipulated prices, but no blame should be placed on the Exchanges which merely act as a clearing house for the transactions.

If you could find out the rules the master market makers use to make money, you would buy and sell when they do and make profits, wouldn't you? If you knew what the big operators were doing, you certainly would follow them. People often ask me: "How can I make some easy money?" or "How can I make some money quick?" There is no way to make easy money and there is no way to make money quickly until you have acquired knowledge yourself. You must pay for whatever you get. What is worth having is worth paying for. Getting money quick and easy does more harm than good.

You can learn what the big operators are doing by being a good Wall Street detective. You can detect what the "powers that be" are doing, by a study of Supply and Demand. The records of the total sales and the high and low prices of every stock are published daily in the newspapers throughout the country. There is no secret about it. It is just up to you to follow rules. If you study Supply and Demand and apply my rules, you can detect the trend and make money.

How New Deal Has Changed Conditions

The New Deal in Washington and the laws passed have changed stock trading so far as the public is concerned. Washed sales under the Securities Exchange Law are no longer permitted. The specialist is restricted on trades that he can make for himself. Short selling has been curtailed. A heavy increase in the amount of margin required to carry stocks has reduced the volume of trading. Taxes have been increased, both income taxes and other taxes, which causes traders and investors to hold on longer and not sell out their stocks because they would have to pay such a large amount of their profits to the Government. This changes the technical position of the market; makes it stronger at times but eventually will make it much weaker and stocks will decline much faster because the short interest in the future will be limited, pool operations will be smaller, and the support in the market by the specialist will be much smaller than it has been in the past.

There will come a time when the market will run into real heavy selling; bids and offers will be far apart. It will be hard to sell stocks when everybody wants to sell and nobody wants to buy. Another thing, heavy margins will work against the market and cause a greater decline, because when people put up 40 to 60% margin, they will hold on longer, or until the margin is nearly exhausted, then everybody will want to sell at the same time and there will be few buyers. It is my opinion that the laws passed to regulate the Stock Exchange will not prove beneficial to the public in the future, just as many laws already passed by the Administration under President Roosevelt have already proved to be detrimental and the Supreme Court has found it necessary to declare them unconstitutional.

CHAPTER II

FOUNDATION FOR SUCCESSFUL TRADING

"Wisdom is the principal thing:
therefore get wisdom: and with
all thy getting get understanding."—PROVERBS 4:7.

Have you ever stopped to think and make a careful analysis why you have lost money in stocks or why you have been wrong when you made a trade? If you have, you have probably found that you traded on hope, bankers' opinions, brokers' opinions, or relied on tips, or you guessed yourself. Another reason, because you did not admit to yourself that you could be wrong and did not protect yourself when you made the trade. But regardless of how you made the mistake and had the loss, the fault was your own, because you had no definite rule or plan or way to know just when to buy and sell.

You should learn to trade on knowledge, which will eliminate fear and hope. Then, when hope or fear no longer influence you, knowledge will give you nerve to trade and make profits. You should learn the truth about a stock, then learn how to apply all the rules that I have given in my books TRUTH OF THE STOCK TAPE, WALL STREET STOCK SELECTOR and in this book, NEW STOCK TREND DETECTOR. Then you will have a knowledge of trading and an education that you never had before, and when you make a trade, it will be for a good and sufficient reason and on definite rules. You will neither hope nor fear then. You will trade on facts. You will protect your capital and profits by the use of stop loss orders and will make profits.

There is one way to always correct a mistake if you buy or

sell a stock against the trend, and that is to place a *stop loss order*. A stop loss order protects you in many ways. When you buy a stock, place a stop loss order 1, 2 or 3 points away. Then if you are out of town or out of reach of your broker and some sudden, unexpected event happens to cause a sharp decline and the stock reaches your stop loss order, you are automatically sold out. The stock might go 10 points lower the same day before they could reach you. Yet, you are protected because you had your order with the broker to sell. You did not have to be there to watch it and did not have to be where the broker could reach you.

There is nothing that will give you more valuable information or enable you to tell more what a stock is going to do than to study its past actions and apply the rules that I give in my books. If you know what a stock has done in the past, it will help you to determine what it will do in the future. All of the buying and selling is recorded and registered in the price of the stock, which is influenced by Supply and Demand. Price movement, if studied correctly, will tell you more about the stock than brokers can tell you, or newspapers or any other kind of so-called "inside" information.

Learn To Be Independent

The greatest help that one man can give another is to show him how to help himself. The man or woman who depends on others for advice, for inside information or what others think about the stock market, will never make a success of speculation or anything else. You must learn to be independent. Learn to do by doing and to know by study and application. Then you will have confidence and courage that no one else can give you.

An intelligent man will not follow blindly the opinion of others without knowing what their opinion is based on, but when he himself sees, understands and knows the rules that forecast stock market trends, then he becomes a good Wall Street detective. He detects the future trends and follows them with confidence. He no longer says, "If I knew the information I get on Chrysler was right, I would buy 500 shares instead of 100." When he sees and understands why Chrysler gives a definite indication of an advance, he then has no fear and no hope, but has confidence and courage to buy 500 shares.

No matter what business you are interested in, learn all you can about it. The most important thing, outside of your health, for you to protect is your money. Therefore, take time to study and prepare yourself to handle your money yourself and do not depend forever and entirely upon others.

A Definite Plan

Make up your mind now to have a definite plan or aim in the future. Decide to follow rules when you buy or sell stocks, but first prove to yourself that the rules are good and that they will work.

The rules given in my books are good practical rules. You can prove them to your own satisfaction in a short period of time. Many men and women who have bought my books, TRUTH OF THE STOCK TAPE and WALL STREET STOCK SELECTOR, have learned the rules, followed them and made a success, and you can do the same if you will work and study hard.

I have studied and improved my Methods every year for the past thirty-five years. I am still learning. Some of my greatest discoveries were made between 1932 and 1935. After long years of study and research, I have simplified and made my rules practical so that others can apply them as easily as I can. I have eliminated unnecessary details; have cut down the work so you can get results quicker; and have made profits by following strictly the same rules.

Knowledge Brings Success

The door that opens to big profits has but one key to unlock it and that key is Knowledge. You cannot get that knowledge without work.   I have made a success by hard work and you, too, can make plenty of money out of the stock market if you study and work hard enough.   Work is the way to find the Royal Road to riches in Wall Street.

When the Queen of Sheba visited King Solomon, she did not go for his bank-roll or jewelry.   It was his wisdom that she sought, and his ‘great wisdom won her love, so Arthur Brisbane says, and I have a great respect for Mr. Brisbane’s opinion.   If you get practical knowledge on stocks and commodities you will have no trouble in getting capital to make more money with.   Money always comes to knowledge; without knowledge money is worthless.   You can increase your money and make wise investments when you have acquired knowledge.

Qualifications for Success

1st: KNOWLEDGE

First and most important—You must get Knowledge.

Make up your mind to spend thirty minutes to one hour per day studying stock market movements for the next five years.   Then you will get knowledge of how to detect stock market trends and will make money.   You will not be looking for a quick and easy way to make money.   You will have paid in advance with time and study.   The more time you put in in getting knowledge, the more money you will make later.

2nd: PATIENCE

This is one of the very important qualifications for success.   When you buy or sell you must have the patience to wait for opportunities to get in right.   Then, you must have the patience to wait until there is a change in trend before you close a trade or take profits.

3RD: NERVE

I can give a man the best gun in the world and if he hasn't the nerve to pull the trigger, he will never kill any game. You can have all the knowledge in the world and if you haven't the nerve to buy and sell, you cannot make any money, but Knowledge does give a man nerve; makes him bold and enables him to act at the right time.

4TH: GOOD HEALTH

After you have gained knowledge, acquired patience and developed nerve, the next important quality is good health. No man can have patience and nerve and do his best unless his health is good. If you are in bad health, you become despondent, you lose hope, you have too much fear, and you will be unable to act. I have been through the game for all these years; have tried to trade when I have been in bad health and have seen others try to trade, but I never saw a man yet make a success speculating when his health was bad. The thing to do if your health gets bad is to quit business, quit speculating and get your health back, for health is wealth.

5TH: CAPITAL

With all of these qualifications for making a success, you must have capital, but if you have knowledge and patience, you can start with a small capital and make a lot of money, provided you use stop loss orders, take small losses, and do not overtrade.

Remember, never buck the trend: after you detect the trend, go with it regardless of what you think, hope or fear and you will make a success. Read and follow the "Twenty-four Never-failing Rules" on pages 18-19 of WALL STREET STOCK SELECTOR.

CHAPTER III

HISTORY REPEATS

Future stock market movements can be forecast by a study of past history and past movements. By knowing the time when the greatest advances have taken place and the times when the greatest panics and declines have occurred and the time periods to watch for major and minor changes in trend, you can detect what to expect in the future. Just remember one thing, whatever has happened in the past in the stock market and Wall Street will happen again. Advances and bull markets will come in the future and panics will come in the future, just as they have in the past. This is the working out of a natural law and the balancing of time with price. It is action in one direction and reaction in the opposite direction. In order to make profits, you must learn to follow the trend and change when the trend changes.

War in the past has always had a great effect upon stocks and commodity prices. The starting of wars often has produced panics or sharp declines followed by booms, and after the war was over, there was another sharp decline or a panic, followed by another boom with probably higher levels than occurred during the war days. It is important, therefore, to study the action of stocks and commodities around the beginning of war periods and after the ending of wars in order to detect what may happen in the future when these same conditions repeat.

It is important to study the time that has elapsed between bottoms and tops and the greatest duration of any bull campaign as well as the greatest duration of any panic or decline.

12

W. D. GANN AVERAGES

1856–1874

1856—If you will refer to my averages in WALL STREET STOCK SELECTOR, you will see that in February, 1856, stocks reached a high of 95½. Then followed a period of distribution.

1857—In January, the last high was reached at 92, from which a panicky decline started. This was the 1857 panic, which culminated in October, 1857, with the Averages down 58 points in a period of six months.

1858—A rally followed to March, 1858, lasting five months.

1859—The market declined and made low in June, down 15 months.

1860—In September, the high was made again, 15 months up.

1861—Last low on the Averages at 48 in March. Time of decline, 7 months, the last low before the Civil War boom. At this point watch the length of time period to compare with other war booms.

1864—In April the Averages reached a high of 155. Time, 36 months from the last bottom and at no time did they decline more than two consecutive months.

1865—March, low 88, down 67 points in 11 months; October, high 121; time, 7 months.

1866—February, low 100; time, 4 months; October, high 125, 8 months from the low and 19 months from 1865 low.

1867—April, low of reaction 104; time, 6 months. From this low the big after-war boom followed.

1869—July, high 181; time, 27 months from April, 1867; 50 months from March, 1865 low; and 99 months from March, 1861 low, which was the most important time period to measure from, being 8 years and 3 months. The last stage of the boom lasted 27

months. This ended the great after-war boom, and
a panic followed.

1873—November, low 84, a decline of 96 points from the
high of 1869. Time of bear campaign, 52 months,
but from August, 1870 to May, 1871, there was a
rally of 9 months and from January to June, 1872,
a rally of 6 months; and from November, 1872 low,
a rally to January, 1873, a two months' rally, which
indicated a weak market, just as we had in 1931 and
1932.

1874—February, high 107. Time of the rally, 3 months.
In June and October, lows were reached; time period,
4 months and 8 months. Then the rails rallied to
May, 1875.

12 Industrial Stock Averages

1875–1896

Here we begin with 12 Industrial Stocks which were
about the same as the Dow-Jones Averages, which started
in 1897.

1875—March, high 53; October, low 48.

1876—February, high 52.

1877—October, low 36, a decline of 16 months without
much rally.

1879—A real bull market began in August, 1879 and lasted
until June, 1881, a period of 22 months.

1881—June, high 72, an advance of 47 months with a
6-months' reaction in 1878 and 1879, and 2 to 3
months' reaction several times.

1881–1885:

From June, 1881 to June, 1884, there was an extreme bear campaign with the Averages down from
72 to 42. The Bear Campaign lasted 36 months
with only a 2 months' rally, like the rally from July
to September, 1932. Then, from the top of a rally
in August, 1884, there was a decline to January,

1885, making a double bottom at 42 against the low
of June, 1884.

1885—November, high 57, up 10 months.

1886—May, low of reaction at 53.

1887—End of bull market in May; time, 34 months from
1884 low and 27 months from the secondary bottom of January, 1885.

1888—April, low of bear market at 51. Time, 11 to 12
months.

1889—June and September highs at 63.

1890—A third top at 63 was reached in January, 1890,
making this almost a triple top and selling level.

1888–1890—The time from April, 1888 to January, 1890
was 21 months.

1890—December, low of decline at 49. Time, 11 months
from last high of January, 1890.

1893—January, high of bull market at 72. Time, 25
months from 1890. Then followed the panic of
1893. August, 1893, bottom of bear market at 40,
down 32 points in 7 months.

1895—High of the bull campaign in June at 58; time, 22
months. This was really a rally in a bear market,
for the main trend was still down.

1896—Bryn Silver Panic:
August, 1896, low of the Dow-Jones Averages at 29.
Time, 14 months from the top of 1895, and 43
months from January, 1893 top. After this panicky
decline was over, the McKinley boom started, which
lasted for several years.

Dow-Jones Industrial Averages

1897–1935

1897—September, high 55. Time, 12 months.

1898—March, low 42. Time, 6 months from the previous
top.

1899—April, high 78. Time, 13 months. A sharp decline

followed in May; then a slow advance. September,
high 78, same as the April high. Time, from 1896,
37 months and from March, 1898, 18 months.

1900—September, low 53. Time, 12 months. End of bear
market.

1901—June, high 78, same as top in 1899, a third top and
the end of the bull market. December, low 62.
Time, 6 months.

1902—April, high 69. Time, 4 months.

1903—October and November, low 42½. Time, 28 to 29
months from 1901 top; 8 months from top of last
rally in February, 1903. After 1903, the Industrial
Averages became more active and were leaders,
whereas previous to this time the railroads were the
most active and leading stocks. The rails did lead
from 1896 to 1906, which was the last high until
1924-29 boom, when the rails reached the highest
in history. We will now continue with the industrials.

1906—January, high 103. Time, 27 months from 1903
low and never reacted more than 2 months, an indication of a strong bull market. Low of reaction at
86 in August. Time, 6 months. October, high 97.

1907—January, high 97, from which a big decline started.
March 14, 1907, a panicky decline known as the
"silent panic." Stocks declined 20 points that day.
Low of the Averages was 76. Rallied to 85 in May,
then declined to 53 in November. Time, 22 months
from January, 1906 high. Accumulation took place
and a bull market started from November.

1909—October, high 101, top of bull campaign. Time, 23
months. Never reacted more than 3 months.

1910—July, low 73, bottom of decline. Time, 9 months.

1911—June, high 87. Time, 11 months. A sharp decline
followed. September, low 73, same low as July,
1910.

1912—October, high 94, top of bull wave. Time, 13 months.

1913—June, bottom at 53. Time, 8 months, the third time at the same level. This is very important and always indicates that an advance should follow as long as the third bottom is not broken. September, high 83. Time, 3 months. December, low 76.

1914—March, high 83, same as September, 1913. War was declared in Europe in the early part of July and the Stock Exchange closed at the end of July and remained closed until December, 1914. After the Exchange opened in December, 1914, the Industrial Averages declined to 53½, the same low level reached in 1907. Time from October, 1912, 26 months.

1915—December, high 99½, just under the top of 1909. Time, 12 months from 1914 low.

1916—April, low 85. Time of reaction, 4 months. November, high 110, top of bull campaign. This was a new high level for the Dow-Jones Industrial Averages. Time, 23 months from December, 1914.

1917—February, low 87. June, high 99. Time, 4 months. Then a big panicky decline followed. December, low 66, bottom of bear campaign. Time, 13 months.

1919—November, high 119½, top of bull campaign. Time, 23 months from December, 1917 low. No reaction lasted more than 3 months.

1920—December, low 66, same low as 1917. Time from top, 13 months.

1921—May, high 79. August, low 64, not 3 points under the 1917 and 1920 lows, which was a sign of good support and indicated that a bull market would follow. Time from 1919 top, 21 months.

1921–1929 Bull Campaign

From the low in August, 1921, followed the greatest bull market in the history of the United States, culminating in September, 1929.

1923—Top of first section of this great bull market was reached in March, 1923, with the Averages at 105. Time, 19 months. Low of reaction at 86 in October. Time, 7 months.

1924—February, high of rally, 105, from which a 3 months' reaction followed. May, low 89. May, 1924 was the real beginning of the Coolidge Bull Market.

1925—In January the Dow-Jones Averages crossed 120, the high of 1919, which indicated much higher prices because the volume of trading was heavy and stocks were very active.

1926—February, high 162. Time from last low, 21 months. March, bottom of a sharp decline, the Averages declining to 136 and some stocks declining 100 points in this short period. The Averages held for a few months in a narrow trading range and then started up again. After that no reaction lasted more than 2 months until 1929.

1929—On September 3, 1929, when final top was reached the Industrial Averages made 386, up 322 points from the 1921 low and 300 points from the 1923 low. Time from 1921 low to 1929 high, 97 months. (Refer to 1861–1869 and you will see how this compares. The Bull Campaign at that time lasted 99 months, which was one of the greatest in history until 1929.) The time from the 1923 low to 1929 high was 71 months, and from the 1924 low, 64 months; from March 1926 low, 42 months; and from the last low of October, 1926, 35 months.

It is before and after wars that you can determine the greatest length of time a bull market may run and the greatest length of time a panicky decline may run. The culmination of the bull market in September, 1929 was really the result of a long-trend business cycle which began in August, 1896 and continued for 33 years, with each campaign in the market making higher prices, which showed that the long-trend was up. It was only natural that after the greatest bull market in history, the greatest bear market in history must follow, and to determine how long the bear campaign might run, you would look back to see what had happened after previous war booms!

1869–1873: From 1869 to 1873 we find that the time period was 53 months and that the market had a 9 months' rally, a 6 months' rally and a 2 months' rally during that period.

1871–1873: May, 1871 top to November, 1873 low. Time, 30 months.

1881–1884: Then we refer to 1881 to 1884 and find that the bear market lasted 36 months.

1893–1896: Then we refer to 1893 to August, 1896 and find that the bear market lasted 43 months.

Going back over all the records, we find that the greatest bear market had lasted not more than 43 months and the smallest had been as short as 12 months. Some of them had culminated around 27 months, 30 months, 34 months and in extreme declines, anywhere from 36 to 43 months.

Therefore, from 1929, based on past records, we would begin to watch for bottom around the 30th to the 36th month and then again around the 40th to 43rd month.

1929–1932 BEAR MARKET

First Section of The Great Bear Market—September 3, 1929 to November 13, 1929.

The Dow-Jones 30 Industrial Averages declined from a high of 386 on September 3, 1929 to a low of 198 on November 13, 1929, a decline of 188 points in 71 days—the greatest decline in the history of the New York Stock Exchange in the shortest period of time.

A secondary rally culminated on April 17, 1930 with the averages at 297, up 99 points in 155 days. The volume of sales decreased in April. The top of a secondary rally is always an important point to watch.

Second Section of The Great Bear Market—April 17, 1930 to December 17, 1930:

From the top on April 17, 1930 there was a decline to December 17, 1930. The averages declined from 297 to 155, a decline of 142 points. Time, 244 days or 8 months.

The second rally carried prices to top on February 24, 1931, with the averages at 196, up 41 points in 69 days. This shorter time period and smaller number of points indicated weakness and showed main trend down.

Third Section of The Great Bear Market—February 24, 1931 to January 5, 1932:

After top in February, 1931 a decline started and in April, 1931 the Average broke the lows of December, 1930. On June 2, 1931 declined to 120, the top of November, 1919. My rule is that old tops become bottoms and old bottoms later become tops; therefore, from the old top level a rally could be expected. From June 2nd to June 27th the Averages advanced to 157½, up 37½ points in 25 days. This was a quick rally in a bear market and showed weakness since stocks could not rally one full month. After this rally there was a decline to October 5, 1931, with the Averages at 85½, down 72 points in 100 days. A quick rally followed to November 9, 1931, with the price at 119, up to the bottom of June 2, 1931. Here we would expect selling under the old bottom, according to my rule of old bottoms becoming tops. This was a rally of 35 points in 35 days. The main trend down was resumed and on December 17, 1931, just one year from the low of December, 1930, the Averages reached 72; had a quick rally to 83 on December 19th and declined to 70 on January 5, 1932, down 49½ from the last high of November 9, 1931. This decline lasted 57 days, but was 192 days from June 27, 1931 and was really the end of the Third Section of the Great Bear Market because after the low of January 5, 1932, the market rallied to March 9, 1932. The Averages reached 89½, up 19½ points in 64 days, a very feeble rally for the time required, which showed that liquidation had not run its course.

Fourth Section of The Great Bear Market—March 9 to July 8, 1932:

The fourth and last section of the great Bear Market lasted four months, from March 9, 1932 to July 8, 1932, or 121 days, a shorter time period with a price decline of 49 points. Note that this was about the same number of points as the decline from November 9, 1931 to January 5, 1932. From March 9 to July 8, 1932, when the final wave of liquidation was taking place, the greatest rally on Averages was 7 points, and each decline from the small rallies got shorter and the volume of sales less, which showed that liquidation was about over. The last decline from June 16th to July 8th was 11 points. Then the Great Bear Market ended and the trend turned up.

On July 8, 1932, the Dow-Jones Averages made low at 40½, down 34 months from the 1929 top and 27 months from April, 1930 top, which were time periods when we would expect a sharp, panicky decline to end, especially a decline which had carried the Averages down 345 points in 34 months and wiped out the gains of 33 years in many stocks.

Note that in April, 1897, the last low was 40½, from which the real bull market started, and in July, 1932 the Averages reached this same level, 40½, although there was a different number of stocks.

Previous to the bottom in July, 1932, the volume of sales

and time periods all indicated that the market was near the end of the bear campaign.

1932–1935 BULL MARKET

First Section of Bull Market—July 8 to September 8, 1932:

From the low of 40½ on July 8, 1932 the Dow-Jones 30 Industrial Averages rallied to 81 on September 8, 1932, an advance of 40 points in 62 days. This was a fast advance on short covering and some good buying, but when stocks could not hold and go higher in the third month, it was an indication of lower prices. The large volume also made it plain that this was only the first rally in the bull campaign, from which a secondary decline must follow.

Secondary decline—Just as the Bear Market had a secondary rally from November, 1929 to April, 1930, so after the market had given a signal that the Bear Market was over, there was a secondary decline, which lasted until February 27, 1933, with the Averages at 49½, down 31 points from the top of September 8, 1932 in 172 days, but 9 points above the 1932 lows. At this time President Roosevelt was inaugurated and banks closed. The New York Stock Exchange closed for one week. The volume of sales was very small, which indicated liquidation was over. When news is the worst, it is time to buy stocks, as a Bull Market begins in gloom and ends in glory with nothing but good news.

Second Section of Bull Market—February 27, 1933 to July 17, 1933:

The averages advanced from the low at 49½ in February, 1933 to a high of 110½ on July 17, 1933, up 61 points in 141 days. Time, 12 months from July, 1932 low and 5 months from February, 1933 low. My rule tells you to always watch for a change in trend one year, two years, etc., from any important top and bottom. The sales during May, June, and July were larger than at the end of the Bull Market in 1929. This enormous volume was an indication that the market was reaching a culmination and a sign of top.

A reaction followed. The Averages reached bottom at 82½ on October 21st, 1933, down 28 points in 96 days. The volume of sales was small. In view of the fact that the Averages declined only 2 points under the low point of July 21, 1933 and did not decline to the top of 81½ made on September 8, 1932, indicated that the main trend was still up.

Third Section of Bull Market—October 21, 1933 to February 5, 1934:

From the low at 82½ on October 21, 1933, the Averages worked up to 111½ on February 5, 1934, just one point above the top of July 17, 1933, a double top on large volume of 5 million shares per day. This was an advance of 29 points in 107 days. Time, 19 months from July, 1932 low and 4 months from October, 1933 low. Since the Averages failed to go through 112, the market indicated top.

Then there was a reaction to July 26, 1934, with the Averages declining to 84½, a decline of 27 points in 171 days, the same length of time as the reaction from September .8, 1932 to February 27, 1933. Time, from February, 1934 top, 5 months. The volume of sales on July 26 was 3 million shares and the Averages were 2 points above the low of October 21, 1933. This large volume and higher support level was an indication of bottom.

Fourth Section of Bull Market—July 26, 1934 to November 20, 1935:

The 30 Industrial Averages advanced from 84½ on July 26, 1934 to 149½ on November 20, 1935, an advance of 65 points in nearly 16 months. Time, 40 months from July, 1932 low; 33 months from February, 1933 low; 25 months from October, 1933 low.

The greatest reactions were from August 25, 1934 to September 17, 1934, a decline of 12 points, and from

February 18, 1935 to March 18, 1935, a decline of 12 points on the averages, and as this reaction lasted only one month, it showed main trend was still up. After March 18, 1935 lows, there was no reaction of over 8 points and none lasted more than 2 weeks until top was reached on November 20, 1935. Then a reaction followed to December 19, lasting one month, a decline of 11 points. The volume of sales in October and November were 104,000,000 shares, which in-dicated at least temporary top, with the Averages up 109 points from 1932 low, and up 53½ points from March 18, 1935 low in a period of 247 days.

At this writing, December 31, 1935, it is my opinion that the Averages will not cross 150 and when they decline to 138, will indicate 120, possibly 112, the old top of 1933–1934, but as I have said before, follow the trend of in-dividual stocks when you trade as many of them will go op-posite to the trend of the 30 Industrial Averages.

TIME PERIODS TO WATCH FOR FUTURE CHANGES IN TREND

January, 1936 will be 42 months from 1932 low; March, 1936 will be 37 months from February, 1933 low; July, 1936 will be 36 months from the 1933 top and 48 months from the 1932 low. Therefore, these months will be very important in 1936 to watch for changes in trend.

CAUSE OF THE 1929–1932 PANIC

The price decline from 1929 to 1932 was so drastic because people who bought at high levels held on and hoped and bought more to average on the way down. They were wrong at the time they bought the first stock and continued to be wrong by bucking the trend and buying more to aver-age, the worst thing that any trader can do. Remember, average your profits, but never average a loss.

After stocks had declined 100 points or more, other peo-ple began to buy stocks, because they thought they were cheap—and the only reason they thought they were cheap was because they were down 100 points compared with high levels. This was the worst reason of all for buying stocks. Later, when stocks were down around 150, 250 and 300 points from 1929 top levels, other people bought for the same reason, that they were a long distance down from the top and looked cheap. They were wrong because there had been no change in trend. The time period had not run out and the market had not given buying signals.

If these buyers had only waited, and had known how to follow the rules laid down in my books, WALL STREET STOCK SELECTOR and TRUTH OF THE STOCK TAPE, they could have determined when the trend changed and could have bought stocks at low levels and made big profits, but most of them were buying on guesswork and hoping that the stocks would go up. Many of these people, no doubt, made up their minds to sell out when a rally came, but fixed a price at which stocks never rallied to. They hoped for a rally, but the hope was not based on any sound reasons and there was no sound reason for expecting a rally or an advance that would let them out.

Hope Gives Way to Despair:

Finally, in the Spring and Summer of 1932, when stocks had declined to what looked like ridiculously low levels, they continued to decline from 25 to 50 points more. This caused all kinds of buyers and investors to lose hope. Their hearts grew sick. Fear supplanted hope. They saw things in the very worst way and all sold out. Some sold because they were forced to sell, because they could not put up margins to carry their stocks; others sold because they feared stocks would go lower, which was no reason for selling, no more than when they bought because they hoped they would go up, which was no reason for buying.

"WHO BOUGHT STOCKS IN THE PANIC?"

Many people ask this question. The people who bought stocks at low levels were those wise ones who sold out in

1928 or early 1929, or sold after the first break in September, 1929, when the signs were plain that the trend had turned down. These people kept their money and waited until conditions looked the worst; then bought stocks when they were far below their actual value. They received a rich reward for their patience, knowledge and nerve, for it took nerve to buy when everything looked the worse, just as it took nerve to sell in 1929 when everything looked the brightest and one could hear nothing but optimistic talk.

"WILL STOCKS GO BACK TO 1929 HIGHS?"

This is another question that I have been asked from time to time. Why do people ask this question? Because many of them hold stocks bought at very high levels and hope that they will go up so they can get out without a loss. I am confident that the Dow-Jones 30 Industrial Averages will never sell at 386 again. I am also confident that the Railroad Averages will never sell at 189, the high of 1929, and that many of the public utility stocks will never reach the 1929 levels again. Why? Because at the time they sold at these abnormally high levels, their selling price was not based on value or earning power. Prices were forced to these high levels for the simple reason that everybody was gambling mad and buying regardless of price or value. They will not buy stocks again like that for a long time to come because high margin requirements will restrict larger buying operations.

While I do not expect the Averages and old-time leaders to reach the 1929 highs again, yet many individual stocks will advance above their 1929 highs. During the 1932–1935 Bull Market new leaders developed that went far above the 1929 highs. In another chapter we give you examples of stocks that crossed 1929 highs and show you their position and how plain the indications were that they were going higher and the ones to buy. Other stocks, later on, will go above their 1929 highs, as will be explained in the following chapters.

CHAPTER IV

INDIVIDUAL STOCKS *vs.* AVERAGES

For years the Dow-Jones Industrial Averages, Railroad Averages, and Public Utility Averages have been a reliable guide to the trend of the market. Years ago when there were 12 Industrial Stocks which were representative, they were a guide to the trend of industrial stocks. When Railroads were the leaders and active, the 20 Railroad Averages were a good trend indicator. But now, since more than 1200 stocks are listed on the New York Stock Exchange, the 20 Railroad Averages and the 30 Industrial Averages are no longer representative or a guide to the average trend of the entire market.

Various industries throughout the country are affected by changing conditions and are also affected by varying conditions in foreign countries. One motor company may be prospering and making money while another one is going into bankruptcy and out of business. Cross-currents in the stock market, due to various influences, cause some stocks to decline while others advance. These changed conditions began in 1928 and 1929, but have been more pronounced since stocks made low in July, 1932. Therefore, in order to make money trading in the stock market, you must study and apply rules to individual stocks and not depend on Averages.

We do not have a universal bull market any more, when all stocks advance at the same time. We have a mixed trend, the main trend being up on some stocks and distinctly downward on others. The majority of stocks reached low levels in July, 1932, and started working higher. The Dow-Jones 30 Industrials made low in July, 1932. The 20 Railroad

Averages made lows in June and July, 1932. In 1935, at the time the Dow-Jones 30 Industrial Averages were up 80 points, the Public Utility Averages reached a new low level. This was brought about by adverse legislation.

By studying and applying the rules to the individual stocks, you would have found that the Public Utility stocks showed downtrend while other stocks advanced. A study of the chart of American Telephone & Telegraph, which held up better than the other Public Utilities in 1935, revealed that it was in a stronger position. One reason was that during the entire depression American Telephone and Telegraph never passed its dividends and continued to pay $9 a share per year, while other Public Utility stocks passed their dividends. During the boom, which culminated in 1929, the Public Utility stocks had been watered; stock dividends had been declared; there had been numerous splitups. The result was that no other stocks had been more overbought than the Public Utilities.

You cannot detect the best stock to buy by following the averages of any group of stocks. Some of the stocks in a group will make new highs every year in bull markets while others will make new lows in bull markets or go into receivership or be taken off the Exchange. For example: In 1932 when the average of all airplane stocks showed uptrend, if you had selected Curtiss Wright "A" as the best airplane stock in this group to buy just because it had been a leader in a previous campaign, you would have made a mistake. In August, 1932, Curtiss Wright "A" sold as low as 1½, in April, 1934, made a high of 12. Now compare Douglas Aircraft and make a study of its position. In 1932, Douglas made a low of 5; in February, 1934 reached a high of 28½; in September, 1934 declined to 14½, a decline of about 50% from the top. In July, 1935, when Curtiss Wright "A" was still selling 4 points under the 1934 high, Douglas crossed its 1934 top, which showed that it was in a strong position and much better to buy, even at 28½, than Curtiss Wright

"A." In December, 1935, Douglas crossed 45½, the 1929 high, and advanced to 58 while Curtiss Wright "A" only advanced to 12¼. Curtiss Wright "A" never showed the activity or power to advance as Douglas and some other airplane stocks. Douglas was making higher bottoms and higher tops right along while Curtiss Wright "A" was moving in a narrow trading range, so Douglas was the stock in this group to buy. This is proof that you must study each individual stock in a group in order to detect its trend.

THE DOW THEORY OBSOLETE

To make a success, you must be up to date; must discard old theories and old ideas when they become obsolete and follow new rules and new stocks in order to make a success trading in the stock market.

During recent years the Dow Theory has spread all over the country. People have begun to regard it as very valuable and infallible, but in fact, it is now practically of no value to a trader. With so many stocks listed on the New York Stock Exchange, 30 stocks or 20 stocks are no longer a representative of the trend. Besides, you cannot trade in averages. You must follow the trend of individual stocks in order to make money.

The Dow Theory worked quite well up to 1916, when the World War changed everything. Then this country changed from an agricultural country to a manufacturing country. In 1916, when the Dow-Jones 30 Industrial Averages advanced to new high levels, which was 7 points above the highs of 1906, the Railroad Averages at that time were 24 points under the 1906 record high. The man who waited for the Rails to confirm the upward trend in Industrials certainly got left and missed opportunities and probably lost money.

In 1917 the Government took over the Railroads, and in December, 1917, the Dow-Jones 20 Railroad Averages declined to 69. The Industrials at the same time made a low of 66. This was the first time that the Rails were as low as they were in 1897, while the Industrials were 13 points above the 1907 panic lows.

In 1918 and 1919 the Rails failed to follow the Industrials and were no good as a guide or confirmation according to the Dow Theory. In July, 1919, the Industrials made a new high record while the Rails were making new low levels. In November, 1919 the Industrials reached a new high at 119½. In the same month the Railroad Averages reached low of the year, only 3 points above the 1907 lows. The Rails were going exactly opposite to the trend of Industrials and the Dow Theory was not working.

In June, 1921, the Railroad Averages reached a low of 64. In August, 1921, the Industrial Averages reached the same low of 64. The Industrial Averages were only 2 points under the 1907 lows. Then followed a big bull market in Industrial stocks and the Rails were laggards.

In January, 1925, the Industrial Averages crossed 120, the record high of 1919 and the Rails were still 38 points below the 1906 highs and 12 points below the 1916 highs. If you had waited for the Rails to confirm the Industrials by making new highs before buying industrial stocks, you would have missed big opportunities and would have had to wait until July, 1927 when the Rails crossed the highs made in 1906. The Industrial Averages, at that time, were 63 points above the 1909 highs and 80 points above the 1906 highs for Industrial Stocks.

On September 3, 1929 the 30 Industrial Averages reached the highest price in history at 386 and the Rails reached a high of 189. After the panicky decline to November, 1929, the Industrial Averages rallied nearly 100 points. The Rails rallied only 29 points. After April, 1930, the Rails were weaker than Industrials and had smaller rallies.

In November, 1931 the Rails broke 42, the low made in August, 1896. In June, 1932, the Rails declined to 13⅛, while the 30 Industrial Averages declined to 40½. The Industrials were 12 points above the 1896 lows, while the rails were 29 points under the 1896 lows.

In July, 1933, the Industrials rallied to 110 and the Rails rallied to 58.

In October, 1933, the Industrial Averages reacted to 82½ and the Rails to 33. The Industrials never broke the 1933 lows until they advanced to 149½ in November, 1935.

In March, 1935, the Rails sold at 27 while the Industrials were at 96. The Industrials were 13 points above the lows of October, 1933, while the Rails were 6 points below. This again proved that you could not depend upon the Dow Theory.

From March, 1935 to November, 1935 the Industrials advanced 53½ points while the Rails rallied only 12 points. You would have missed profits of anywhere from 50 to 75 points if you had waited to buy Industrial stocks until the Rails made new highs and confirmed the advance.

This is plenty of proof that the Dow Theory is now obsolete and that you cannot depend upon it to work in the future.

CHANGE WITH THE TIMES

In order to make money under the changed conditions, you must study individual stocks and follow their trend. Don't let the Averages fool you. When one stock shows a change in trend, go with it regardless of the action of others in the same group and regardless of the action of the Averages.

Years ago Stage Coach Stocks advanced and you could have made money buying them, but stage coaches went out of business and so did the stocks. Then there were Canal Stocks that advanced and you could have made money buying them, but other modes of transportation reduced the business on canals. The automobiles came along and took business away from the railroads. Now the airplane is coming along and taking business from the railroads and will later take it from the automobiles and trucks. The airplane will be the future mode of transportation. You will have to watch airplanes in future for a guide, the same as you watched automobile stocks a few years ago, because the money will be made trading in airplane stocks rather than rails or automobiles.

Keep up to date; be progressive. Do not cling to old theories or ideas. Learn to follow the trend of individual stocks and you will make profits.

CHAPTER V

NEW RULES TO DETECT TREND OF STOCKS

The rules which I give in my books, TRUTH OF THE STOCK TAPE and WALL STREET STOCK SELECTOR, are all good. They will work in future market moves for 100 years but under the changed conditions stocks will move up slower the greater part of the time and on a smaller volume. (Compare present volume of U. S. Steel and General Motors with volume of former years.) The rules in my books are based upon Supply and Demand; have been tried and tested. Whether stocks advance on buying by the public, pools or investors, it is after all the result of Supply and Demand. When buying power is greater than selling power, it forces stocks higher right along. Then when the reverse takes place and the selling pressure is greater than the buying, stocks work lower.

The new rules that I give you in this book, if used with the rules in my other books, will help you to make a success trading in individual stocks.

Just as detectives learn the habits of a certain gang of criminals from the clues that they leave behind them, so can a Wall Street detective find a clue to what the "powers that be" or master market manipulators intend to do with the stocks. The movement of a stock, up or down, is made by human minds who buy or sell it with the intention of closing the deals later at a profit. What one man's mind can devise, another mind can figure out, for after all, human nature never changes. By studying individual stocks and following the rules for detecting and determining the trend, you will be able to make large amounts of money.

Best Way to Detect Trend

Years of experience have convinced me that the trend can be detected by a study of charts.

Monthly Chart: The best chart to use for detecting the main trend of a stock is the Monthly high and low Chart.

Weekly Chart: The Weekly high and low Chart is the next best guide to the real trend of a stock.

Daily Chart: When a market is moving very fast and is very active on large volume, the Daily high and low Chart is a good guide and trend detector.

To detect when a stock is getting into a strong position and ready to advance, look up the Monthly Chart. If there is good support and good buying, then the stock will gradually be absorbed and as it grows scarcer and the demand increases, it will work higher and receive support at a higher level, making higher bottoms and higher tops.

When a stock is getting ready to change trend to the downside, it will start making lower tops and lower bottoms; then when it breaks below the point from which it made the last run up to the top, it will be an indication that the main trend has turned down.

Kind of Stocks to Trade in

The kind of stocks to trade in are those that are active and those that follow the rules and a definite trend. There are always queer acting stocks and some stocks that don't follow the rules. These stocks should be left alone. Stocks that hold in a narrow trading range for a long time should not be traded in until they break out on the upside or break bottoms on the downside and show increased volume of sales and activity.

Where to Buy and Sell

You should buy a stock near a single bottom, a double bottom, or a triple bottom and place a stop loss order not more than 3 points away. By buying near a single bottom, I mean that after a reaction you should wait until a stock holds around a level for 2 to 3 weeks, then buy and protect with a stop loss order 3 points under the lowest week, or in active markets if a stock reacts and then holds around a level for 2 to 3 days, buy and protect with a stop loss order not more than 3 points under the lowest day.   When a stock sells around the same price level several weeks, several months or a year or more apart, it forms a double bottom and is a buy.   If it sells around the same level the third time, it is a triple bottom.

When a stock advances to a new high level or crosses a former old top by 3 points then if it is going higher, it should not react back 3 points below the former old high.   Then you should buy on a slight reaction of 1 to 3 points and place a stop loss order 3 points under the old top.

After a bull market gets started, buy on a reaction and place a stop loss order 3 points under the previous support level.

After a stock crosses the top of a previous year by 3 points, it is a buy on any little reaction.   For example:

Douglas Aircraft: 1932 high 18⅝.   1933 high 18¼. In 1934 when it crossed this double top, according to the rule you would buy.   Refer to Chart No. 1 on page 36.   The stock advanced to 28½ in 1934.   Then in 1935 after Douglas Aircraft crossed 28½, it never reacted lower than 26½. Therefore, when it reacted back below 28, it was a buy with a stop at 25½.   It is significant to note that after Douglas crossed the old high of 28½, it never reacted 3 days (the reactions only lasting about 2 days) before the stock resumed its upward trend.   When it crossed the 1929 high at 45½, you would buy again and continue to pyramid as long as it showed uptrend.   The stock advanced to 58⅜ in December, 1935.

Reverse the above rules on the selling side.   You should sell against single tops, double tops, or triple tops, or at some point where you can place a stop loss order not more than 3 points away, or wait until a stock shows distribution

CHART No. 1—DOUGLAS AIRCRAFT
Monthly High and Low: 1928-1935

CHART No. 2—UNITED FRUIT
Weekly High and Low: 1935

and breaks the last important bottom by 3 points, then sell short on a small rally and place a stop loss order 3 points above the old bottom. After a stock breaks the bottom of a previous year by 3 points, it is a short sale.

In a bear market when a stock declines and breaks an old bottom by 3 points or more, then if it is going lower, it should not rally 3 points above the bottom before it goes lower. For example:

United Fruit: This stock made a low of 84⅞ in May, 1935 and a low of 84¼ in June, 1935; rallied to 90¾ in July, and after it broke 81 or 3 points under these previous lows, it never rallied 3 points above them until it declined to 60½ in October, 1935. Refer to Chart No. 2 on page 37.

Whatever you do, it should be according to a definite rule and after the market shows a definite trend. Wait for as sure an indication to buy or sell as you can possibly get. Don't get impatient and jump into the market just because you want to make a trade. Remember, a stock is never too high to buy so long as the trend is up, provided you place a stop loss order for protection in case the trend reverses. A stock is a short sale at any time and at any price so long as the trend is down, regardless of how high it has been previously.

PRICE AT WHICH FAST MOVES START

The higher the price, the faster a stock moves and the wider the fluctuations. Stocks move up faster after they sell above 50 and even faster after they sell above 100, and when they get above 150 and 200 per share the fluctuations are very wide and rapid. You can prove this to yourself by going over any of the stocks that have been active and had big advances and see what happened after they crossed 50, after they crossed 100, and after they went above 150 and 200.

The same on a decline: Stocks move down rapidly from extreme high prices in the first 50 to 100 points' decline from the top. After a stock gets below 100 the moves are somewhat smaller and when it gets below 50, they are even smaller and rallies are also smaller, especially if the stock has had a big decline. The lower they get, the less they rally.

TIME TO HOLD AFTER BUYING OR SELLING

After you make a trade, if the stock closes showing you a loss the first day, you are apt to be wrong and trading against the trend. If it closes against you the third successive day, you are wrong nine times out of ten and should get out of this trade immediately.

When you buy or sell and the trade immediately moves in your favor and closes with a profit the first day, you are right and with the trend. At the end of three days if it still shows you a profit, it is almost a sure sign that you are right and with the main trend.

Therefore, get out at once when you see that you are wrong and hold when you see that you are right.

BUYING OUTRIGHT FROM 1929 TO 1932

I have written in all of my former books that it never pays to buy stocks outright because it does not help any if the trend happens to go against you. I have stated that the only time it is safe to buy stocks outright is when they are selling around $10 per share or lower. So many people get the mistaken idea that because they have a stock paid for they cannot lose on it. That is just where they are wrong. When you buy a stock outright, you do not worry because you think you will not have a margin call, but you also fail to realize the fact that you can lose all the money that you pay for the stock, because it can go to nothing and be assessed. Therefore, when you make a trade, the idea is to know what you are going to do if it goes against you. You should protect it with a stop loss order and limit your risk. Holding on and hoping never helped anyone and never will. When you are wrong, get out at the market and take a small loss, but when the market moves in your favor, hold on for big profits.   Don't think that because you are well acquainted with a stock and because it has gone up for many bull campaigns in the past, that it will go up in the future, because old leaders go and new ones come to take their places. You must keep up to date in the market and buy and sell the new leaders in order to make profits.

WATCH BOTTOMS AND TOPS OF PREVIOUS CAMPAIGNS

When a stock breaks the bottom of the previous bear campaign by 3 points, then you should watch for support around the bottom of the next former campaign.   For example :

When stocks started down in 1929, you should watch the bottoms of 1923-24, the previous campaign.   Then if those lows were broken, you should watch the bottoms of the 1921 campaign, from which the great Bull Market started. If these bottoms were broken by 3 points the next lows would be 1917, then 1914, and after that the 1907 panic lows, then 1903-04 and 1896 extreme lows.

You should look up each individual stock and see what years it made its previous extreme lows.   When you find that a stock has reached the extreme low of its history and then holds for several weeks or several months and fails to break the old bottom by 3 points, you judge that it is in a strong position and time to buy with a stop loss order 3 points under the old low level.

Industrial Averages: In 1932, after the Averages broke the low of 85, which was made in 1931, the next important bottom to watch was the low of 64 in 1921.   The Averages declined to 70 in 1932, and held for some time, but finally declined and broke the low of 64.   Then you would look for the next bottom and would find that in 1907 and 1914 these Averages made a low at 53.   When they declined and broke 53 in 1932, the support level of these two panicky declines, you would have to look for the next bottom, which was 43 in 1903, from which a big bull campaign started. In July, 1932 the Dow-Jones Industrial Averages declined to 40½, failing to get 3 points under the 1903 low, a sign of support. The market became dull and narrow, the volume of sales dropped to the lowest of any time since 1929, accumulation took place and the trend turned up again from that point.

In an extreme bear campaign, like 1929-32, when a stock declines back to the old levels made 20 to 30 years before, then holds without breaking these previous panic levels by 3 points, it indicates that it is receiving support and that it is a buy with a stop loss order 3 points under the old low level.

U. S. Steel is an example. In June, 1932, it declined to 21¼, which was only ⅝ point lower than the extreme low in the 1907 panic. It was a buy protected with a stop loss order at 19. A rally followed from that level, but U. S. Steel did not have so big an advance from 1932 to 1935 as other stocks because it had been split up and the amount of stock increased from 5 million shares to over 8 million shares.

It is just as important to watch old tops of previous campaigns. The further back they are, the more important when they are crossed by 3 points. For example:

Westinghouse Electric made a low of 38½ in 1918 and a low of 40½ in 1919. In 1921 the low was 38⅞, selling around the same level for 3 years. This showed strong support and indicated that the stock was being accumulated for much higher prices. It continued to work higher and in 1925 crossed the 1915 high at 74⅞ and advanced to 84, which showed that it was going higher. The next top to watch was the high of 116½ in 1902, the highest of its history up to that time. When it crossed this level, it indicated much higher prices, and according to the rule you would continue to pyramid all the way up. The stock sold at 292⅝ in 1929.

Follow the trend of each individual stock in the same way and when it crosses the top of a previous year or the tops of previous campaigns by 3 points, it is an indication that the stock is going higher.

In a bear campaign you should watch tops of former campaigns as well as bottoms of previous campaigns. In the bull market that culminated in November, 1916, the Dow-Jones Industrial Averages reached a new high level of 110, then followed a sharp decline. In 1919 these averages made another new high just under 120; then in the panicky decline in 1921 reached 64. After the bull market culminated in 1929, there was a sharp decline in October, 1931 and the averages broke 3 points under 120, the old 1919 top, which was an indication of lower prices. Then we would watch the next top at 110. When the averages broke 3 points under that top, they declined to 85 in October, 1931. Then on November 9, 1931, rallied back to 119 or around the old top at 120. When they failed to cross this old top, it was an indication that stocks were still in a bear market and that prices were going lower.

How to Detect Early Leaders in a Bear Market

Stocks which advance fast and make top and are distributed before other stocks reach top indicate that they will be early leaders in a bear market.

When stocks break the bottoms of previous years or the low point for several months previous, ahead of other stocks, they indicate that they will be early leaders on the decline.

In every bear market there are early leaders or stocks that decline first and reach bottom ahead of the general list of stocks. For example:

Chrysler Motors: In March, 1926, Chrysler Motors sold at 28½. The big bull market followed and in October, 1928 it reached extreme high at 140½. This was 11 months before the Dow-Jones Averages and the general market made top in September, 1929. You could have been short of Chrysler while other stocks were advancing. Many motor stocks did not reach high until August and September, 1929.

It is important to study and see what happened to Chrysler in 1929 while the big advance in other stocks was taking place. Look at the Monthly and Weekly Charts. In January, 1929 Chrysler high 135; trend turned down and in May, 1929, it declined to 66, down 74½ points from the 1928 high. August, 1929, high of the rally 79, still down 61 points from October, 1928 high. Then, when the great crash followed in October and November, Chrysler which already showed downtrend and was in a weak position, declined to 26 in November, 1929. On April, 1930, high of the rally 43, which showed weakness because it failed to have any big rally. June, 1932, low 5. Stayed around the low level for 3 months, down 135 points from the high of October, 1928.

When a stock advances sharply in the first or second year of a bull market and makes top and then fails for two years to cross the top made in the first or second year of the bull market, it is a sign of weakness and the stock should be sold short when it shows that the trend has turned down again. You can detect this change in trend by watching the Monthly and Weekly Charts. For example:

Corn Products was one of the stocks that was an early leader in 1933. In August and September, 1933, Corn Products advanced and made top at 90⅝. In August, 1934, it declined to 56; then showed accumulation and the trend turned up again, but when the advance started in March, 1935, Corn Products moved up slower than it had in 1933. In July, 1935, it reached a high of 78⅜. By studying the Weekly Chart and the Daily Chart, it was easy to see that Corn Products had made top. Refer to weekly charts on pages 44–45. It failed by 12 points to reach the high of August and September, 1933, which showed that the selling was better than the buying. In October, 1935, it declined to a low of 60, down 18 points from the high of July, 1935,

CHART No. 3a—CORN PRODUCTS
WEEKLY HIGH AND LOW: 1933–1934

CHART No. 3b—CORN PRODUCTS
WEEKLY HIGH AND LOW: 1934–35

while the averages and other individual stocks were advancing during August, September and October, 1935. This proves that by following the rules you could have been short of Corn Products and making money and at the same time could have been buying Westinghouse and other stocks and making money on the long side.

Note that Corn Products during the week ended July 13, 1935 held in a narrow trading range. Then, in the week ended July 20, there was a sharp decline to 70½ on a larger volume. This was a sure indication that the trend had changed and turned down and that you could sell it short. At the same time, the Dow-Jones Averages showed strong uptrend, but just because the Averages showed uptrend was no reason that you should buck the trend and buy Corn Products when it indicated that it was a short sale.

How to Detect Early Leaders in a Bull Market

Stocks which decline and make bottom and show accumulation before other stocks reach bottom indicate that they will be early leaders in a bull market.

When stocks cross the tops of previous years or the high point of the past few months ahead of other stocks, they indicate that they will be early leaders.

In every bull market there are early leaders or stocks that advance first and then make tops ahead of other stocks. The stocks that made bottom early and accumulated in 1931 while other stocks were declining were among the first to advance in 1932 and 1933. For example:

American Commercial Alcohol: April, 1929 extreme high 90; October, 1931 extreme low, 5, making bottom 8 months before the low of the general list in 1932. Note the narrow range and big accumulation. In May, 1932, when other stocks were making new lows, this stock crossed all tops of the past year and showed uptrend. September, 1932 high 27; February, 1933 low 13, two points higher than the previous bottom. In May, 1933 crossed the 1932 high and in July, 1933 reached a high of 90, the same as in 1929, and failed to cross this level.   This being a double top, is where you should have sold out longs and gone short with a stop 3 points above the 1929 high.   July, 1934 low 20¾ ; December high 34¾ ; June, 1935 low 22½.   Holding 1¾ points above the previous bottom, it showed good support.   It held for 7 months between 23 and 28, and in October, 1935 crossed 28, showing uptrend; in November, 1935 crossed the December, 1934 high at 34¾.   It will have to advance 3 points above that level to indicate higher prices.

U. S. Smelting: This was another early leader that showed plainly ahead of time that it was going to have a big advance.   April, 1929 high, 72⅞ ; September, 1931 low 12⅜ ; in November rallied to 26; June, 1932 extreme low 10, which was the lowest in its history.   Note the Yearly Chart: 1907 low 24¼ ; 1915 low 20; 1916 high 81½, the record price up to that time; 1923 low 18; 1929 high 72⅞, making lower tops since 1916; then in June, 1932 made a new all-time low.

Big accumulation took place in a narrow trading range. In April, 1933 U. S. Smelting crossed 26, above all tops back to 1930.   See Chart No. 4 on page 48.   Here you should start buying and would pyramid as the stock worked higher. A fast advance followed.   In July, 1933, it crossed 73, the 1929 high, a sure indication for much higher prices and a place to buy more; then crossed 81, the high of 1916, the highest in its history.   Here would have been the place to buy more stock and continue to pyramid.   In 1933, September, October and November made highs around 105, and in February, 1934 crossed 105, where you would buy again.   It reached extreme high of 141 in July, 1934, up 131 points from its low, at the time when other stocks were making bottoms.   After this quick advance against the trend of the general market, the stock worked lower, showing downtrend, while other stocks still showed uptrend.   In September and December, 1935 it sold at 92.

CHART No. 4—U. S. SMELTING
MONTHLY HIGH AND LOW: 1924–1935

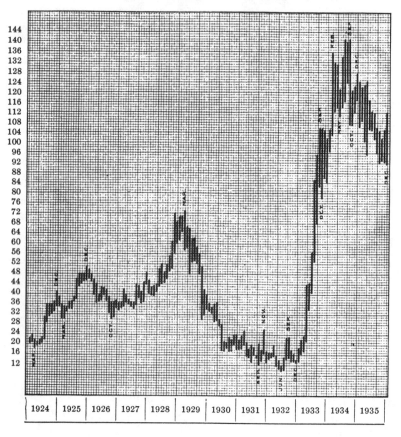

U. S. Industrial Alcohol: In June, 1932, it made a low of 13¼; advanced in September, 1932 to 36; then on the secondary decline in February, 1933 declined to a low of 13½, holding one-half point above the 1932 low. This double bottom was a sign of strength and a place to buy. In 1933, in July, U. S. Industrial Alcohol advanced to 94. This was due to the Repeal of the 18th Amendment and an overestimate by the public of the earnings that whiskey stocks and other industrial alcohol companies could make. The public went wild and bought too high.   This sharp advance from a low of 13½ in February, 1933, to a high of 94 in July, 1933 was entirely too fast and the movement collapsed. In September, 1934, U. S. Industrial Alcohol declined to 32. The Dow-Jones Industrial Averages reached low on July 26, 1934.   In December, 1934, U. S. Industrial Alcohol rallied to 47.   After that it was a slow mover, lagged behind the market and did not cross 47 again until September, 1935.

If you had followed the trend, you would have bought this stock all the way up in 1933 and then as soon as the trend turned down on the Weekly Chart, you would begin to sell it short.

United Fruit: In June, 1932, extreme low 10¼. Showed good accumulation, turned trend up and indicated that it would be an early leader when it crossed the 1932 high at 32⅜ in March, 1933.   It was a good leader in 1933, 1934 and early in 1935.   1933 high 68; 1934 high 77; May, 1935 high 92¾.   As long as it continued to make higher bottoms and higher tops, you would buy, but when the trend turned down in July, 1935, ahead of other stocks, you would follow the trend and sell it short.

Chrysler Motors: In June, 1932, extreme low 5; September, 1932, high 21¾.   March, 1933 declined to 7¾, a higher bottom than 1932 by 2¾ points, a sign of strength and accumulation and a good place to buy.   April, 1933, Chrysler started activity on increased volume and in May crossed the 1932 top, a sure sign of higher prices.   Then crossed the 1931 high at 25¾ and the 1930 high at 43.   February, 1934 high 60⅜ on big volume of sales.   The Daily and Weekly Charts showed that this was top and the trend turned down.   August and September, 1934, Chrysler sold at 29¼. As it held nearly half of the advance from the 1932 low to the 1934 high, it was in strong position.   March, 1935, made another bottom at 31, holding 1¾ points above the 1934 level, a double bottom, a sign of good support and time to buy.   August, 1935 it crossed the old 1934 top at 60⅜, a sure indication of higher prices and a place to buy more. December, 1935, advanced to 93⅞. From the low in March, 1935 to the high in December, 1935, Chrysler advanced 62⅞ points and at no time reacted more than 9 points, a wonderful opportunity to pyramid, which was plainly shown all the time by the strong uptrend.

How to Detect Stocks in Strong Position

It is easy to pick the stocks in strong position if you follow the rules laid down in TRUTH OF THE STOCK TAPE and WALL STREET STOCK SELECTOR and the rules in NEW STOCK TREND DETECTOR. Example:

Westinghouse: June, 1932, low 15⅝, the same low as 1907. According to our rule, this was a place to buy with a stop 3 points under the old bottom. September, 1932, high 43½; February, 1933, low 19⅜, a higher bottom by 3¾ points, showing good support. The stock remained in a dull, narrow trading range for some time and by the rules for detecting a change in trend you would discern that this was accumulation and would buy the stock. One reason why you should be watching Westinghouse was that this stock was never splitup and never declared a stock dividend during the 1929 boom.

In July, 1933, Westinghouse crossed 43½, the top of September, 1932. This was an indication for higher prices and you should have bought more when it crossed the old top. It advanced to 58¾ in July, 1933. The Daily and Weekly Charts showed at that time, that it was making top and you would sell out and go short. In October, 1933, it declined to 28⅝, making a higher bottom by 9¼ points than February, 1933, still showing a strong uptrend. Then it held for a long time in a narrow trading range with a small volume of sales, a sign of accumulation, and failed to break the bottom at 28⅝.

It advanced in February, 1934 to a high of 47¼, where

again there was large volume and the Daily and Weekly
Charts showed that it was making top and that it was time
to get out and go short, as the trend of most stocks turned
down after February, 1934, when the trading was running
at the rate of 5,000,000 shares per day after stocks had had
a big advance.   In July, 1934, Westinghouse declined to
27⅞ only ¾ point lower than the bottom of October, 1933,
and if you bought around 29, the old bottom, with a 3-point
stop loss order at 26, the stop wauld not have been caught.
After the low of July, 1934, Westinghouse remained in a
narrow trading range until December, 1934, a sign of accumulation.   A detective who had been watching this stock,
would have seen clear signs of accumulation when it failed
to break the old bottom by one point, and would have bought
the stock.

In March, 1935, when most all of the stocks reacted and
the Dow-Jones Industrial Averages made bottom, Westinghouse declined to a low of 32⅝; then activity started and
volume of sales increased. In April, 1935, it crossed 47¼,
the 1934 top, a strong indication of higher prices and a place
to buy more.

In July, 1935, Westinghouse crossed 58¾, the 1933
high, another strong indication of higher prices and a place
to buy.   According to our rule, it should not decline 3 points
under this old top, which would be 55, in order to maintain
a strong uptrend.   After it crossed 58¾ it reacted to 57
only, and then advanced to 98¾ in November, 1935.   This
was a good stock to pyramid as it showed uptrend all the
way from March, 1935 to November, 1935.

New Lows Late in a Bear Campaign

When stocks decline late in a bear campaign, or after a
prolonged decline which has run two or three years, and
break into new low levels, they are not likely to decline as
far as they would if they broke into new low levels early in
the campaign.   Your rule should be that after a stock de-

clines to new low levels and then rallies back 3 points above the old bottom, it is an indication that the decline is over, that liquidation has been completed, and that the stock is getting ready to turn up again.

American Tel. & Tel.: 1907 panic low 88. In June, 1932 it broke 88 after the bear market had run 33 months and in July, 1932, declined to 70¼, or 17¾ points lower than the old low of 1907, but later in that same month rallied and closed at 89½, above the old low·of 88. The decline below 88 was a final wave of liquidation and the quick rally that followed was an indication that final bottom had been reached. In August the stock advanced to 91, or 3 points above the old low of 88, an indication of higher prices; then in September, 1932, advanced to 121. Following the rule, you would have bought American Tel. & Tel. at 91, when it was 3 points above the old bottom at 88, even though it was up 20 points from the extreme low, and then would have made 30 points on it in less than 2 months. Another proof that you should always follow the rules and go with the trend of an individual stock and change when the trend changes.

Consolidated Gas: This is another stock that had a final wave of liquidation in 1934–1935 when other stocks had crossed previous highs. 1923 low 56⅛. In 1932, it broke 56⅛ and declined to 32; rallied to 66 in September, 1932. Then in July, 1934, it broke 32, the low of 1932, and declined to 15⅞ in February, 1935; rallied to 34½ in August, 1935 and 34¾ in November. When it failed to get 3 points above the 1932 low of 32, a sign of weakness, you should have sold out and gone short. It declined to 25⅝ in September, 1935. When it can cross 35, or get 3 points above the old low, it will then indicate higher prices.

New Highs Late in 1929 Bull Market

The Dow-Jones 30 Industrial Averages made the extreme high on September 3, 1929 and U. S. Steel and many other leading stocks reached high on that date, but very few people know who do not take the trouble to keep up records, that after the big crash in September, 1929, some stocks were still working higher and made the high of the year in early October, 1929.

Timken Roller Bearing: The high for Timken during September, 1929, was 119½. Extreme high of 139⅜ reached in October, 1929: It made 20 points higher in October, while the Averages had declined 100 points from the high in September.

U. S. Industrial Alcohol: September, 1929 high 226½. Early October, 1929, high 243⅝, making a top 17 points higher in October than in September, despite the heavy selling and the smash in the general market. The time was not yet up for this late mover to make top, and, therefore, it advanced against the trend of the Averages.

You would have made a mistake if you had sold Timken Roller Bearing and U. S. Industrial Alcohol short just because the Averages and other stocks had turned down and were short sales, but if you had followed the rule and bought these stocks according to the trend, as indicated, you would have been long of them until they reached top and gave a signal for downtrend.

New Highs Following Year After End of Bull Campaign

After a market reaches final top of a bull campaign, usually there is a sharp, quick decline, then a secondary rally, from which a prolonged bear market follows. After the extreme top in September, 1929, there was a panicky decline in October and November, one of the worst in history. Then stocks advanced and made a secondary top in April, 1930, with the Dow-Jones Industrial Averages nearly 100 points lower than the 1929 tops. Yet, a few stocks made these extreme highs in April, 1930.

It is interesting to study what kind of stocks recorded

new highs and determine why they made them. Most of the stocks which advanced into a new high territory in April, 1930, were stocks that had a small amount of stock outstanding and were easy to manipulate. When these stocks crossed the 1929 highs, they certainly indicated higher and you should have followed their trend up until they indicated top, even though other stocks were still in a bear market and selling far below the 1929 highs.

Coca Cola: This stock which had been split up in 1929, advanced in 1930 and did not reach high until June, 1930. It recorded a high of 191⅜ at that time. In view of the fact that it had been late in making its top, it would naturally be late in making a bottom. While many stocks, in fact the majority of stocks, made low in June, 1932, Coca Cola declined and did not make low until December, 1932, when it sold at 68½; then showed accumulation and the main trend turned up. It continued to work higher each year, making higher bottoms and higher tops, until it advanced to 298½ in November, 1935 and was again split up 4 for 1.

Electric Power & Light: In the panicky decline of November, 1929, this stock sold at a low of 29⅛; in April, 1930, made a high of 103½, up 17 points above the high of September, 1929. After it crossed the September, 1929, high, you should have followed the trend up until it showed definite signs of turning down. Then, when it broke back under the September, 1929, top and showed downtrend, you should have followed it down on the short side just the same as any other stock.

In July, 1932, Electric Power & Light declined to 2¾. In September, 1933, it advanced to 16; then worked lower in 1933, 1934 and 1935. When other stocks advanced in 1934 and 1935 and this stock failed to cross the high of September, 1933, it indicated a short sale. In March, 1935, when the Public Utility Stocks were under pressure due to adverse legislation, Electric Power & Light reached an extreme low of 1⅛. Therefore, as this stock was working down and making new lows from time to time, showing downtrend, you should have been following its trend and selling short.

Vanadium Steel: February, 1929, high 116½. April, 1930, high 143¼. April, 1935, low 11¼. One of the reasons why this stock advanced to such a high level in April, 1930, was because there was a small available supply of stock and a small number of shares outstanding. At that time the directors of the Company made a lot of money speculating in stocks. Then followed poor business and the company during the depression got into a bad financial condition. After the stock declined to 11¼ in April, 1935, it worked up very slowly, being a late mover in working up just as it was in 1930, because the steel business was slow and the last to recover from the depression.

National Steel: It is important to compare the position of this stock, which has a small floating supply, with other steel stocks. This company showed good earnings during the depression, much better than Vanadium or even U. S. Steel. National Steel was a late mover and made top in April, 1930, at 76½. July, 1932, low 13½. It made higher bottoms in 1933, 1934 and 1935. In July, 1935, it crossed the top of February, 1934, an indication of higher prices and a point to buy more. In November, 1935, advanced above the top of April, 1930. This company with its small capitalization is well managed and has a better future than U. S. Steel, Bethlehem Steel and some others, but you must always follow the trend of a stock, regardless of what you think about it, and when the trend turns down, you should follow it down.

STOCKS THAT CROSSED 1929 HIGHS

I have stated before that I did not expect the Averages to ever sell at the 1929 high again, but that individual stocks from time to time would cross their 1929 highs and make new highs. For example:

American Safety Razor: June, 1932, low 13⅜. It worked higher during 1933 and 1934 and never had more than two or three months' reaction. In 1935, February, March and April, held around 75, the 1929 top. May, 1935, crossed 75, which was a sure sign of higher prices as it was in new high territory. July, 1935 advanced to 95¾. This stock showed uptrend all the way from 1932 and was an early leader. You should have bought it right along and then bought more when it crossed the 1929 high.

By comparing Gillette with American Safety Razor, you will see what would have happened if you had bought this stock to follow American Safety Razor. In December, 1933, Gillette made a new low at 7⅝; then held in a very narrow trading range. It reached a low of 12 in August, 1935.

Columbia Pictures: April, 1930, high 54¾. December, 1931, low 2⅝. This stock made low six months before other stocks. In July, 1932, when other stocks reached extreme low, Columbia Pictures crossed tops and already showed uptrend. March, 1933, low 6⅝, showing good support 4 points higher than the 1931 low. In May, 1933, crossed the 1932 high, a sure sign of much higher prices. It continued to work higher, making higher bottoms and higher tops and in May, 1935, crossed 55, above the high of 1930. This was another sure sign of higher prices. In July, 1935, it sold at 81. While Paramount, Radio-Keith-Orpheum, and Warner Brothers' stocks in the moving-picture line were in the hands of receivers and holding at low levels, this stock was working up. Always buy the stocks in strong position and leave those in weak position alone.

Congoleum: December, 1930, low 6¼. It showed a long level of accumulation and made last low at 7½ in March, 1933; then continued to make higher bottoms and higher tops until July, 1935, when it crossed the 1929 high at 35¾.

McKeesport Tin Plate: June, 1932, extreme low 28; September high 56⅝; December low 40⅛; and in Febru-

ary, 1933, when other stocks were at low levels, it advanced
to 57, above the September, 1932 top, a sure sign of much
higher prices. Extreme high had been 103½ in 1931. It
showed in the early stages of the campaign that it was in
a straight-up bull market and a real leader. In August,
1933, it made a high of 95¾; in October reacted to 67¼;
February, 1934 high 94¼; July, 1934 low 79, raising bottoms all the time. In April, 1935, when it crossed the 1931

CHART No. 5—NATIONAL DISTILLERS
MONTHLY HIGH AND LOW: 1925-1935

high, it was easy to detect that it was in a strong position and making for a new high. Refer to Chart No. 5 on page 57.

National Distillers: June, 1929 high 58½; October, 1929 low 15; June, 1932 low, 13, making a double bottom against May, 1926 low at 12½ and holding only 2 points under the low of October, 1929, an indication of strong support. Big accumulation took place, and while other stocks were making new lows right along, this stock was holding up. August, 1932 high 27¼; February, 1933 low 16⅞. This higher bottom indicated that it was getting ready to advance to higher levels. In April, 1933, it crossed the 1932 high at 27¼ and 1931 high at 36⅜, another sure sign for higher prices, where you should buy it and then pyramid all the way up. In May, 1933, it crossed the 1928 and 1929 highs around 58 and in July, 1933 reached a high of 124, when everybody got bullish and was talking 500 to 1000 for this stock; then was the time to sell out and go short. A sharp decline followed.

This shows the wisdom of following the trend of an individual stock and not the trend of the Averages or just any stock in a group.

STOCKS THAT DID NOT ADVANCE MUCH FROM 1932 TO 1935

By going over a large list of stocks, you will find many that did not advance much from 1932 to 1935; in fact, during that period some of them made lower prices than in May to June, 1932. For example:

American International: July, 1932 low 2½. July, 1933 high 15⅛. 1933 low 4¼, 1934 low 4¾, 1935 low 4½. In December, 1935 it was selling at 10, while other stocks that made lows around 3 to 5 in 1932 had advanced 25, 50 and 75 points. By looking at the Monthly Chart on American International you will see that it never showed that it was going to follow the advance in other stocks.

Therefore, you would leave it alone and buy those that were making higher bottoms and higher tops.

Standard Gas & Electric: June, 1932 low 7⅝. March, 1933 low 5⅛. December, 1934 low 3⅝. March, 1935 low 1½. This stock made new low levels each year while other stocks were advancing and crossing former highs. It sold at 6⅜ in December, 1935.

National Dairy: In June, 1932, it sold at 14⅜ and in February, 1933 sold at 10½. It was almost 4 points lower than the 1932 low while the Dow-Jones 30 Industrial Averages were selling 9 points higher than their 1932 lows. Then you certainly would not have bought National Dairy in March, 1933, as an early leader or a stock that would advance fast, because it showed that it was in a weak position. However, it did advance in 1933, but not nearly so much as other stocks which had sold around the same low price as National Dairy.

In July, 1933 it reached high at 25¾. Again the trend turned down and in December, 1933, it declined to a low of 11¼, making a double bottom or slightly higher than the low of February, 1933. This was a place to buy if you wanted to buy this class of stock, which is a slow mover. In July, 1934, it made a high of 18¾; then in March, 1935, declined to a low of 12⅞ and held in a slow trading range. The fact that it was 2 points higher than the low of December, 1933, showed the stock was getting support and would eventually work up. It did not cross the 1934 high until November, 1935. Therefore, you would not expect this stock to decline just because the Averages or some other stocks which had had a big advance, declined, because National Dairy had just advanced to a new high. Regardless of whether it goes very much higher or very much lower, it is not likely to decline as other stocks which have had big advances or those that are up 75 points or more from the lows of 1932 and which may decline sharply.

U. S. Realty: 1929 high, 119½; June, 1932 low 2; July, 1933 high 14½; March, 1935 low 3, only one point above the 1932 low; December, 1935 high 11½. As this stock controls New York real estate and as real estate is one of the last things to move up, U. S. Realty may be one of the late movers, but will have to cross 1933 highs before it shows strong uptrend again.

Loft Candy, Continental Motors and other stocks did not show activity or cross the high levels of previous years as other stocks did. You should always trade in stocks that cross former highs and make higher tops and higher bottoms, as they are the best to buy, and leave the dead, inactive ones alone.

Stocks in Weak Position in a Bull Market

After an extreme low has been reached in a bear market and stocks start to rally, those that rally only 2 to 3 months in the beginning of the next bull campaign and then never cross the top levels of the first rally are in a very weak position.

From July, 1932 to September, 1932 some stocks had a sharp rally of 2 months, then never crossed the top of that rally. The cause of this was short covering in these weak stocks and after a sharp recovery there was not enough buying demand to keep these stocks moving up with the trend and they gradually worked lower or remained in a narrow trading range. For example:

American Home Products: This stock declined to 25 in June, 1932; then rallied two months to 43¾ in August, 1932; and declined to 25 again in December, 1933. At the end of 1935, it was selling around 36. It never crossed the top of the two months' rally in 1932, which showed that it was in weak position and not one of the stocks that you would select for a leader.

How to Detect Independent Movers

Auburn Motors: Auburn Motors has often been an independent mover, that is, moving opposite to the trend of motor stocks. It advanced when other motor stocks were declining and declined when other motor stocks were advancing.

May, 1933 low 28¾; August, 1932 high 81; February, 1932 low 31, a higher bottom by 2¼ points than the 1932 bottom, a sign of support. July, 1933 high 84¼, only 3¼ points above August, 1932 high. Then the trend turned down, and Auburn declined swiftly to October, 1933, reaching 31, the same level as February, 1932. March, 1934, rallied to 57⅜, making a lower top and showing weakness. June, 1934, broke all lows around 31 to 29, and declined to 17 in July, 1934. October, 1934, rallied to 30. It met selling right under the old bottoms and when it could not get through, it showed a weak position and indicated lower. 1935, in March, made a new low for all time at 15; then started up and in August crossed 30, above two former tops, and got through the old bottoms, an indication of higher prices. In October, 1935 it advanced to 45½.

Chrysler Motors: Compare the position of Chrysler and Auburn at different times and see how one began to show weakness while the other was showing strength:

1932—In June Chrysler sold at 5, and in the same month Auburn advanced to 77⅛.

1933—In February Chrysler made a low of 7¾ and Auburn made a low of 31¼.

In September Chrysler advanced to 52⅞, while Auburn was selling at 45, down 39 points from its high of 84¼ in July. Auburn was then showing weakness while Chrysler was getting stronger.

1934—In August Chrysler made low at 29¼, Auburn low 17.

1935—In July Chrysler crossed the 1934 tops at 60⅜

CHART No. 6

UNITED FRUIT   CHRYSLER MOTORS while Auburn was far below the 1934 top. While Auburn moved up in October, 1935 to 45, Chrysler advanced to 88¾, selling at a higher level than Auburn sold in July, 1933.

This is more proof that you must follow the trend of the individual stocks and buy those in the strongest position and sell short those in the weakest position.

Why did Chrysler move up much faster during 1935 than Auburn and other motor stocks? Because it had made high early in the previous bull campaign, reaching high in October, 1928; therefore, its time period was different than other stocks. Auburn made high late in the 1929 campaign; reacted to 60⅜, and then advanced to 295½ in April, 1931, while other stocks were on a decline. This again proves that you must trade according to the trend of the individual stocks.

BUYING ONE STOCK AND SELLING ANOTHER SHORT AT THE SAME TIME

UNITED FRUIT AND CHRYSLER MOTORS COMPARISON

A comparison of these two stocks and their weekly high and low movements for the year 1935 is to prove to you how important it is to study individual stocks and trade according to the trend of the individual stock and not buy one stock just because some other stock is going up or sell one stock short because some other stock happens to be declining. Judge each stock according to its position and determine its individual trend and go with it.

1935
Week
ended

Jan.   5   United Fruit high 75½; Chrysler Motors high 42½. United Fruit 33 points higher than Chrysler.

Mar. 16   Chrysler reached low of the year at 31; United Fruit selling at 75⅛, or 44⅛ points higher than Chrysler.

May 18   United Fruit reached extreme high of 92¾. At this time Chrysler was selling at 49⅜. United Fruit 43 points higher than Chrysler.

At this point if you had followed the trend on Chrysler, which showed up, and had bought Chrysler, and then, when the trend showed down on United Fruit, had gone short, you would have made big profits on both deals.

Aug. 10   United Fruit 72, down 20¾ points from the high of week ended May 18.

Chrysler 62¾, up 13⅜ points from the high of week ended May 18. At this time United Fruit was only 9¼ points higher than Chrysler.

Aug. 24   On a reaction Chrysler sold at 57½.

United Fruit was selling at 65, only 7½ points above Chrysler.

Sept. 14   Chrysler 74, United Fruit 74. United Fruit down 18¾ points from the top of May; Chrysler up 24⅝ points from high of week ended May 18. Here you would have had a profit of 24 points in Chrysler if you had bought it at the time you sold United Fruit short and you would have had 18 points' profit in United Fruit. The trend was still down on United Fruit and the trend was still up on Chrysler. You would trade in both stocks according to their individual trend.

Oct. 5   Chrysler low 69. United Fruit extreme low of the decline 60½, down 32¼ points from the high. At this time Chrysler was selling 8½ points higher than United Fruit.

Nov. 23   Chrysler high 90, United Fruit 73½. Chrysler 16½ points higher than United Fruit.

Dec. 28   Chrysler reached extreme high of the year at
93⅞. United Fruit again declined to 60⅞. At
this time Chrysler was 33 points higher than
United Fruit.

The Weekly Swing Chart on United Fruit and Chrysler
on page 62 shows you how these stocks were far apart and
then how they worked and came together; then one worked
lower and the other worked higher.

This is not the only comparison of this kind that can
be made. There were many other stocks in 1935 that were
declining while other stocks were advancing, but this is ample
proof of the large profits that you could have been making
by keeping short of United Fruit right along and at the same
time pyramiding on the long side of Chrysler, buying all the
way up.

By selling stocks short that are in weak position or show
downtrend and buying the stocks that show uptrend, you can
often make money on the short side and the long side at
the same time.

Stocks That Rally or Decline Only Two to Three Months

As a rule, in a bull market a stock that is going higher
will not react more than two to three months and should
resume the upward trend in the third month. If a stock is
going lower it will continue the decline in the third month.

Chrysler: After it sold at 28 in March, 1926, it never
had more than two months' decline at any time until it advanced to 140½ in October, 1928. After it reached top at
140½ it never rallied over two months until it sold at 26
in November, 1929, which shows you how important this
rule is. In April, 1930, the high was 43 and it never rallied
over two months until the time it sold at 5 in June, 1932.

Dow-Jones Railroad Averages:

The Dow-Jones 20 Railroad Averages reached the highest in their history in September, 1929 when they sold at 189. They declined sharply in the panic of November, 1929; then rallied to 158 in April, 1930; and declined to 13 in June, 1932. The lowest price at which these Averages sold in August, 1896, was 42. Therefore, when they broke their lowest average level in history, they indicated much lower prices and you should have sold railroad stocks short and followed them down until the Averages and the individual stocks that you were short of showed that they had reached bottom and that a change in trend was taking place.

One of the signs of weakness in a bear market is a rally of only six to seven weeks or not more than two months, not getting higher in the third month. From March, 1930 to the low in 1932 at no time did the Railroad Averages advance over two months; and from February, 1931, when the high was 111, until they declined to a low of 13, they never rallied more than one month. This was a sign of great weakness, indicating heavy liquidation and a real panicky bear market.

Should Stocks with Small Number of Shares Outstanding Be Sold Short?

In a bear market or when the trend of a stock is down, it is just as safe to sell short stocks with a small number of shares outstanding as it is to sell short stocks with a large number of shares outstanding, because they all go down after distribution has been completed, and stocks that have sold very high go very low, as was proved in the great panic of 1929 to 1932. Example:

Case Threshing Machine: With only 130,000 shares outstanding, Case advanced to 515 in November, 1928; then declined to a low of 16¾ in May, 1932. This stock had many sharp rallies. If you had followed the trend, sold it short as long as the trend was down, covered and went long when the trend showed up, you would have made a large amount of money as it worked down nearly 500 points from the top.

Auburn Motors: This is another example of a stock that sold at 514 in September, 1929 and declined to 15 in March, 1935.

Auburn had only 166,000 shares outstanding, yet it declined 499 points from the extreme high in 1929 to the extreme low in 1935.   How many people would sell Auburn short after it was down to 100 and after it sold at 50?   Yet, as long as the trend was down, it was a short sale even at 25 or 20.   The same on the long side!   A stock is good to buy no matter how high it goes as long as the trend is up. Auburn was just as good to buy at 400 when the trend was up as it was to sell short at 40 when the trend was down.

Radio Common: While this was not a stock with a small number of shares outstanding, it reached extreme high at 549 in March, 1929; was split up 5 for one; declined to a low of 2½ in June, 1932.   How many people in 1929 dreamed that Radio would ever decline to 2½ again?   Probably not one in a million.   This decline of 546½ points in 32 months was the greatest decline in any stock from 1929 to 1932, which is certainly convincing proof that buying stocks outright never pays because they can go down to nothing.   There is only one way to trade, that is, to place stop loss orders and limit risks to a few points on every stock you buy.

No matter how small or how large the volume, when the trend turns down, stocks go down, and when the trend shows up, stocks go up.

Wait for Definite Buying Signal at Bottom

At the end of a panic or a long decline, there is always plenty of time to buy stocks near low levels.   All you have to do is to study past records and how stocks acted at the bottom in 1932 to prove to yourself that it requires a long time for accumulation to take place at the bottom before

stocks start up.   You can make money much quicker by waiting to buy when the trend turns up.   After you have allowed
several weeks or several months to elapse, if a stock holds
bottom levels, it shows accumulation and you can buy with a
stop loss order under the bottom.

Johns-Manville: This is a good example of how long a
stock, that has sold at very high levels, can hold at low levels.
Johns-Manville sold at 242¾ in 1929.   It declined to 10 in
April, 1932 and held around 10 during April, May, June
and July, 1932, accumulating for nearly 4 months at low
levels.   In the latter part of July, 1932, Johns-Manville
showed uptrend by crossing the tops of previous months and
in September, 1932, advanced to a high of 33⅜.   This was
an opportunity to make more than 20 points' profit in 60
days after you had waited three to four months to see if it
would hold the bottom.   You could have bought it at 10,
or just above 10, and placed a stop loss order at 9, which
would have held. Johns-Manville was one of the good stocks
to pyramid in 1934 and 1935 because it continued to cross
tops and make higher bottoms and higher tops, reaching a
high of 99½ in November, 1935.

It takes time for accumulation to be completed.   Do not
make the mistake that is made by so many traders who hang
over the tape and try to catch the bottom eighth and the
top eighth.   They never do it and lose all of their money in
the end.   Do not guess and try to anticipate what the market
is going to do.   Wait until you detect a definite indication of
a change in trend and get a definite buying signal.   Do not
pay any attention to averages or stocks in the same group.
Remember, you must follow the trend of the individual stock.

CHAPTER VI

VOLUME OF SALES

The *Volume of Sales* is the real driving power behind the market and shows whether Supply or Demand is increasing or decreasing. Large buying or selling orders from professional traders, the public or any other source of supply and demand, are bound to be registered on the tape and shown in the volume of sales.

Therefore, a careful study of the *Volume of Sales* will enable you to determine very clearly a change in trend, especially if you apply all the other rules for detecting the position of a stock.

RULES FOR DETERMINING CULMINATIONS BY VOLUME OF SALES

Rule 1—At the end of any prolonged bull campaign or rapid advance in an individual stock, there is usually a large increase in the volume of sales which marks the end of the campaign, at least temporarily. Then, after a sharp decline on heavy volume of sales, when a secondary rally takes place and the volume of sales decreases, it is an indication that the stock has made final top and that the main trend will turn down.

Rule 2—If the stock holds after making a second lower top and gets dull and narrow for some time, working in a sideways movement, and then breaks out on increased volume, it is a sign of a further decline.

Rule 3—After a prolonged decline of several weeks, several months, or several years, at the time a stock is

69

reaching bottom, the volume of trading should decrease and the range in fluctuation should narrow down. This is one of the sure signs that liquidation is running its course and that the stock is getting ready to show a· change in trend.

Rule 4—After the first sharp advance (when the trend is changing from a bear market to a bull market) the stock will have a secondary reaction and make bottom, just the same as it had a secondary rally after the first sharp decline. If the volume of sales decreases on the reaction and then the stock moves up, advancing on heavier volume, it will be an indication of an advance to higher levels.

These rules apply to the general market, that is, to the total sales traded in on the New York Stock Exchange— daily, weekly or monthly—as well as to individual stocks.

Summary: *Sales increase near the top and decrease near the bottom,* except in abnormal markets, like October and November, 1929 when the market was moving down very fast and culminated on large volume of sales, making a sharp bottom, from which a swift rebound followed. As a rule, after the first sharp rally, there is a secondary decline on decreased volume, as described above under Rule 4.

MONTHLY RECORD OF VOLUME OF SALES ON NEW YORK STOCK EXCHANGE

1929–1935

To understand the importance of Volume, a study of the total number of shares traded in on the New York Stock Exchange is necessary.

In July and August, 1921, at the bottom of the Bear Campaign, the volume of sales was around 10,000,000 to 12,000,000 shares per month. In March, 1928 sales reached 84,000,000 shares per month for the first time in history.   After that the volume of sales was very large, with this group of stocks working higher right along after the reaction in June, 1928.   The volume increased enormously in November, 1928, reaching 114,000,000 shares, the largest for any month up to that time. Sales continued heavy in December, 1928, and, in fact, right up to the top in 1929.

1929

September Sales were over 100,000,000 shares.   The Averages reached 386, the highest price in history.

October For the first time since May, 1929, the Averages broke under the low level of a previous month, which showed that the trend had turned down.   All records for volume of sales were broken in October, sales reaching ·141,000,000 shares.

November At the bottom of a panicky decline in November sales dropped down to 72,000,000 shares.

December Sales 83,000,000 shares.

1930

January Sales 62,000,000 shares.

February 68,000,000 shares.

March Volume of sales reached 96,000,000 shares.

April Total volume reached 111,000,000 shares on a very small gain in price of the Averages.

May In the early part of the month the Averages broke under the April low, which was the first time that they had broken a monthly low since bottom was reached in November.   Sales for May were 78,000,000 shares.   A sharp decline followed.

June   Sales were 80,000,000 shares, with the market moving lower.

July &   On a small rally the total sales were only
August   80,000,000 shares for two months.

September   The market was slightly higher early in the month, then a decline started, which carried prices to new low levels, sales of 50,000,000 shares being recorded.

October   The market broke to new low levels. Stocks at this time broke the low levels of November, 1929 and sales increased to 70,000,000 shares.

December   The Dow-Jones Industrial Averages declined 46 points under the low levels of November, 1929. Total sales this month were 60,000,000 shares.

1931

January   A rally started and in January, 1931 the sales were 42,000,000 shares.

February   The market made top of the rally on sales of 64,000,000 shares, which showed that the volume of trading was increasing on the rally and that stocks were meeting resistance. Note that this top was just under the low levels of November, 1929, which showed that stocks met selling when they moved up under the old low levels of the panic.

March   A decline started in March and the sales were 64,000,000 shares, a heavier volume, with prices moving lower.

April   Sales were 54,000,000 shares.

May   Sales 47,000,000.

June There was a sharp decline on a volume of sales totaling 59,000,000, which carried the Averages down to new low levels, reaching 120, the old top of 1919 and the last low of May, 1925. A quick rally followed to the end of June and early July, the Averages ·reaching 157½, but failing to cross the high level made in May, 1931.

July The sales were smaller, only 33,000,000, and the market narrowed down.

August The sales were 24,000,000, still a narrow, dull market, not making much progress on the upside.

September Activity started and sales reached 51,000,000. On this increased volume the Averages declined 45 points during the month of September. This showed great weakness and indicated a further decline.

October A sharp decline occurred which carried the Averages down to 85 on sales of 48,000,000 shares.

November A rally followed, culminating on November 9. The Averages reached 119½, back to the old top of 1919, to the last low of 1925, and to the bottom of a previous rally. Failing to penetrate these old bottoms and cross the previous top, the market showed weakness and indicated that the trend was still down. Sales in November were 37,000,000, the volume decreasing on the rally.

December The Averages declined to a new low for the move, making 72 on sales of 50,000,000 shares, the largest since September, 1931. This indicated that big liquidation was still going on.

1932

January   The Averages reached a low of 70 on sales of 44,000,000 shares for the month.

February   Rallied to 89¾ on sales of 31,000,000 shares.

March   The Averages made about the same high on sales of 33,000,000 shares. Then the market went dead on the rally, stocks narrowing down.

April   The Dow-Jones 30 Industrial Averages broke 70, the low of January, and declined to 55 on sales of 30,000,000 shares.

May   The Averages broke 53, the old low levels of the panic of 1907 and 1914, which indicated lower prices; then declined to 45 on sales of 23,000,000 shares.

June   The range between extreme high and extreme low averaged 10 points and the Averages reached a new low on sales of 23,000,000 shares.

July   On July 8, 1932, the extreme low was reached, with the Averages down to 40½. The volume was very small and the Averages and individual stocks moved in a very narrow trading range, indicating the last stages of a bear market. Late in the month the Averages crossed the high of June, which indicated that the trend was turning up. Sales were 23,000,000 shares. The range was about 13 points on Averages.

            At the low in July the Averages were down 345 points from 1929 high. The volume of sales for the three months—May, June and July—aggregated only 69,000,000 shares, the smallest since 1923, in contrast to over 100,-000,000 shares per month at the top in September, 1929 and 141,000,000 in the month of October, 1929. This indicated that after such a drastic decline, liquidation had run its course and the trend was changing. The market really had been sold to a standstill. Traders and investors sold out everything because they feared things were going to get worse. It was the same old story: A bull market begins in gloom and ends in glory. All of the indications were plain: The small volume of sales and narrow range of fluctuations indicated that the end had been reached and that a change in trend was certain.

During the latter part of July, 1932, the advance started.

August   There was a sharp rally in August on sales of 83,000,000 shares, more than for the entire three months past. This was on short covering and wise investment buying.

September Top of the rally was reached on sales of 67,-000,000 shares, with the Averages up 40 points from the low of July 8. After this advance to September on a large volume, distribution took place and the trend turned down. (Note that the total volume from July 8 to the top in September was 168 million shares.) The Averages failed to go higher in the third month. At no time from April, 1930 to July, 1932 had the Averages or most of the individual stocks rallied over two months. Therefore, to show a change in trend to a prolonged bull market, they would have to advance three full months or more.

October After September stocks worked slowly down on a smaller volume of sales. In October the sales were 29,000,000.

November   Sales were 23,000,000.

December   Sales 23,000,000.

1933

January   Sales were 19,000,000 shares.

February   The whole country was in a state of panic. Banks were failing right and left. People were panic stricken and selling stocks and bonds regardless of price. There were business failures, and when President Roosevelt was inaugurated on March 4, he immediately acted and closed all the banks in the United States. This marked the end of the secondary decline and started a constructive movement.

The Dow-Jones Industrial Averages declined to 50 in February, which was 9 points higher than the low of July, 1932. Sales were only 19,000,000 shares, the smallest volume of any time in over 10 years and the smallest volume for any month since the top in September, 1929, a sure sign of bottom.

March   A rally started on increased sales. The volume was 20,000,000 shares.

April   The United States went off the gold standard. This started a rapid advance in stocks and commodities. Sales on the New York Stock Exchange were 53,000,000 shares this month.

May   The advance continued and the volume of trading reached 104,000,000 shares.

June   The volume increased to 125,000,000.

July   The sales were 120,000,000 shares.

From March low to July high, 1933, the total number of shares traded in on the New York Stock Exchange was 422,000,000 shares and the Averages at the top in July were up 60 points from the low of February, 1933. Very few people keep records and study enough to understand what the enormous volume of 422,-000,000 shares meant. This was the greatest volume of sales of any bull campaign in the history of the New York Stock Exchange. It was greater than the last advance in 1929. (From the last low in May, 1929 to September, 1929, the Averages advanced 96 points and the total sales on the New York Stock Exchange were 350,000,000 shares.) It was one of the wildest buying waves in history. Commodities advanced by leaps and bounds. People bought stocks regardless of price. Just think about it: Sales of 350,000,000 in three months—May, June, and July, 1933—equal to the volume from May, 1929 to September, 1929. The signs were plain that volume was telling the story of a wave of inflation. Commodities and stocks had advanced so rapidly and everybody had bought on such thin margin that a wide-open break occurred in four days from July 18th to 21st, carrying the Dow-Jones Averages down 25 points to 85. Cotton and Wheat broke badly at the same time on heavy liquidation. At this time Dr. E. A. Crawford failed. He was involved in commodities, said to be the largest amount carried ever known.

August & September   After the sharp decline in July, a rally followed in August and September, which carried the Averages to within two points of the July high, making a double top. The volume of sales on this second rally was smaller. In August the sales were 42,000,000 and in September 43,-000,000 shares. In these two months the volume was only two-thirds of the total volume for July, 1933.

October   The Dow-Jones 30 Industrial Averages declined to 82½, the last low before the start of a long advance.   Sales decreased to 39,000,000 and the market became very dull and narrow.   A slow rally started from the October lows.

November   Sales were 33,000,000 shares.

December   Sales 35,000,000.

1934

January   The sales this month were 54,000,000.

February   Sales 57,000,000 shares, with the top in February only slightly above the high of January. The Averages failed to get over one point above the high of July, 1933, making a double top. Sales of 111,000,000 shares in two months and the third time at the same level was a signal of top.   Individual stocks especially showed plainly by the large volume and the slow progress they were making in February that they were getting ready to start down.   The trend turned down in the latter part of February.

March   Sales reached 30,000,000 shares.

April   There was a slight rally on 29,000,000 shares.

May   Prices were lower on 21,000,000 shares.

June   There was a small rally and the volume decreased to 16,000,000 shares for the month.

July   On July 26, 1934, stocks made bottom on sales of nearly 3,000,000 shares for the day, with the Dow-Jones Averages down to 85, slightly above the low level of October, 1933.

            For the month of July, 1934 total sales were

only 21,000,000 shares. Individual stocks moved in a narrow trading range, which showed that bottom was being made and the foundation laid for another bull campaign. The fact that an extreme high was reached in July, 1933 was an indication that you should watch for a change in trend in July, 1934, according to my rule to watch for a change in trend one year, two years, or three years from any important top and bottom.

August   The market rallied 11 points on Averages; sales 16,000,000 shares.

September   The market reacted within one point of the July low. Sales were down to 12,000,000 shares, a sure sign of bottom, being the smallest sales per month in many years.

October   The market rallied in October on a slightly increased volume of sales, 15,000,000 shares.

November   The sales increased to 21,000,000 shares.

December   Prices were higher; sales 23,000,000 shares for the month.

1935

January   There was increased activity on sales of 19,-000,000 shares.

February   The market reached the top of the rally. Sales only 14,000,000 shares, which was a sign that there was not enough buying power to carry prices through.

March   There was a big decline, which was the last before the market advanced to new highs. Sales were 16,000,000 shares.

April   Increased activity shown and stocks started advancing. Volume of sales was 22,000,000 shares, which showed that a bull market was under way.

May   The Dow-Jones 30 Industrial Averages crossed the high levels of 1933 and the top of February, 1934, on sales of 30,000,000 shares. Individual stocks showed increased volume and many of them moved up to new high levels.

June   The Averages crossed 120, which was above the last high of November 9, 1931, a sure indication of higher prices. The sales for June were 22,000,000 shares.

July   New highs were reached by individual stocks and the Averages. Sales for the month were 29,000,000 shares.

August   More new highs for individual stocks and new highs for the industrial Averages. Sales reached 43,000,000 shares, the highest since January and February, 1934.

September   The advance continued and sales were 35,000,000 shares.

October   The Dow-Jones 30 Industrial Averages advanced to 142. The total sales for the month were 46,000,000 shares.

November   Sales 57,000,000 shares, practically the same as February, 1934 when stocks made top. The Averages reached 149½, up 109 points from the low of July, 1932. During the week ended November 23, 1935, when the Averages reached top, the total volume of sales was nearly 19,000,000 shares, the largest since the week ended February 10, 1934 when top was reached. After such an enormous volume, with the Averages up 53 points since March, 1935, according to my rule it was time to watch for top and a change in trend in stocks that had had big advances.

December   A reaction followed which carried the Averages down over 10 points from the November high. The volume of sales for the month was 45,-000,000 shares.

JULY, 1934, TO NOVEMBER, 1935

The total sales from the low of July 26, 1934 to the high of November 20, 1935 were 407,000,000 shares. The total number of points which the Dow-Jones Industrial Averages advanced from July, 1934 to November 20, 1935 was 65 points. Note that the total advance from the low of March, 1933 to the top in July, 1933 was 60 points: Therefore, with the averages in November, 1935 up 65 points, 5 points more than in the 1933 campaign, it was time to watch for at least a temporary change in trend.

Note that the volume of sales during the 16 months' campaign from July, 1934 to November, 1935 was about 15,000,000 shares less than during the 5 months' campaign from March, 1933 to July, 1933. This shows that after the Security Administration Law became effective, it reduced trading considerably.

If you continue to study the Volume of Sales on the New York Stock Exchange and watch the position of the Dow-Jones Industrial Averages, you will be able to detect culminations with greater accuracy.

CHAPTER VII

A PRACTICAL TRADING METHOD

To be profitable, a method for trading in the stock market must work in practice as well as in theory. Several years ago I originated a practical trading method and since 1932 have made some important improvements which I have tested in my actual trading. I am giving my readers the benefit of this valuable discovery.

With this method you use the Weekly High and Low Chart, which is the best chart for trading purposes, but when stocks are very active and selling at very high levels you can use the Daily Chart and apply the same rules to detect a change in trend, buying and selling levels, and points for stop loss orders.

I am giving the rules and making the trades on paper covering a period of more than 10 years to prove to you that big profits can be made by following these rules:

Rule 1—Amount of Capital Required:

To make speculation or investment a successful business, you must know the amount of capital required to begin trading and continue to trade. To be safe, I consider that at least $3,000 should be used for trading in each 100 shares of stock and if you follow the rules you will make money. For trading in 10-share lots, a capital of $300 should be used.

Never risk more than 10% of your capital on any one trade. If you have as many as two or three losses, then reduce your unit of trading, risking only 10% of your remaining capital. In this way you will never lose all of your capital and can continue to trade and make profits.

When profits have increased to the amount of your capital, say $3,000, then you can increase your trading unit to 200 shares, but after you have accumulated a large amount of profits, keep a larger amount of capital behind each trade.

Safety must be your first principle at all times. When large profits have accumulated, establish a reserve fund for protection, placing this money in a savings bank, first mortgages or gilt-edge investments for income.

Rule 2—Always Use Stop Loss Orders:

Never fail to place a stop loss order on each trade that you make, and let these stop loss orders be 1, 2 or 3 points away from the price at which you buy or sell, and under any conditions—even when stocks are at very high levels—on your first trade never risk more than 5 points or $500 on each 100 shares.

As a rule, a 3-point stop loss order is the safest to use as it will be caught less than any other.

After a prolonged advance, when stocks are advancing very fast and at high levels, if you have big profits then follow up with a stop loss order 5 points below the high price of each day or 1 to 3 points under the low or closing price of the day. In case a stock is selling at very high levels, follow up with a stop loss order 10 points under the high price of each day.

When you make initial trades, never risk 10 points of your capital on any one trade. Five points must be the limit, and when it is possible, always try to make a trade where your risk is only 2 or 3 points.

Follow up profits with stop loss orders 1, 2, 3 or 5 points under each week's bottom on the long side, and follow down with a stop loss order 1, 2, 3, or 5 points above the top of each week on the short side.

Rule 3—How to Detect Buying Points:

Buy against double or triple bottoms and place a stop loss order 1, 2, or 3 points below them.

Buy when a stock holds 1, 2, 3, or more weeks around the same low level, and place a stop loss order 1, 2 and never more than 3 points under the lowest weekly bottom.

Buy when a stock crosses the previous high levels by 1 to 3 points. In most cases it is safer to wait until it advances 3 points above an old top before you decide that the trend has given a definite indication that it is going higher. Then, after it has crossed an old top by 3 points, it should not react 3 points under the old top. For example: If the old top is 50 and it advances to 53, then it should not react to 47 again. Therefore on a reaction to around 51 to 48, you should buy and place stop loss order at 47, or 3 points under the old top.

When a stock advances into new high territory, that is, crosses the highest price of its history, it usually indicates higher prices and is safe to buy. If it is going higher the stock seldom reacts 3 points under the old high level.

Watch the tops of previous years. When a stock crosses the top of a previous year by 3 points, it is nearly always safe to buy, especially if it reacts back to the old top or slightly under it.

In a bull market reactions only last 2 or 3 weeks before the main uptrend is resumed, therefore it is safe to buy at the end of two or three weeks' reaction after the stock shows that it is making bottom by holding 2 to 3 days.

Rule 4—How to Detect Selling Points:

Sell against double and triple tops and place a stop loss order 1, 2, or 3 points above them.

When old bottoms or low levels of previous movements are broken, sell short and place a stop loss order 1, 2, and never more than 3 points above the old bottom. It is always safest to wait until a stock breaks 3 points under an old bottom, then sell at the market or on a small rally and protect with a stop loss order 3 points above the old bottom.

Then, after a stock has broken to new low levels, follow

down your short position with stop loss order one point above the high of the previous week and watch for a point where there is an old bottom or previous low level to cover shorts and buy again.

As a rule, a rally in a bear market only lasts two to three weeks, therefore at the end of the second or third week, it is safe to go short with a stop loss order 3 points above the high of the previous week.

Watch the bottoms of previous years. When a stock breaks the bottom of a previous year by 3 points it is nearly always safe to sell short, especially if it rallies up to the old bottom or slightly above it.

Rule 5—How to Pyramid:

It is important to know how and when to pyramid. When stocks are at low levels, between 20 and 50, you can buy or sell every 5 points apart if your capital and margin warrant it, that is, when you have 5 points' profit on the first trade, buy or sell an additional amount and place a stop loss order so that you will not have any loss on the two trades if the market should reverse and catch the stop.

When stocks are selling between 80 and 200 per share, you should only buy or sell 10 points apart. After you make the first commitment, then wait until you have 10 points' profit, then buy or sell a second lot. After you have bought or sold the fourth or fifth lot in a pyramid, then you should decrease the trading unit. For example:

If you have been buying 100 shares each 5 or 10 points up and have accumulated 500 shares, then it is safer to reduce your trading to 50 shares every 5 or 10 points up. If you have been trading in 200 shares and have bought 4 or 5 lots, then reduce your trading to 100-share lots. Reverse this rule on the short or selling side.

The big money is made by always following the main trend of a stock. Never buy a second or third lot unless the first trade has moved in your favor.

Never average a loss. To average a loss is the greatest mistake that any trader can make.

Rule 6—When to Reverse Position:

By reversing position, I mean that if you have been buying and pyramiding, then, when there is a change in trend and an indication to sell out long stocks, you should also sell short. For example:

If a stock advances to around 75, where there is an old top, and holds 1 or 2 weeks, you should sell out longs and go short and place a stop loss order at 78 or 3 points above the old top. Then, if the stop at 78 is caught, you should cover shorts and go long again because you must keep with the trend all the time.

Apply the same rule when a stock is declining. When there is a change in trend and the time comes to cover shorts, then you should buy for long account again, just as I show in all the trades made in Chrysler Motors.

Rule 7—Volume of Sales:

By following the rules given in my books on Volume, you will be able to detect when tops and bottoms are reached and a change in trend takes place.

Nearly always when stocks are advancing rapidly and reach high levels, the Volume of sales increases. After the first quick, sharp reaction, there is a secondary rally, and if the main trend is going to turn down, the Volume will be smaller than it was on the advance when the final top was made. (See example of Volume on Chrysler at the end of this Chapter.)

After a prolonged decline, a decrease in Volume is an indication that liquidation has about run its course and a change in trend is due.

In panicky markets, when stocks have sharp declines, they often make bottom on large Volume and a rally follows on fair-sized Volume, then there is a secondary decline when the Volume falls off considerably.

Look up the Volume of each individual stock and judge its position according to the amount of stock outstanding. For example: General Motors with 44,000,000 shares must move much slower and require more time to advance a point than Auburn Motors or J. I. Case which have such a small number of shares outstanding. Chrysler Motors has only 4½ million shares compared with 44,000,000 of General Motors, which is the reason Chrysler made a greater range during 1932 to 1935 than General Motors.

The Following of Rules Makes Profits

The human element beats most traders. The market does not beat them. Eliminate human judgment and guess-work. Do not buy or sell on hope or fear.

The man who will make up his mind to follow rules strictly to the letter will make profits. Prove to yourself that the rules work which I give you and then follow them. Buy or sell when the rules indicate that it is time to buy or sell and then do no close trades and take profits until the rules indicate that it is time for a change in trend; then make your trades accordingly and you will make a success.

CHAPTER VIII

FUTURE OF STOCKS

FULFILLED PREDICTIONS

When I wrote the TRUTH OF THE STOCK TAPE in 1923, I said that chemicals, airplane and radio stocks would be the leaders in the next bull market. They did lead in the 1924–1929 Bull Campaign and these groups of stocks showed some of the greatest advances.

In the chapter on "Stocks of the Future" on page 191 of WALL STREET STOCK SELECTOR, which I finished in April, 1930, I said that chemicals, radio stocks, airplane and moving picture stocks would be the leaders of the future bull campaign. This prediction has been fulfilled. Radio "B" sold at $3 per share in 1932 and advanced to $92 per share in December, 1935. United Aircraft sold at 6½ in 1932 and later advanced to 46⅞. Allied Chemical sold at 42½ in 1932 and advanced to 173 in 1935. Air Reduction sold at 30⅞ in 1932, then advanced to 171 in 1935. In this new book, I show you how easy it was to detect these stocks that developed into early leaders and had big advances while others held in a narrow trading range, or declined during the bull market.

In Chapter IX, page 198 of WALL STREET STOCK SELECTOR, written in April, 1930, I wrote as follows:

"The public learned about automobile stocks in 1915 and 1916, when they had their big advances and again in 1919, but from 1924 to 1929 the public bought automobile stocks on a scale greater than ever before in any group of stocks. Therefore, the motors are greatly overbought and most of the companies are greatly overcapitalized. They have paid stock dividends and increased their stock to such an extent that they cannot pay dividends during the years of depression to come. Therefore, the automobile stocks will be among the best short sales in the coming bear market."

This prediction was amply fulfilled. Auburn Motors whicn sold at 514 in 1929; 263¾ in April, 1930 and 295½ in April, 1931, declined to 15 in March and April, 1935. Chrysler Motors which sold at 140½ in October, 1928 and 43 in April, 1930, declined to 5 in June, 1932, a decline of 135½ points. General Motors, which sold at a high of 54¼ in April, 1930, declined to 7⅝ in June, 1932. Certainly, these declines were drastic enough to prove that I knew what I was talking about when I said in 1930 that motors were the best short sales.

On pages 203–204 of WALL STREET STOCK SELECTOR, I wrote as follows:

INVESTORS' PANIC

"About every 20 years there is an investors' panic or a severe depression, brought about by investors selling stocks at low levels. This is due to a prolonged decline and loss of confidence. Buying power having been reduced and investment selling continually coming into the market, force prices lower and lower, until banks call loans on high-class investment stocks, with the final result of a wide-open break or a sharp, severe decline. This occurred in 1837 to 1839, 1857, 1873, 1893, 1896, 1914 and 1920 to 1921. The panic of 1929 was not an investors' panic. It was a gamblers' panic.

"Various causes have produced these different panics, but the real basis behind all of them has been the money market. The banks, having become overloaded with loans during periods of prosperity, forced selling and produced the panic. Most bankers get too optimistic after a prolonged period of prosperity; then after a prolonged decline and business depression they become too pessimistic and are afraid to make loans. In fact, instead of making new loans they call old loans, which makes the situation worse than it would be otherwise. It is the same with most of the newspapers. They know that it is popular to talk optimistic and they go to the extreme in good times and then when conditions get bad, they generally paint the picture blacker than it really is.

"Certainly, during all of these panics, some of the brokers and banks must have seen the handwriting on the wall and have known just exactly what was coming, but they never told their customers about it. Then the investors must *stop, look,* and *listen.* He must think for himself and not depend upon his banker or his broker to get him out of the market at the right time, because past history proves that their advice at critical times cannot be depended upon.

"The coming investors' panic will be the greatest in history, because there are at least 15 to 25 million investors in the United States who hold stocks in the leading corporations, and when once they get scared, which they will after years of decline, then the selling will be so terrific that no buying power can withstand it. Stocks are so well distributed in the hands of the public that since the 1929 panic many people think that the market is panic-proof, but this seeming strength is really the weakest feature of the market. The public has never been good leaders and never will be, because their hopes and fears are easily excited. If stocks were all in the hands of a few strong men, then investors and the country would be safe, but when they are in the hands of millions of people who are unorganized and without leadership, then the situation is dangerous. A wise man will sell before it is too late. The public will hold on and hope; then all will become scared at the same time and sell when nobody wants to buy, thus precipitating a panic. This was what caused the 1929 panic. The speculators and gamblers all got scared and sold at the same time.

"Greed and love of money will cause the next panic and the love of money will be the cause of the next war. 'War is hell!' You might ask what that has to do with stocks. War has always caused panics. War is coming and a panic is coming in stocks, and this time the panic in stocks may be the cause of war. People often get a misconception of an idea or quote things wrong. We often hear people say, 'Money is the root of all evil.' They think they are quoting the Bible, but they are not. The Bible says, 'The love of money is the root of all evil.' In fact, the love of money and the quest for power has been the cause of all wars, as history proves. Love of money has been the cause of all financial troubles and depressions in the past, and the coming panic will be the greatest the world has ever known, because there is more money in the United States than ever before, therefore more to fight for. Men fight harder for money than anything else, once they see it slipping away."

It is a matter of record that the panic of 1931–1932 was the greatest in history with the most severe declines ever recorded in the history of the New York Stock Exchange. This prediction was based on my Master Time Factor, which enables me to tell months and years in advance when certain time cycles repeat and cause extreme high and low prices. This is enough to convince any man that my discoveries, based on mathematical science, can be depended upon to forecast future market movements.

How Traders and Investors Were Fooled in 1930 to 1932 Panic

Investors and traders lost money in this great panic because they listened to other people who knew less about the market than they did and who were simply guessing. Many a so-called wise economist said that the bottoms in November, 1929, would not be broken and that this decline had corrected all the weak spots in the market and that the bull market would be resumed. They said the same thing about the breaks in 1930, 1931 and 1932. When the market actually reached bottom, they did not know what to say because they had been fooled so long. They had not studied past history enough to know that after the greatest advance in history had culminated in 1929, the greatest panic in history must follow and that it would require a long time to liquidate stocks. Every time stocks made bottom, the newspapers, government officials and economists said that it was the last bottom, but stocks went down, down, down, until people lost faith and hope in everything. They went lower than anybody dreamed they could go. That is what happens when everybody decides that stocks cannot go down or that stocks cannot go up—they always do the opposite. The public is always wrong, because they follow no well-defined rule and are not organized. People believed that the Government by buying cotton, wheat and loaning money could stop the depression, but when once a cycle is up and prices are due to decline, nothing can stop them until it has run its course. The same when the main trend turns up, neither government interference nor anything else can stop the advance until it runs its course.

Every investor and trader should do his own studying and learn rules and apply them and not rely on other people who know no more about the market than he does.

How Traders and Investors May Be Fooled in the Future

During the year 1935, especially the last half of it, newspaper writers, statisticians and economists were all writing and talking about the abundance of cheap money and the large bank reserve. They talked about inflation and led people to believe that the Government had changed conditions and money rates and that stocks must continue to go on up and up just because it is easy to get money. They forget the fact that this money, in many cases, is held by people who are too smart to buy stocks when they are too high.

Another fact they have overlooked is that the money is not in liquid form. A large amount of money on deposit in the banks and held by insurance companies and savings banks is not in cash, but in government bonds, which if forced upon the market would break the bond market to pieces and result in a panic. When everybody is convinced an event is going to happen, it usually has already happened or has been discounted. People talk about inflation and how high stocks and commodities are going. My opinion is that we have had inflation ever since 1933 and that everything is discounted and that the market is getting ready to discount deflation before the election in the Fall of 1936.

WHAT HAS HAPPENED TO CAUSE THE NEXT BEAR MARKET

The present Administration at Washington with its New Deal, or I think it would be more proper to name it the "raw deal," decided to make it their business to run every other man's business, regardless of whether they knew anything about it or not. Most politicians and "brain-trusters" know nothing about running any kind of business. All they know or have is a theory on paper which will not work in practice. Their idea was to "crack-down" on business. If they could have had their way and General Johnson could have "cracked-down," as he tried to, on Henry Ford, his factory would have been closed and thousands of people would have been put out of business and men out of employment. The New Dealers assume the attitude that from him that hath it shall be taken and given to him that hath not and does not work. Their policy is creating a nation of loafers. They are teaching people to depend upon the Government and to depend upon other people who pay the taxes, which is the worst thing that could happen and must result in serious consequences sooner or later for the entire country. This country was developed by men who had the courage and the confidence to work from sun to sun. They were progressive and went into a new country and built up this country by work, and we can never build this country up by spending and not working. You cannot take the fruits of one man's labor and give it to another. You cannot tax one man who works and runs a successful business and give the money to other people who fail in business. It would be just as logical to tax one line of manufacturing business and give it to another business that is failing as it is to tax people who buy goods and give the money to farmers for ploughing up crops, destroying cattle and hogs and forcing the price so high that people who really work to pay for what they get, cannot afford to eat pork. The farmer can run his own business. He has always been able to run his business. If he cannot, then he will have to go down just the same as any other man who fails in business. It is a question of the old law of the survival of the fittest and the reward must go to those who work. No one has ever yet been able to get something good without paying for it. It cannot be done. We cannot beat the law of compensation. Nature pays off for work done and the more work done, the more a man receives.

No one man or set of men is greater than all of the people of this country. The majority of the people voted to elect Roosevelt and did not know they were electing him to direct a lot of "brain-trusters" to run the country. Congress has submitted to Roosevelt and permitted "brain-trusters" to run things. The Government is no different from any other business or individual who spends two or three times as much as it earns and may eventually go bankrupt. Government's interference with business and the Government's heavy expenditures simply mean trouble ahead and a day of reckoning must come and the bill must be paid by the taxpayers, just the same as in the last panic which was the result of the World War and other foolish acts by our own Government and foreign governments. We had to pay with the worst depression the world has ever seen. We cannot escape it in the future. It will cause another panic in stocks. When it comes, both traders and investors will sell stocks, as usual, after it is too late or in the last stages of the bear market, although stocks will decline on a smaller volume than in previous campaigns due to the restrictions of the Securities Exchange Law.

If the policies that are now being pursued in Washington continue for another four years, this country will be ruined. Banks that are loaded up with billions of bonds forced on them by the Government, will be unable to sell them to pay their depositors. Savings banks, insurance companies and trust companies loaded up with government bonds will find them depreciating 15 to 30 per cent and then just suppose the Government inflates and prints paper money, what will the money be worth? There is only one hope for this country and that is to stop this reckless spending and get down to business and work out of it. Governor Landon of Kansas has demonstrated that he can run the state government economically and has reduced the debt and is not spending more than they are taking in. This country will recover from the mistakes that have been made by the Roosevelt Administration if the spending is stopped and the budget is balanced. In future instead of taxing business to death, business men should be allowed to run their own business to support legitimate expenditures of the Government and not a nation of loafers.